W9-BAR-065

TURING

Jack Copeland FRS NZ is Professor of Philosophy at the University of Canterbury, New Zealand, where he is Director of the Turing Archive for the History of Computing. He is an authority on Turing's work, and his books include *The Essential Turing* (OUP, 2004), *Colossus: The Secrets of Bletchley Park's Codebreaking Computers* (OUP, 2010), and *Alan Turing's Electronic Brain* (OUP, 2012). He has published over 100 articles on the philosophy and history of computing, as well as on mathematical and philosophical logic.

B. JACK COPELAND

TURING

Pioneer of the Information Age

OXFORD
UNIVERSITY PRESS

OXFORD
UNIVERSITY PRESS

Great Clarendon Street, Oxford, OX2 6DP,
United Kingdom

Oxford University Press is a department of the University of Oxford.
It furthers the University's objective of excellence in research, scholarship,
and education by publishing worldwide. Oxford is a registered trade mark of
Oxford University Press in the UK and in certain other countries

© B. Jack Copeland 2012

The moral rights of the author have been asserted

First published 2012
First published in paperback 2014

Impression: 1

All rights reserved. No part of this publication may be reproduced, stored in
a retrieval system, or transmitted, in any form or by any means, without the
prior permission in writing of Oxford University Press, or as expressly permitted
by law, by licence or under terms agreed with the appropriate reprographics
rights organization. Enquiries concerning reproduction outside the scope of the
above should be sent to the Rights Department, Oxford University Press, at the
address above

You must not circulate this work in any other form
and you must impose this same condition on any acquirer

Published in the United States of America by Oxford University Press
198 Madison Avenue, New York, NY 10016, United States of America

British Library Cataloguing in Publication Data
Data available

ISBN 978–0–19–963979–3 (Hbk.)
ISBN 978–0–19–871918–2 (Pbk.)

Printed and bound in Great Britain by
Clays Ltd, St Ives plc

Links to third party websites are provided by Oxford in good faith and for
information only. Oxford disclaims any responsibility for the materials
contained in any third party website referenced in this work.

This book is dedicated to all Turing's friends and (in memoriam)
to Robin Gandy, Jack Good, Peter Hilton, and Donald Michie.

I am grateful to Ralph Erskine, Andre Haeff, Brett Mann, Diane Proudfoot,
Bernard Richards, Martin Sage, Oron Shagrir, Edward Simpson, and Eric Steinhart for
their helpful comments on parts of the manuscript. Special thanks to Latha Menon
for her constant encouragement, good advice, and patience.

TABLE OF CONTENTS

1

CLICK, TAP, OR TOUCH TO OPEN

Three words to sum up Alan Turing? Humour: he had an impish, irreverent, and infectious sense of humour. Courage: both intellectual and physical. He would need courage when put on trial for being gay. Isolation: he loved to work alone. Reading his scientific papers, it is almost as though the rest of the world—the busy community of human minds working away on the same or related problems—simply did not exist. Turing was determined to do it his way.

Three more words? Patriotic. Unconventional: he was uncompromisingly unconventional, and he didn't much care what other people thought about his unusual methods. Genius. Turing's brilliant mind was sparsely furnished, though. He was a Spartan in all things, inner and outer, and had no time for pleasing decor, soft furnishings, superfluous embellishment, or unnecessary words. To him what mattered was the truth. Everything else was mere froth. He succeeded where a better furnished, wordier, more ornate mind might have failed. Alan Turing changed the world.

What would it have been like to meet him? Turing was tallish (5 feet 10 inches) and broadly built.[1] He looked strong and fit. You might have mistaken his age, as he always seemed younger than he was. He was good-looking but strange. If you came across him at a party, you would certainly notice him. In fact, you might ask, 'Who on earth is that?'[2] It wasn't just his shabby clothes or dirty fingernails. It was the whole package. Part of it was the unusual noise he made. This has often been described as a stammer, but it wasn't. It was his way of preventing people from interrupting

Figure 1. Turing aged 16

Credit: Sherborne School

him, while he thought out what he was trying to say.³ 'Ah…Ah…Ah… Ah…Ah.' He did it loudly.

If you crossed the room to talk to him, you would have probably found him gauche and rather reserved. He was decidedly lah-di-dah, but the reserve wasn't standoffishness. He was shy, a man of few words. Polite small talk did not come easily to him. He might—if you were lucky—smile engagingly, his blue eyes twinkling, and come out with something quirky that would make you laugh. If conversation developed, you'd probably find him vivid and funny. He might ask you, in his rather high-pitched voice, whether you think a computer could ever enjoy strawberries and cream or could make you fall in love with it. Or he might ask if you can say why a face is reversed left to right in a mirror but not top to bottom.

Once you got to know him, Turing was fun—cheerful, lively, stimulating, comic, brimming with boyish enthusiasm. His raucous crow-like laugh pealed out boisterously. But he was also a loner. 'Turing was always by himself,' said codebreaker Jerry Roberts. 'He didn't seem to talk to people a lot, although with his own circle he was sociable enough.' Like everyone else, Turing craved affection and company but he never seemed to quite fit in anywhere.[4] He was bothered by his own social strangeness—although, like his hair, it was a force of nature he could do little about.[5] Occasionally he could be very rude. If he thought that someone wasn't listening to him with sufficient attention, he would simply walk away. Turing was the sort of man who, usually unintentionally, ruffled people's feathers—especially pompous people, people in authority, and scientific poseurs. He was moody too. His assistant at the National Physical Laboratory, Jim Wilkinson, recalled with amusement that there were days when it was best just to keep out of Turing's way.[6] Beneath the cranky, craggy, irreverent exterior there was an unworldly innocence, though, as well as sensitivity and modesty.

Turing died at the age of only forty-one. His ideas lived on, however, and at the turn of the millennium, *Time Magazine* listed him among the 20th century's hundred greatest minds, alongside the Wright brothers, Albert Einstein, DNA busters Crick and Watson, and the discoverer of penicillin, Alexander Fleming. Turing's achievements during his short life were legion. Best known as the man who broke some of Germany's most secret codes during the war of 1939–45, Turing was also the father of the modern computer. Today, all who click, tap, or touch to open are familiar with the impact of his ideas. To Turing we owe the brilliant innovation of storing applications, and all the other programs necessary for computers to do our bidding, *inside the computer's memory*, ready to be opened when we wish. We take for granted that we use the same slab of hardware to shop, manage our finances, type our memoirs, play our favourite music and videos, and send instant messages across the street or around the world. Like many great ideas, this one now seems as obvious as the wheel and the arch, but with this single invention—the stored-program universal computer—Turing changed the way we live. His universal machine caught on like wildfire—today personal computer sales hover around the million-a-day mark. In less than four decades, Turing's ideas transported us from an era where 'computer' was the term for a human clerk who did the sums in the back office of an insurance company or science lab, into a world where many young people have never known life without the Internet.

But a biography should begin at the beginning. Alan Turing was born just over a century ago, on 23 June 1912, about half a mile from London's Paddington Station, at 2 Warrington Crescent. His mother, Sara Stoney, came from a family of engineers and scientists. Sara was educated at Cheltenham Ladies' College and at the Sorbonne in Paris.[7] His father, Julius, had a position in the Indian Civil Service, in what was then the imperial city of Madras, now Chennai. The young Alan grew up in the south of England in a privileged world: cooks, maids, holidays abroad. But he lived the life of a near orphan, lodging with carers, and seeing his parents only when they returned from India on leave. Sara describes how she came back from one absence of many months to find Alan profoundly changed. 'From having always been extremely vivacious—even mercurial—making friends with everyone, he had become unsociable and dreamy,' she said.[8] As she departed again for her next stint in India, she was 'left with the painful memory of his rushing down the school drive with arms flung wide in pursuit of our vanishing taxi'.[9]

The school was Hazelhurst, near Tunbridge Wells, a prep school for sons of the upper classes. The unsociable and dreamy child was thrust into boarding-school life at the tender age of nine. An adolescence of persecution and fagging awaited him. It was at Hazelhurst that Turing the inventor began to emerge. He wrote a letter to his parents with a fountain pen of his own devising, even supplying a detailed diagram of his invention.[10] Subsequent inventions reported by letter included an unusual form of typewriter and an accumulator to power his bicycle lamps. Six years later he moved on to Sherborne School in Dorset. Founded in 1550 and built in the shadow of Sherborne Abbey, the place looked like a monastery. Turing arrived by bicycle, alone and dishevelled. 'I am Turing,' he announced.[11] Britain was in the grip of the General Strike and no trains were running. 'Landing from France at Southampton, he bought a map, bicycled to Blandford and after spending the night at the best hotel duly reported the following morning,' recollected Turing's housemaster, Geoffrey O'Hanlon.[12] His epic journey was even mentioned in the local *Western Gazette*. The dreamy boy was turning into a courageous and independent-minded young man. He seemed resigned to the prospect of incarceration at Sherborne. 'You have to have cold showers in the morning,' he reported to his mother. 'Fagging starts for us next Tuesday,' he wrote. 'It is run on the same principle as the Gallic councils that tortured and killed the last man to arrive.'[13]

At Sherborne, Turing became a mathematician. His maths teacher was Donald Eperson, a priest who admired Lewis Carroll's *Alice in Wonderland*. Eperson published *The Lewis Carroll Puzzle Book* and also made a short film entitled *Alice in Numberland*. Turing, he recalled, was 'difficult to teach, as he preferred his own independent methods'.[14] These, Eperson said, were 'sometimes clumsy and cumbersome and sometimes brilliant but unsound'. Turing loathed having to take anything for granted or second-hand. Sherborne's headmaster nicknamed him 'The Alchemist' and labelled him 'definitely anti-social'.[15] Another master promised to give a billion pounds to any charity named by Turing if he passed his Latin exam.[16] In 1929 his ambitious parents paid to put his name down for entrance to King's College, Cambridge.[17] Two years later their dream came true. Turing won a scholarship and in the autumn of 1931 he shambled through the imposing front gateway of King's.

He was soon punching above the weight of any normal maths fresher, coming up with an interesting theorem that, as it turned out, had previously been proved by the famous Polish mathematician,

Figure 2. Turing

Credit: King's College Library, Cambridge

Wacław Sierpiński. Inspecting the older proof, Turing observed that Sierpiński had employed 'a rather difficult method'. 'My proof is quite simple so Sierpiński is scored off,' he gloated.[18] At King's he fitted in better than he ever had before. The college became his intellectual home. Young Turing rowed, played bridge and tennis, networked, enjoyed the theatre and opera, played his second-hand violin. He skied, slept under canvas, dreamed of buying a small sailing boat, travelled in Europe, joined the Anti-War Movement. But mainly he worked on mathematics. In 1934 he passed his finals with flying colours, earning the whimsically named Cambridge grade of 'B Star Wrangler'—a first-class honours with distinction. In March of the following year he was elected a fellow of King's, at the age of only twenty-two. His ascent of the greasy academic ladder was off to a flying start. 1935 also saw the publication of his first piece of research, in the august journal *Proceedings of the London Mathematical Society*.

It was while a new fellow that he invented the universal Turing machine, as the next chapter relates. The invention came about while he was investigating an abstruse philosophical problem in the foundations of mathematics—ironically, his universal machine emerged from utterly abstract research that nobody could ever have imagined would lead to anything of practical use, let alone to a machine that would affect all our lives. He wrote up his research under the opaque title 'On Computable Numbers, with an Application to the Entscheidungsproblem' and published it in 1936, again in the *Proceedings* of the LMS. Today this paper is regarded as the foundation stone of modern computer science. Turing, still a graduate student, had no idea of the fame that this obscure and difficult paper would ultimately bring him. Stretching his wings, he set off to America with an invitation to Princeton University in his pocket. There he picked up a PhD in just over eighteen months—lesser mortals usually take a minimum of three years. He might have liked to stay longer in this new world, but war in Europe was on the horizon, and in the summer of 1938 he returned to his fellowship at King's.[19] For the next sixteen short years, as he pioneered the information age, his career moved from crescendo to crescendo.

In 1939, on the first day of war with Germany, Turing took up residence at Bletchley Park, a Victorian mansion in Buckinghamshire. There he was a key player in the battle to decrypt the coded messages generated by Enigma, the German military's typewriter-like cipher machine. Turing pitted machine against machine. The prototype model of his anti-Enigma 'bombe' was installed in the spring of 1940. His bombes turned Bletchley Park into a codebreaking factory. As early as 1943, Turing's machines were cracking a staggering total of 84,000 Enigma messages each month.[20] Turing personally broke the form of Enigma that was used by the U-boats preying on the North Atlantic merchant convoys. It was a crucial contribution. He also searched for a way to break into the torrent of messages suddenly emanating from a new, and much more sophisticated, German cipher machine that the British code-named 'Tunny'. The Tunny communications network, a harbinger of today's mobile phone networks, spanned Europe and North Africa, connecting Hitler and the Army High Command in Berlin to the front-line generals. Turing's breakthrough in 1942 yielded the first systematic method for cracking Tunny messages. His method was known at Bletchley Park simply as 'Turingery', and the broken Tunny messages gave detailed knowledge of German strategy—information that changed the course of the war. Turing's work on Tunny was the third of the three strokes of genius that he contributed to the attack on Germany's codes, along with designing the bombe and unravelling U-boat Enigma. Turing stands alongside Churchill, Eisenhower, and a short glory-list of other wartime principals as one of the leading figures in the Allied victory over Hitler.

Turingery was the seed for the sophisticated Tunny-cracking algorithms that were later incorporated in Colossus, the first large-scale electronic computer. With the installation of the Colossi—there were nine by the end of the war—Bletchley Park became the world's first electronic computing facility. The designer of these ultra-secret computers, Thomas Flowers, was aware of Turing's 1936 idea of storing programs in digital form inside a computer's memory, but he didn't incorporate it in Colossus. Turing knew as soon as he saw Flowers's racks of electronic equipment in operation that the time had come to build his stored-program universal machine.

Turing was a theoretician's theoretician, yet, like Leonardo da Vinci and Isaac Newton before him, he also had immensely practical interests. In 1945 he designed a huge stored-program electronic computer called the Automatic Computing Engine—or ACE. The name was a homage to 19th-century visionary and computing pioneer Charles Babbage, who had proposed giant mechanical calculating 'engines'. Turing's ACE design achieved commercial success as the English Electric Company's DEUCE, one of the earliest electronic computers to go on the market. In those days—the first eye-blink of the information age—the new machines sold at a rate of no more than a dozen or so a year. One top government advisor even argued that a single one should be sufficient for all Britain's scientific needs. In fact, Turing's sophisticated ACE design went on to become the basis for the world's first personal computers.

Turing was not the only one to have made the connection between his universal machine of 1936 and electronics. As soon as the war ended, his codebreaking colleague, Max Newman, left Bletchley for the University of Manchester, taking a dismantled Colossus with him, and lost no time in setting up a Computing Machine Laboratory. With Turing's ACE project in London bogged down by delays, the race to build the first electronic universal stored-program computer came to an end in June 1948, when the Manchester group succeeded in running a simple program on their cranky prototype. They called their computer the 'Baby'. It was the first of a new species of machine.

That same year Turing himself moved to Manchester. At last he had his hands on a universal Turing machine. He spent the next years of his life programming the Manchester computer, and also carried out pioneering research into Artificial Intelligence (AI). 'Can machines think?' he asked.[21] In posing this question he was years ahead of his time, and he is now viewed as the founding father of the controversial field of AI. He even suggested computing with a network of artificial neurons—a computer modelled on the human cortex. The phrase 'thinking computer' still strikes many as an impossible pairing, but Turing predicted that soon 'one will be able to speak of machines thinking without expecting to be contradicted'.[22] He created the world's first AI program—it played chess—and he wrote the first manifesto of Artificial Intelligence, a far-sighted report titled 'Intelligent Machinery'.

In his final years, Turing pioneered the field now called Artificial Life. He focused on the question of how growing organisms develop their form and structure. What are the underlying chemical mechanisms that produce the regular arrangement of petals on a daisy, or the intricate spirals of a fir cone, or the complex structure of the human brain? At the dawn of the information age, Turing was using the Manchester Ferranti computer to simulate growing tissue. Other people were still trying to take on board the idea that electronic computers were the new way to do office arithmetic. Today, researchers who have far more computing grunt at their disposal than Turing's Ferranti was able to muster are extending his biological investigations. Their explorations of his mathematical equations are producing leopard spots, giraffe stripes, structures reminiscent of reptile skin, corals, sponges, sea shells, fungi, and—most excitingly of all—neurons. Turing died while in the midst of his groundbreaking work on biological growth.

My account of Turing's short but brilliant life draws on many years of conversations with his closest friends and colleagues. I hope it captures something of the complex character of this shy genius, as well as describing the breadth and importance of his legacy.

2

THE UNIVERSAL TURING MACHINE

It was the Cambridge Lent term of 1935 and the tail end of winter. Cambridge's ancient spires and walled colleges looked even older in the bleak grey light. In this damp and chilly corner of England the weather was unremittingly overcast, even though the winter had been unseasonably mild. Across a courtyard beyond St John's College, the Trinity bells were striking 10 a.m. noisily from the clock tower—ten thought-shattering chimes, followed by another ten at a higher pitch, in what the poet Wordsworth called the Trinity bells' 'female' voice.[1] Max Newman, a fellow of St John's, strode energetically into the college lecture room. St John's, located a short distance away from King's College along narrow medieval streets, was said to be the second-richest college in Cambridge, after the fabulously wealthy Trinity. According to a rumour of several centuries' standing, it was possible to walk all the way from St John's as far as the other St John's College in distant Oxford without once stepping off St John's land. Newman, bespectacled, balding, and almost forty, was a rising star of British mathematics. His academic gown flapped around him as he walked. The lecture room, which was several centuries old, felt as though it might be part of an ancient cathedral or monastery. There were not very many students there. Newman's topic, the foundations of mathematics, was renowned for its difficulty. Turing sat attentively in the audience.

The grand finale of the lecture series would be an exposition of some spectacular results recently obtained by Kurt Gödel, a silent but exceptionally brilliant twenty-five-year-old mathematician at the University of Vienna.[2] Soon, in 1940, Gödel would flee from Vienna and the Nazis to the United States[3]—the Nazis, despite his various illnesses real and imagined, having declared him fit to join the military. Gödel wasn't having that; he preferred to become a refugee. The prowling German submarines made crossing the Atlantic too risky a proposition, so he escaped eastwards through Russia by the Trans-Siberian railway, and then by boat from Japan to San Francisco. He was taken in by the Princeton Institute for Advanced Study, already home to some of Europe's greatest scientists and mathematicians, among them Albert Einstein and also John von Neumann, who would later become deeply involved in the Los Alamos atomic bomb project.

In 1931, Gödel had proved that arithmetic was incomplete, and this sensational and curious fact would be the topic of Newman's final lectures. Known simply as 'Gödel's incompleteness theorem', Gödel's result remains to this day one of the most stunning discoveries ever made about mathematics. Nowadays his result is put like this: he showed that no matter how the formal rules of arithmetic are laid down, there would always be some arithmetical truths—complicated relatives of simpler truths like $2 + 2 = 4$—that *cannot* be proved by means of the rules.[4] It is a bit like discovering that your jigsaw puzzle has been deliberately manufactured with some pieces missing, or that your exotic new carpet is never going to fit into all four corners of the room simultaneously. The only way to eradicate the incompleteness appeared to be to arrange the rules so that they are actually *self-contradictory*, but that was hardly an appealing escape route.[5]

What Gödel showed is that more is *true* in mathematics than can be *proved*. His result shocked and even angered some. Mathematicians had tended to think not only that everything true *could* be proved but also that everything that matters *ought* to be proved, because only rigorous proof by transparent and obvious rules brings certainty. But Newman's lectures on this awe-inspiring topic would come in a few weeks' time. In that day's lecture, he was talking not about Gödel but about David Hilbert, a famous professor of mathematics at Göttingen, one of Germany's leading universities. Hilbert, more than forty years Gödel's senior, was virtually the pope of European mathematics. 'In mathematics,' Hilbert famously declared, 'there is no *ignorabimus*'—no *we shall not know*.[6] In 1900, in a lecture delivered in Paris, the magisterial Hilbert had set the agenda for much of 20th-century mathematics. Turing, a fidgety Cambridge graduate student, was about to prove Hilbert fundamentally wrong.

Newman was telling his audience about the idea of a 'systematic' procedure in mathematics, a concept central to Hilbert's whole approach. The well-known rules for long multiplication that we all learn at school are a good example of what mathematicians mean by a systematic procedure. A systematic procedure is simply a paper-and-pencil method that anyone can carry out, step by mechanical step, without the need for any creativity or insight. Nothing like ingenuity or intuition is required. A well-trained clerk who carries out the procedure need not even know what the procedure is for; the clerk can carry it out accurately, by following the instructions to the letter, without necessarily understanding the purpose of the procedure or how or why it works. In fact, this was not merely an abstract concept. In business, government, and research establishments, there were actually many thousands of calculating clerks carrying out systematic procedures. They did the mathematical drudgework nowadays done by electronic computers. Amusingly, these clerks were themselves called computers. At this time, a computer was not a machine at all, but a human being, a mathematical clerk who worked by rote.

Newman informed his audience that the basic feature of all these systematic mathematical procedures is that a *machine* can do them. At that time it was a novel way of putting the idea, and Newman's words fired Turing's imagination. Many years later, reminiscing about Turing's invention of the universal machine, Newman said: 'I believe it all started because he attended a lecture of mine on the foundations of mathematics and logic.'[7] The suggestion that a machine could carry out systematic procedures, Newman explained, inspired Turing to 'try and say what one would mean by a perfectly general computing machine'. What Turing heard in Newman's lecture fascinated him so greatly that it came to dominate his working life for many months. He thought furiously.

Characteristically, he doesn't seem to have discussed his ideas much with others, or told people what he was thinking about—not even Newman. This was *his* problem, and he didn't feel any need to talk about it.

One day at dinner at High Table in King's, another fellow of the college, Richard Braithwaite, managed to get Turing talking about what he was working on. Braithwaite said thoughtfully that he could see connections with what Gödel had shown. But he found Turing unresponsive, and he later wrote in a letter of 'Turing's complete ignorance of Gödel's work'.[8] Braithwaite added: 'I consider I played some part in drawing Turing's attention to the relation of his work to Gödel's.' Maybe Turing had been bitten so deeply by the machine bug that he had never even bothered to turn up to Newman's subsequent lectures on Gödel. Or perhaps it was an example of what Newman later called, rather snippily, 'a defect of his qualities', namely that 'he found it hard to use the work of others, preferring to work things out for himself'.[9] Gödel certainly had no such defect, and was unstinting in his praise for what Turing achieved during his year of deep thought. Gödel generously said that Turing brought him 'to the right perspective'.[10] Using Turing's discoveries, he was able to extend the scope of his incompleteness theorem to cover *all* formal mathematical systems containing some basic arithmetic.[11] Incompleteness was virtually *everywhere* in mathematics.

Once Turing was good and ready, towards the end of April 1936, he called in on Newman and gave him a lengthy draft of 'On Computable Numbers'.[12] Newman must have got a shock when he read it. Turing had invented a universal machine. This idealized machine consisted of a limitless memory—an endless paper tape—and a 'scanner' that moved backwards and forwards along the tape, reading what it found printed there, and in turn printing further letters and numbers on the tape. The machine's program, and whatever data it needed for the computation, were printed on the tape before the computation started. By placing different programs on the memory tape, the operator could make the machine carry out *any* procedure that a human computer could carry out. That is why Turing called the machine *universal*.

A 'computing machine', as the term was used in those days, was a machine capable of doing work normally done by a human computer, and Turing referred to his invention as the *universal computing machine*—although it soon became known simply as the 'universal Turing machine'. In the now vast literature about his machine, its name is sometimes misprinted as the 'Turning' machine, or the 'Türing' machine, and even the universal 'touring' machine. It was the modern computer in essential outline, the single slab of hardware that, by making use of programs stored in its memory, could effortlessly change itself from a tool dedicated to one task into a tool for a completely different task—from calculator to word processor to chess opponent, for example.

The universal Turing machine was, in fact, a highly abstract idealization of a human computer. But it was also something utterly new, a machine of unsuspected versatility. Moreover, Turing had daringly introduced concepts smelling of *engineering* into a discussion of the most fundamental parts of mathematics. Newman later wrote: 'It is difficult to-day to realize how bold an innovation it was to introduce talk about paper tapes and patterns punched in them, into discussions of the foundations of mathematics.'[13] The appendix at the end of this book describes a very simple Turing machine—in fact, one of Turing's own examples from 1936—complete with paper tape, read–write scanner, and Turing's first published computer program.

For Turing, engrossed in his attack on Hilbert's pontifical opinions about the nature of mathematics, the universal computing machine was one major step on the road that led ultimately to Hilbert's refutation. By reasoning about the behaviour of the universal machine, Turing was able to show that there are well-defined mathematical problems that the universal machine *cannot solve*. This result was as astounding as Gödel's incompleteness theorem. As we would express it nowadays, Turing had shown that there are well-defined mathematical problems, admitting of a straightforward yes-or-no answer, that no finite computing machine can possibly solve—not even if the computer is given unlimited blank memory and is able to continue computing forever. Exuberant computer programmers sometimes think that computers can solve any mathematical problem, just so long as the problem is stated precisely enough to enable a suitable program to be written. But Turing's result shows that this optimism is unfounded.

Turing gave several examples of well-defined mathematical problems that cannot be solved by a finite computing machine.[14] One of these is called the *printing problem*. The problem is this: to work out about any given Turing machine program whether or not running the program will cause the Turing machine ever to print '0' on its tape.[15] Many programs will print a zero at some point, whereas others never do so. In principle, it is possible to tell which of these is the case without even running the Turing machine, just by reasoning about the nature of the program. To be able to solve the printing problem is to be able to say, after some finite amount of reasoning, which is the correct alternative—and, moreover, to give the correct answer no matter what Turing machine program is being investigated. Remarkably, no computer can possibly solve this simple-looking problem.

Between them, Gödel and Turing delivered a double whammy from which Hilbert's account of the nature of mathematics never recovered. Gödel's incompleteness result had dealt the first blow to Hilbert's view that mathematics is essentially about *proof*. Five years later, Turing sawed another leg off Hilbert's teetering throne. Gödel's attack had focused on a very specific system of arithmetical rules, while Turing attacked on a much broader front, using the universal machine as his weapon. By making use of the fact that his machine is capable of carrying out any and every systematic procedure—a proposition nowadays known simply as 'Turing's Thesis'—he was able to establish results that are more general than Gödel's.[16] Turing had developed the tools required to redraw the map of mathematics, pinpointing mathematical problems that, like the printing problem, are so difficult as to be incapable of being solved by any systematic procedure.[17]

Hilbert thought there must be a single supreme systematic procedure for settling truth or falsehood in mathematics. Equipped with this procedure—'this new philosopher's stone', Newman called it, in a mocking allusion to the mythical substance that enabled alchemists to turn lead into gold[18]—anyone would be able to tell, of any given mathematical statement, and without any need for insight, intuition, or creativity, whether the statement is true or false. Hilbert said that the existence of a supreme systematic procedure was required in order to place the whole of mathematics 'on a concrete foundation on which everyone can agree'.[19] Gödel's work had shaken belief in the existence of a supreme systematic procedure, and now Turing produced a completely convincing argument that no supreme procedure could exist. If it did exist, then the universal Turing machine could carry it out, since the universal machine can carry out every systematic procedure. And then, equipped with the new philosopher's stone, the universal Turing machine would be able to solve all yes–no mathematical problems. Yet Turing had shown beyond any shadow of doubt that the universal machine *cannot* solve all yes–no mathematical problems. It follows inexorably that Hilbert's supreme systematic procedure cannot exist.

Although correcting Hilbert was important to Turing at the time, from a modern standpoint this aspect of his work was really little more than a side story when compared with his wonderful invention of the universal computing machine. He was interested right from the start in actually building a universal machine[20] but he knew of no suitable technology. In the Victorian era, the far-sighted Charles Babbage had dreamed of building a gigantic all-purpose digital calculating machine, an 'Engine' he called it, that could take over the work of hundreds of human calculators (see Fig. 3). If Turing is the father of the modern computer, then Babbage is undoubtedly its grandfather.[21] A small model of Babbage's ambitious 'Analytical Engine' was completed just before his death, but the full machine was never built.[22] According to Babbage's design, the Analytical Engine would be fed instructions punched into cards connected together with ribbons—an idea that Babbage borrowed from the Jacquard automatic weaving loom. Although the Analytical Engine was designed to store data in its internal memory (which Babbage called simply the 'Store'), there was no provision for also storing the instructions themselves. Babbage's machine lacked Turing's stored-program set-up, the essential feature of modern computers. As for how Babbage planned to

Figure 3. Part of Babbage's Difference Engine

Credit: © Science Museum/Science & Society Picture Library – All rights reserved

construct his machine, he lived in the railway age, and he intended to build his calculating engines from the kinds of mechanical components that were used in railway engines and other Victorian industrial machinery: brass gearwheels, rods, ratchets, pinions, and so forth.

Babbage's steam railway technology was of no use at all to Turing, even though small special-purpose computing machines had recently been built successfully from Babbage-like mechanical components. One was the analogue Differential Analyser, completed at Massachusetts Institute of Technology (MIT) in 1931.[23] This computer required a skilled mechanic equipped with a lead hammer to 'program' it for each new job! Turing, on the other hand, needed a form of technology that was capable of operating at very high speed, and that would enable him to store the instructions and the data in a reasonably compact volume. Mechanical cogwheels were just not up to the job.

In 1936 the leading technology for building electrical information-processing devices, such as telephone switchboards and equipment for sorting punched cards, was the electromechanical *relay*. This was a small electrically driven switch, consisting of a metal rod that was moved by an electromagnet and a spring. As the rod moved in one direction it completed an electrical circuit, and when it sprang back in the opposite direction the circuit was broken again. Relays were large, slow, clunky, and none too reliable. Turing joked that a universal Turing machine built out of relays would need to be about the size of the Albert Hall, a large building in central London.[24] It was not until during the war, when they were working as codebreakers at Bletchley Park, that Turing and Newman learned how a universal Turing machine could be built. The secret was electronics. Electronic 'valves', as the British called them—they are known as 'vacuum tubes' in the United States—operated very many times faster than relays, because the only moving part was a beam of electrons. The two codebreakers became gripped by the dream of building a miraculously fast *electronic* universal computing machine.

In the spring of 1936, however, Turing's main focus was on getting an academic paper into print detailing his mathematical results. He titled this 'On Computable Numbers, with an Application to the Entscheidungsproblem'. Publication in a professional journal was the first step to getting his new ideas noticed and understood. Unpublished papers seldom have any impact—and even once published, a paper might receive scant attention—but Turing knew that publication was necessary if there was to be any chance of his discoveries influencing the mathematical world at large. There was a difficulty, however. It arose because, as Turing's lengthy title indicated, he had chosen to focus on what Hilbert called the *Entscheidungsproblem*. This German term translates into English along the lines of 'the problem of mechanical decidability'.

Newman had lectured on this tricky problem at St John's, and Turing confronted it head-on in his research. In 1939 Gödel gave a rather dramatic account of what Turing showed about the *Entscheidungsproblem*. This was during some introductory logic lectures that Gödel gave while visiting the University of Notre Dame, near Chicago.[25] He spoke of an imaginary machine with a crank handle. This machine was something like a typewriter, he said, and you could type mathematical formulae into it. If you typed a formula that was expressed in the notation of what he called the 'calculus of propositions'—an extremely simple part of mathematics—and then turned the crank handle once, the machine would ring its bell if the formula is provable in the calculus of propositions, and would remain silent if the formula is not provable. That is to say, the machine is able to 'decide' whether the formula is a provable one or not. What Turing had shown in his onslaught on the *Entscheidungsproblem* was that if the formulae that were being considered are permitted to come from regions of mathematics lying beyond the simple calculus of propositions, then it is impossible to build any finite computing machine for deciding whether formulae are provable or not.[26] It was another nail in the coffin for Hilbert's view, since he and his followers believed that there should be a systematic procedure for deciding all mathematics.[27] In a final dramatic flourish, Gödel added that Turing's result showed that 'the human mind will never be able to be replaced by a machine'—an intriguing claim that I return to in Chapter 11.

The trouble was that, just as Turing was getting ready to send his manuscript off to the editor of a journal, a copy of a recently published paper by an American logician named Alonzo Church had arrived in Cambridge.[28] Church, a few years older than Turing, was a Young Turk in the mathematics department at Princeton University, and had spent six months studying with Hilbert's group in Göttingen at the end of the 1920s.[29] An examination of Church's brief two pages of mathematical symbols revealed the bitter fact that he had proved and published the same result as Turing's on the *Entscheidungsproblem*. Scooped! It is one of the worst things that can happen to a researcher. True, Church's publication contained nothing like the universal Turing machine and the stored-program concept, but nevertheless there was significant overlap with Turing's manuscript, and the academic rules dictate that once someone has published a mathematical result, no one else shall publish it unless there are some important differences or new insights. Fortunately, Turing had the dynamic Newman on hand to advise him. It was clear to Newman that Turing's paper had a significance going far beyond its narrow application to the *Entscheidungsproblem*.[30] He advised Turing to publish, and even wrote to the editor at the London Mathematical Society, saying that Church's prior publication should not be allowed to stand in the way of Turing's work appearing in the Society's journal.[31] Newman prevailed, as he usually did, and Turing's magnum opus was published at the end of 1936.[32]

Church's approach had not persuaded Gödel, who saw a gap in the argument. Church had failed to argue convincingly that there was *no* possible way of building the decision machine, the typewriter plus crank as Gödel figuratively described it. With the typical bluntness of academics, Gödel told Church that his technical approach was 'thoroughly unsatisfactory' (as Church related in a letter).[33] But when Gödel read Turing's paper, he saw that Turing had managed to supply what Church had not. Turing's 'definition of mechanical computability' was 'most satisfactory', Gödel wrote approvingly, and put matters 'beyond any doubt'.[34]

However, there were some small mistakes in Turing's paper.[35] This is not unknown with mathematical papers of such complexity, and Turing's natural carelessness certainly did not help. He published a correction a few months later, but some minor errors still lay buried. After the war, Donald Davies, Turing's bright young assistant at the National Physical Laboratory in London, discovered these mistakes—'bad programming errors', Davies called them. The young scientist naively thought Turing would be pleased to hear about them.[36] 'I went along to tell him and I was rather cock-a-hoop,' Davies remembered. Turing became angry, however: 'he was very annoyed,' Davies recounted imperturbably, 'and pointed out furiously that really it didn't matter, the thing was right in principle.' This was a character trait that Turing's family knew well.

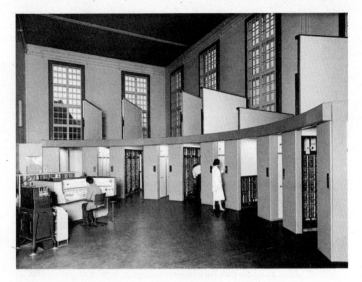

Figure 4. Turing's ACE (Automatic Computing Engine)
Credit: National Physical Laboratory – © Crown copyright

'What made him very angry indeed was to be contradicted on scientific points,' his mother remarked.[37] Sometimes he had to leave the room and walk off his bad mood.

With his paper accepted for publication, it was time for Turing to spread his wings. He chose America, the world's dynamic new player in mathematics and science. He had wanted to visit Princeton University since the previous year, and now that he had discovered Church's existence it made even more sense to go there.[38] Princeton, with its neo-Gothic stone buildings and sheltered quadrangles, was a hothouse world inhabited by some of the planet's greatest mathematicians—a dream-like oasis at the southern fringes of New Jersey's deadening urban sprawl. There were possibilities for joint mathematical work with Church. Church was well aware of Turing, and was responsible for coining the term 'Turing machine' for Turing's invention.[39] Turing packed his bags and left cloistered Cambridge for the land of the free.

AMERICA, MATHEMATICS, HITLER

Turing left the English port of Southampton for America in September 1936, carrying an ancient sextant he had picked up in a second-hand shop in London's Farringdon Road.[1] He travelled on the steamer *Berengaria*, operated by the Cunard White Star line. Turing found himself aboard a vast ship, topped by three gigantic red-and-black funnels, and with a crew of over 1,000 to look after the nearly 5,000 passengers.[2] This floating colossus had room for twice as many people as White Star's earlier flagship, the ill-fated *Titanic*. Like most student travellers, Turing had purchased the cheapest possible ticket, and spent the voyage in 'steerage', the most uncomfortable class of accommodation.

Berengaria's first-class cabins and saloons were modelled on London's most expensive hotels but Turing's cabin in steerage was cramped, with nowhere to put anything.[3] He said peevishly that the cabin steward was 'remarkably lax, and also a bit disagreeable'. Turing didn't feel at home among the fourth-class passengers, and wrote snobbishly in a shipboard letter: 'The mass of canaille [riff-raff] with which one is herded can easily be ignored.' Travelling in discomfort seems to have brought out the worst in him and he condemned his American fellow passengers as 'the most insufferable and insensitive creatures'—although he added hopefully that Americans 'may not all be like that'. The sextant didn't work out very well either, with the constant vibration of the ship's four giant engines preventing him from taking accurate readings of the stars. His uninspiring journey dragged on for almost a week before *Berengaria* tied up at New York's passenger terminal.

'Passing the immigration officers involved waiting in a queue for over two hours with screaming children round me,' Turing grumbled.[4] 'Then,' he continued, 'after getting through the customs I had to go through the ceremony of initiation to the U.S.A., consisting of being swindled by a taxi driver.' In England, complaining is used as a social lubricant, and Turing was yet to learn that this works less well in America. 'These Americans have various peculiarities in conversation which catch the ear somehow,' he whinged. 'Whenever you thank them for any thing they say "You're welcome", I rather liked it at first, thinking that I was welcome, but now I find it comes back like a ball thrown against a wall, and become positively apprehensive.'

It was not a bad time to be in the United States. With the great depression in its final twitches, the economy was still up and down, but things were improving. Americans exuded optimism.[5] Their country was strong and going places. San Francisco's Golden Gate Bridge opened in May 1937, the Fair Labor Act brought in a better deal for workers, and energy-packed tweenie Shirley Temple dominated the movies—the young nation was powering towards a vigorous future of prosperity for all. Not long after Turing arrived, Franklin D. Roosevelt won a landslide election victory with his New Deal policies. 'Tonight is the evening of election day,' Turing wrote, 'and all results are coming out over the wireless ("radio" they say in the native language).'[6] He added drolly: 'My method of getting the results is to go to bed and read them in the paper next morning.' Despite his us-and-them jokes, Turing probably felt quite comfortable in the United States. He never really fitted in at home—Newman's wife, Lyn, said in her amusing way that Turing's 'scattered efforts to appear at home in the upper middle class circles into which he was born stand out as particularly unsuccessful'.[7] In America he was the permanent foreigner, more or less absolved from any expectation to fit in.

Princeton did not disappoint him. 'The mathematics department here comes fully up to expectations,' he said.[8] 'There is a great number of the most distinguished mathematicians here. J. v. Neumann, Weyl, Courant,

Figure 5. Turing in a rocking chair

Credit: King's College Library, Cambridge

Hardy, Einstein, Lefschetz, as well as hosts of smaller fry.' Church was a careful and ponderous man—a bit dull, some said. He liked Turing's 'On Computable Numbers' and took the young Englishman under his wing. 'I get on with him very well,' Turing wrote cheerfully. Things soon took a turn for the worse on the social front, though. Church invited him round for dinner one evening, but afterwards Turing complained. 'Considering that the guests were all university people I found the conversation rather disappointing.'[9] 'They seem, from what I can remember of it, to have discussed nothing but the different states that they came from,' he said critically, adding: 'Description of travel and places bores me intensely.' Also he discovered something about the Church family that he would probably rather not have known. 'I had a nasty shock when I got into Church's house,' he recounted. Both Church and his father suffered from blindness in one eye. 'Any hereditary defects of that kind give me the shudders,' Turing said squeamishly. It was all of a piece with his tendency to become nauseous if the conversation turned to injury or surgical operations.[10] A relationship with Church seems never to have really gelled.

Within a year Newman himself followed Turing to Princeton. He arrived with Lyn and his two boys in September 1937, to spend the university autumn term thinking and networking. 'Max has no job here,' Lyn explained tongue in cheek to her parents.[11] 'He simply sits at home doing anything he likes.' 'This is what the Institute of Advanced Studies exists for,' she said coolly. During his stay at Princeton, Newman discovered what he thought was a proof of Poincaré's famous conjecture in topology, and he was confident enough of the importance of his work to arrange a series of four seminars about it. During these he presented his new proof to the assembled Princeton mathematics professoriate. But he later discovered a terrible flaw in his argument. Fortunately, none of the Princeton mathematicians had noticed the problem, saving Newman considerable embarrassment, but it was still a bitter blow. Lyn woke in the night, recalling half asleep that something dreadful had happened. Was it that one of her children had died? When she remembered that Max's proof had failed, it seemed even worse, she said wryly.[12]

The international situation grew darker by the month, although most Americans felt isolated from the distant events in Europe and the East. As if it were a symbol of all that would soon come, the gigantic passenger airship *Hindenburg*—with swastikas emblazoned on its tail—fell flaming from the sky at Lakehurst in New Jersey, just forty-five miles from Princeton. Also in 1937, the Japanese Imperial Army overran Shanghai and then Nanking, at that time China's capital. General Franco's German tanks poured into Spanish cities loyal to the left-wing Republic. Italian planes bombed Barcelona, and German aircraft destroyed the northern Spanish town of Guernica. The aerial bombing was remote destruction on a seemingly incomprehensible scale, and it prompted Picasso's tormented painting, *Guernica*. Yet the destruction was as nothing when compared to what the future held.

All across Europe, armaments were being manufactured and stockpiled. Each year a vast and increasing crowd of ordinary German people attended the Nazi rally at Nuremburg, where Hitler's oratory held them in thrall. Amid great pomp and ceremony, the German Führer and Italy's fascist leader Benito Mussolini met for the first time, on the platform at Munich railway station. In America, as Boris Karloff chilled the blood of millions in *Frankenstein*, Admiral Claude C. Block took command of the Navy, saying quietly, 'I wish to emphasize that our only justification for being here is to be ready to fight.'[13] Roosevelt's great rival, Herbert Hoover, told American audiences of turmoil all over Europe. 'Free speech, free press, free worship—our great American ideals have died out of three quarters of the population of Europe—and they are gripped with fear,' he intoned in his expressionless way. He went on: 'But we in America must preserve inflexibly our determination that we will not be involved in other people's wars and other people's troubles.'[14]

Britain's monarchy was also in turmoil. The story was all over the American papers for some time before it was allowed to break in Britain. Turing took a keen interest, and sent press cuttings to his mother in England. Edward VIII was in the process of throwing aside the British crown to marry the woman he loved, the divorced Baltimore belle Wallis Simpson. Whatever his failings might have been, Edward was someone who held up his fingers to convention, and this struck a chord with Turing. 'I am horrified at the way people are trying to interfere with the King's marriage,' he said.[15] 'It may be that the King should not marry Mrs Simpson, but it is his private concern.' Turing joked: 'I should tolerate no interference by bishops myself and I don't see that the King need either.'

The sticking point was that the Church of England opposed remarriage after divorce, and the king was duty bound to uphold the principles of the Church. For Edward, the pull of love exceeded the pull of duty. Turing felt divided on the question of whether Edward should be permitted to marry Mrs Simpson while remaining king. 'At first I was wholly in favour of the King retaining the throne and marrying Mrs Simpson, and if this were the only issue it would still be my opinion,' he explained.[16] But there were other matters at stake. 'It appears that the King was extremely lax about state documents leaving them about and letting Mrs Simpson and friends see them,' Turing said. 'There had been distressing leakages. Also one or two other things of same character, but this is the one I mind about most.' Turing's security-mindedness and his ingrained patriotism would soon find their natural home when he entered the secret world of signals intelligence. His patriotism did not, however, stretch as far as unconditional respect for the Archbishop of Canterbury, primate of the Church of England. 'I consider his behaviour disgraceful,' Turing fumed. 'He waited until Edward was safely out of the way and then unloaded a whole lot of quite uncalled-for abuse.'[17] 'He didn't dare do it whilst Edward was King.' Turing railed. 'Further he had no objections to the King having Mrs Simpson as a mistress, but marry her, that wouldn't do at all.' As the Royal soap opera drew to its epic conclusion, Turing sympathized with the King, saying: 'I am sorry that Edward VIII has been bounced into abdicating.' 'I respect Edward for his courage,' he said. Courage was one of the mainsprings of Turing's own life.

In 1937 Turing started work on what quickly developed into his main Princeton project. The focus was what mathematicians call *intuition*. Most people are able to see by intuition that simple geometrical propositions are true, such as the proposition that a straight line and a circle can cross no more than twice. You probably don't need to go through a train of reasoning in order to convince yourself that this is true—it's one of those things that many people can just *see* to be true. 'The activity of the intuition,' Turing explained, 'consists in making spontaneous judgements which are not the result of conscious trains of reasoning.'[18] The more skilled the mathematician, the greater is his or her ability to apprehend truths by intuition.

Hilbert distrusted intuition. He believed that mathematics should proceed 'according to formulable rules that are completely definite'.[19] Intuition was one of the 'mysterious arts' that he thought should be eliminated from modern mathematics.[20] In Hilbert's brave new mathematical world, *systematic procedure* would replace arcane intuition. He dreamed of the 'concrete foundation on which everyone can agree', the single finite system of completely definite formal rules that any human computer could use to prove any and every true mathematical statement—without any need whatever for intuition. Such a foundation would free mathematics from dark arts. Thanks to Turing and Gödel, though, it was now clear that Hilbert's dreamed-of foundation was a figment. No matter which systematic procedure is picked, there will always be statements that mathematicians can see intuitively to be true but which cannot be shown by using the rules. Intuition cannot be eliminated as Hilbert thought.[21]

The idea that came to preoccupy Turing at Princeton was that Hilbert and his followers might be happy enough to settle for the strict *control* of intuition rather than its wholesale elimination. Hilbert had spoken in 1926 of wanting mathematics to be '*kontrolliert*'—controlled.[22] Intuition could be controlled by forbidding its use except in very special circumstances—a bit like forbidding the remarriage of divorcees except to a member of the royal family. Turing saw that in this way it might even be possible to circumvent Gödel's incompleteness theorem by using what he called 'non-constructive' logical systems, in which 'not all the steps in a proof are mechanical, some being intuitive'.[23] So a new form of Hilbert's philosophy was poised to rise from the ashes of the old. Turing leapt forward to slay this phoenix before it had time to take to the air. By extending the arguments of 'On Computable Numbers', he showed that mathematics is just too gloriously unruly for it to be possible to limit the role of intuition like this.

These were the ideas that he wrote up for his Princeton PhD thesis. 'Should have it done by about Christmas,' he said breezily in the autumn of 1937.[24] In this research Turing extended the concept of the mechanical into regions that not even the universal Turing machine was capable of reaching.[25] Unlike 'On Computable Numbers', his PhD thesis, which is off-puttingly titled 'Systems of Logic Based on Ordinals'—and a very difficult read[26]—has never received the attention that it deserves. This may be about to change. The machines that Turing defined in his thesis, which he teasingly called 'oracle machines', are in effect mathematical models of computers, such as laptops or smartphones, that are communicating with an external database, such as the World Wide Web. Emphasizing the modern relevance of this far-sighted mathematical work by Turing, logician Robert Soare said recently that oracle machines provide a mathematical theory for the 'online and interactive computing used in real world computation'.[27] Oracle machines may similarly prove a useful model of the human brain.[28]

Turing's PhD thesis was accepted at the beginning of May 1938, a great event for any young researcher.[29] His time at Princeton had not quite been all work and no play. American hockey was a great discovery, and his tennis addiction kept him busy too, but on the unaccustomed dry earth courts popular in the United States. 'Easier on the feet (and probably on the pocket) than our hard courts, but not very quick at recovering from showers,' he said.[30] He travelled a bit, too, to Washington, Virginia, and South Carolina, and he pottered about New York, exploring the subway and visiting the Planetarium. He was probably surprised by the openness of downtown New York's gay bars and clubs. In Washington he visited the Senate. 'They seemed very informal,' he said. 'There were only six or eight of them present and few of them seemed to be attending.'[31]

His father, Julius, told him that he should find a job in the United States, but with war brewing he was keen to get home. In the summer of 1938 the great John von Neumann did offer him a job as his assistant, at $1,500 a year—roughly the same amount as his King's fellowship—but Turing declined.[32] It would have been a useful start if he had had any thoughts of remaining in America. Von Neumann, a Hungarian emigré, was one of the leading lights of international mathematics, and had himself assisted Hilbert in Göttingen when about Turing's age.[33] Perpetually clad in a business suit, he was an affable, fun-loving party person, and he and his wife Klari held open house for the Princeton intelligentsia. Von Neumann would in any event be an important figure in Turing's future, telling the US electrical engineering community about the universal machine and the stored-program concept. Newman played a similar role in Britain. He and von Neumann were in some ways evenly matched: outstanding mathematicians, both of them movers and shakers, charming and with a tendency to be absent-minded. Von Neumann had never really mastered the automobile, and was often to be seen accelerating along Princeton's streets in bottom gear, with the engine revving wildly. Once he got up to speed, he drove too fast along the centre of the street, dodging fearlessly through the traffic.[34] Newman, fast and nimble in his movements, 'would move the gear lever with a flourish; on a quiet road he preferred to drive in the middle, avoiding oncoming traffic with a quick flick of the steering wheel, as his passengers prepared for death,' his son William recounted. A favourite photograph of von Neumann shows him with a group of horse riders in the American desert. Dressed in his three-piece business suit, he has managed to mount his horse the wrong way round, and faces backwards.

When Turing arrived back in England, later in the summer of 1938, all the talk was of war. As the summer months drew to a close, people began queuing for gas masks at government distribution centres, and there were plans to evacuate children from London. Attempting to avert armed struggle, British prime minister Neville Chamberlain visited Hitler in Munich. Before departing for Germany, he said on British radio: 'How horrible, fantastic, incredible it is that we should be digging trenches and trying on gas masks here because of a quarrel in a far-away country between people of whom we know nothing.'[35] As in America, there was little enthusiasm in Britain for getting pulled into a fight in distant lands. Former king Edward said later: 'I thought that the rest of us could be fence-sitters while the Nazis and the Reds slogged it out.'[36] In Munich, Chamberlain agreed to Germany's seizing part of Czechoslovakia, believing that he could secure peace between Britain and Germany by appeasing Hitler's territorial ambitions. He returned to London to cheering crowds, and newspaper headlines that shouted 'PEACE' in letters several inches high.[37] A bold statement printed right across the front page of the *Daily Express* read: 'Britain will not be involved in a European war this year, or next year either.' From a first-floor window at 10 Downing Street, Chamberlain addressed the large crowds below. 'I believe it is peace for our time,' he told them.[38] The Munich agreement did bring peace, but not for long. Normal life continued for another eleven months.

The start of 1939 found Turing lecturing on mathematical logic at King's, his first experience of teaching. 'My lectures are going off rather well,' he told his mother.[39] He said: 'There are 14 people coming to them at present,' continuing pessimistically: 'No doubt the attendance will drop off as the term advances.' At the same time, Turing was himself attending a course of lectures on the foundations of mathematics given by the philosopher Ludwig Wittgenstein. Wittgenstein presented Turing with a new angle on mathematics, utterly different from his own research. A native of Vienna, Wittgenstein had settled in Cambridge in 1929. One of the 20th century's greatest philosophical minds, he is famous for his pithy and suggestive remarks, such as: 'The limits of my language mean the limits of my world,' and 'If a lion could talk, we could not understand him.'[40] Wittgenstein's lectures—really just freewheeling discussions with his small audience—were held in sumptuous Trinity College, next door to St John's. Wittgenstein told his class: 'Don't treat your commonsense like an umbrella. When you come into the room to philosophize, don't leave it outside but bring it in with you.'[41] His teaching style was distinctive and eccentric. 'What is your aim in philosophy?' he asked rhetorically, answering: 'To show the fly the way out of the fly-bottle.'[42] In one lecture he quoted Hilbert's famous remark: 'No one is going to turn us out of the paradise which Cantor has created.' Wittgenstein said to Turing and the others, 'I wouldn't dream of trying to drive anyone out of this paradise.' 'I would try to do something quite different,' he went on. 'I would try to show you that it is not a paradise—so that you'll leave of your own accord.'

There was an edginess to Wittgenstein's lectures. He would exclaim: 'But I am muddled now and cannot get clear at the moment what I want to say about this,' and 'I am too stupid to begin.' Often the lectures consisted of to-and-fro discussion between Turing and Wittgenstein, and Turing was the class member that Wittgenstein most seemed to want to engage with. One day he announced to the class at large, 'it is no good my getting the rest to agree to something that Turing would not agree to'. In fact, the two men seldom agreed, although Wittgenstein reassured his class: 'Turing doesn't object to anything I say. He agrees with every word. He objects to the idea he thinks underlies it. He thinks we're undermining mathematics, introducing Bolshevism into mathematics. But not at all.' Turing's reply, if he bothered to make one, was not recorded. On another occasion, Turing said to Wittgenstein politely, 'I see your point.' 'I have no point,' Wittgenstein fired back. The discussion was often obscure, even Zen-like. At one stage Wittgenstein began discussing the claim, 'Turing has an invisible telephone.'

Half a dozen of Wittgenstein's lectures concerned the danger of contradictions in mathematics—a topic that had been catapulted into the limelight in 1901 when Bertrand Russell, another Trinity College philosopher, uncovered a contradiction in the theory of classes, one of the most fundamental branches of mathematics. Wittgenstein suggested to his audience that the existence of contradictions in mathematics need not be as harmful as is usually supposed. Turing responded: 'The real harm will not come in unless there is an application, in which case a bridge may fall down or something of that sort.' 'But nothing has ever gone wrong that way yet,' Wittgenstein observed gently. It was an important exchange, that cut right to the heart of the matter. What seemed to many of those working in the foundations of mathematics to be a terrible danger, a danger that could ultimately lead to real damage in the world beyond mathematics, turns out in practice to be entirely innocuous, Wittgenstein believed.

Another groundbreaking sequence of lectures concerned the possibility of *experimental* mathematics. Wittgenstein began the discussion: 'Sometimes it seems as though mathematical discoveries are made by performing what one might call a mathematical experiment.' Turing endorsed the idea of mathematical experiments, but Wittgenstein disagreed, saying that mathematics is 'aloof from experiments—it is petrified'. 'I think that if I could make myself quite clear,' he said, 'then Turing would give up saying that in mathematics we make experiments.' Fortunately, Wittgenstein never did make himself clear enough, and after the war Turing went on to pioneer computer-assisted experimental mathematics at the console of the Manchester computer.

While discussing the nature and foundations of mathematics with Wittgenstein, Turing was also settling down to some seriously hush-hush applied mathematics, throwing his weight now not against Hilbert and the Göttingen School but against Germany's military codes. His first recorded interest in codes was at Princeton in 1936, when he remarked that he had found the answer to the question, 'What is the most general kind of code or cipher possible?'[43] He constructed a number of codes at Princeton, saying 'One of them is pretty well impossible to decode without the key and very quick to encode.' He remarked flippantly, 'I expect I could sell them to H. M. Government for quite a substantial sum, but am rather doubtful about the morality of such things.'

By the end of 1937, as Hitler 'Aryanized' Germany and established the first concentration camps, Turing's moral doubts seem to have dissolved. During his final months in Princeton he designed and partially constructed a relay-based electrical cipher machine. In some respects this resembled the German 'Tunny' cipher machine that he would attack at Bletchley Park in 1942. Tunny, described in Chapter 6, could have been unbreakable if the Germans had used it properly, but Turing and his fellow codebreakers were able to blow it wide open. In both Tunny and in Turing's cipher system, words were represented in the form of binary numbers, as in modern computers. Turing proposed issuing users of his system with a 'dictionary' that listed a number corresponding to each word.[44] Full details of Turing's cipher machine have not survived; probably it was like Tunny in that, once a message had been converted into numbers, the machine encrypted it by *compounding* the message's numbers with other numbers.[45] These were from a stream of numbers known as the 'secret key'. We do not know what method Turing had in mind for creating the secret key. The Tunny machine's engineers used an elaborate system of twelve rotating 'wheels' to produce an ever-changing stream of random-seeming binary numbers.

Once Turing was back in Cambridge, His Majesty's Foreign Office recruited him to work part-time on codes and ciphers. As the last few months of peace ticked by in 1939, Turing was up to his elbows in secret Enigma materials.[46] Behind firmly closed doors in King's, and quite alone apart from the glassy, brown-eyed stare of his studious-looking teddy bear Porgy, Turing made his first explorations of the cipher system that would rule the next years of his life.[47]

Hitler, *Time Magazine*'s 'Man of the Year' for 1938, invaded Poland a few weeks before the first anniversary of the Munich agreement, and Chamberlain finally abandoned his efforts to maintain peaceful relations with Germany. Millions of people sat or stood in their living rooms on a Sunday morning early in September 1939, listening to the crackle and boom of Chamberlain's emergency broadcast. 'This country is at war with Germany,' he announced. He told his listeners, in his hypnotically rhythmic voice, 'The situation in which no word given by Germany's ruler could be trusted, and no people or country could feel itself safe, had become intolerable.' In Washington, President Roosevelt, raccoon-eyed with exhaustion, addressed America. 'Let no man or woman thoughtlessly or falsely talk of sending American armies to European fields,' he exclaimed wearily.[48] 'I hope the United States will keep out of this war,' he said—leaving the door slightly ajar to uncertainty.

DI–DI–DI–DAH—ENIGMA CALLING

During the Second World War, Germany's army, air force, and navy transmitted many thousands of coded messages each day. These ranged from top-level signals, such as detailed situation reports prepared by generals at the battle fronts, and orders signed by Hitler himself, down to the important minutiae of war like weather reports and inventories of the contents of supply ships. Thanks to Turing and his fellow codebreakers, much of this information ended up in Allied hands—sometimes within an hour or two of its being transmitted. The faster the messages could be broken, the fresher the intelligence that they contained, and on at least one occasion an intercepted Enigma message's English translation was being read at the British Admiralty less than fifteen minutes after the Germans had transmitted it.[1]

Some historians estimate that this massive codebreaking operation—especially the breaking of U-boat Enigma, in which Turing played the leading role—shortened the war in Europe by as much as two to four years.[2] If Turing and his group had not weakened the U-boats' hold on the North Atlantic, the 1944 Allied invasion of Europe (the D-Day landings) could have been delayed, perhaps by about a year or even longer, since the North Atlantic was the route that ammunition, fuel, food, and troops had to travel in order to reach Britain from America. Harry Hinsley, a member of the small, tight-knit team that battled against Naval Enigma, and who later became the official historian of British intelligence, has underlined the significance of the U-boat defeat.[3] Any delay in the timing of the invasion, even a delay of substantially less than a year, would have put Hitler in a stronger position to withstand the Allied assault, Hinsley points out. The fortification of the French coastline would have been even more formidable, huge Panzer armies would have been moved into place ready to push the invaders back into the sea—or, if that failed, then to prevent them from crossing the Rhine into Germany—and large numbers of rocket-propelled V2 missiles would have been raining down on southern England, wreaking havoc at the ports and airfields tasked to support the invading troops. In the actual course of events, it took the Allied armies a year to fight their way from the French coast to Berlin; but in a scenario in which the invasion was delayed, giving Hitler more time to prepare his defences, the struggle to reach Berlin might have taken twice as long. At a conservative estimate, each year of the fighting in Europe brought on average about seven million deaths, so the significance of Turing's contribution can be roughly quantified in terms of the number of additional lives that might have been lost if he had not achieved what he did. If U-boat Enigma had not been broken, and the war had continued for another two to three years, a further fourteen to twenty-one million people might have been killed. Of course, even in a counterfactual scenario in which Turing was not able to break U-boat Enigma, the war might still have ended in 1945 because of some other occurrence, also contrary to fact, such as the dropping of a nuclear weapon on Berlin. Nevertheless, these colossal numbers of lives do convey a sense of the magnitude of Turing's contribution.

In 1939, at the outbreak of war, Enigma was the Germans' leading technology for protecting their military communications. The hi-tech Tunny machine did not go into regular service until almost two years later (as Chapter 6 describes). Lightweight and highly portable, the Enigma machine was equally at home in a general's office in Berlin, an armoured vehicle, a submarine, or trench. It looked similar to an old-fashioned typewriter (see Fig. 6). Berlin engineer Arthur Scherbius took out his first patent on his Enigma design in 1918, and the Enigma was sold on the open market from the early 1920s, although the publicly available form of the machine lacked the all-important plugboard shown in the photo. The British authorities rejected this early version of Enigma after one of their experts showed how the code could be cracked (this was Hugh Foss, who more than a decade later would join Turing in the historic battle against the U-boats).[4] Oblivious to British scepticism, the German navy adopted Enigma in 1926, followed by the army in 1928.[5] The plugboard (or *Steckerbrett*), which was added at the request of the German military in 1930, greatly enhanced the security of the system.[6] Like Foss, German cryptanalysts discovered how to break the version without the plugboard, and Germany sold hundreds of these compromised machines to the governments of Switzerland and Hungary, and also to Spain, where they were used during the Spanish Civil War.[7]

Fig. 6 shows the three rotating wheels, the heart of the Enigma machine.[8] An even more complex model used by the Atlantic U-boats from 1942 had a fourth wheel.[9] The three wheels were removable, and a wooden box kept close to the machine contained five (later eight) numbered wheels, each one different. When an Enigma operator started his shift, he consulted a printed booklet that specified how the machine was to be set up on each day of the current month. The same booklet was issued to all the operators in his particular network. Turing and his colleagues gave each of the different Enigma networks a code name—Yellow, Red, Green, Light Blue, Shark, Dolphin, Porpoise, Sucker, Kestrel, Phoenix, Locust, and Snowdrop, to name only a few. The operator dropped the day's three wheels into the machine in the specified order, closed the inner lid, and pulled plugs out of the plugboard and reinserted them according to the day's specification. Sometimes the setting-up would be done by an officer rather than by the lowly Enigma operator himself. Once set-up was complete, the operator began enciphering his first message of the day. To do so, he simply typed the message in plain German at the keyboard.[10]

The keyboard was connected to a lampboard containing 26 torch bulbs, each of which shone through a stencil on which a letter of the alphabet was marked. Every time the operator pressed a letter at the

Figure 6. The Enigma machine, with its wheels, lamps, and plugboard exposed

Credit: © Science Museum/Science & Society Picture Library – All rights reserved

keyboard, some other letter would light up at the lampboard. Typing HITLER might produce the letters FLKPIM, for example. Each time the operator typed a letter, one or more of the wheels inside the machine clicked forwards a notch, and each time a wheel moved it altered the electrical connections between the keyboard and the lampboard. (The wheels could each rotate through a total of 26 positions, A–Z.) Because the pathway of connections was continually changing, typing HITLER a second time would produce a different sequence of letters at the lampboard. Fig. 7 shows how the machine worked.

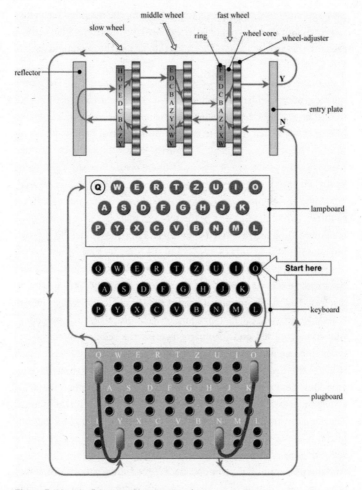

Figure 7. How the Enigma machine encrypts a letter

Credit: Dustin Barrett and Jack Copeland – All rights reserved

The letters that appeared at the lampboard made up the *ciphertext*, the enciphered form of the message. As the letters of the ciphertext lit up one by one, the operator's assistant painstakingly noted them down. Various items were then added as an unencoded 'preamble' to the message, such as the message's time of origin, the intended recipient's radio call sign, and a group of letters identifying the sender's network. A radio operator then transmitted the preamble and the ciphertext itself in Morse code.

At the receiving end, the process was carried out in reverse. The receiving radio operator turned the di–di–dahs of the Morse transmission back into letters of ciphertext, and handed the result to the Enigma operator. The operator typed the ciphertext at the keyboard, having set up his machine identically to the sender's, and the letters of the original German message—the plaintext—lit up one by one at the lampboard. The Enigma was wired so that its letter substitutions were reversible, and this reversibility was the key to the automatic decryption of the message. If, for example, O had produced Q in the sender's machine, then, at the same machine settings, Q produced O in the receiver's machine. Fig. 8 shows how this worked.

The task facing an unauthorized recipient who wanted to decipher the message was daunting. The would-be message breaker needed to discover the Enigma's configuration at the start of the message—which wheels were inside the machine and in what order, how the plugboard was connected up, and to what positions the sending operator had twisted the wheels before he started to type the plaintext. Part of each wheel poked up through a slot in the Enigma's inner lid, so that the operator could rotate the wheels with his thumb or finger before he started typing the message. (In Fig. 6 the three slots are visible above the wheels.) There was an astronomical number of different possible combinations of the machine's movable parts, from which the codebreaker had to select the one combination that was in play at the start of the message. And this presupposes that the codebreaker had already found out, somehow, the basic details of the machine—in particular what the wiring arrangements were inside the wheels. Looking at the left-hand wheel in Fig. 7, the fixed wiring inside takes X across to B and F across to D, for example, and the remaining connections were equally patternless and haphazard. Each of the five (and later eight) possible wheels had different internal wiring. Any would-be codebreaker had to know the wiring of the wheels.

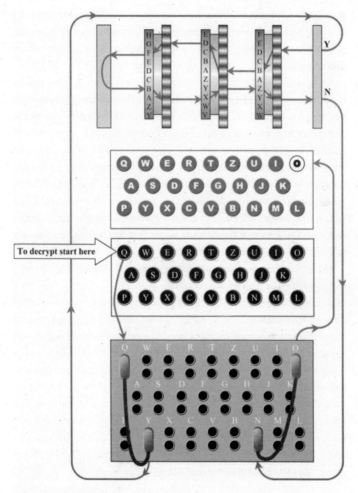

Figure 8. How Enigma decrypts

Credit: Dustin Barrett and Jack Copeland – All rights reserved

The earliest successes against German military Enigma were by the Polish Cipher Bureau or Biuro Szyfrów, located in the city of Warsaw. Around the end of 1932, Polish codebreaker Marian Rejewski, a small, pensive man with owl-like circular spectacles, managed to deduce the wiring inside the wheels.[11] This was one of the greatest feats in the history of codebreaking. Rejewski obtained crucial information from photographs that the French Secret Service passed to their Polish allies. Some of these photos showed pages of Enigma settings for September and October 1932, and this information was 'the decisive factor in breaking the machine's secrets', Rejewski acknowledged.[12] The photos were taken by a German, Hans-Thilo Schmidt, who worked in the cipher branch of the German Army and was spying for the French. Schmidt seems to have been motivated purely by financial gain, and thanks to espionage he enjoyed a high lifestyle—for a while. In 1943, while under interrogation, the man who had recruited Schmidt in 1931 for the Deuxième Bureau, Rudolphe Lemoine, revealed Schmidt's treachery.[13] Schmidt died in a Gestapo prison in Berlin later that year.[14] Although a mercenary, Schmidt was a crucial figure in the Enigma battle. Via Rejewski he profoundly affected the course of European history.

As well as deducing the wheel wiring, Rejewski also uncovered—by a lucky guess—the pattern of fixed wiring across the so-called entry plate of the Enigma (see Fig. 7). The entry plate was an opportunity to introduce an additional layer of scrambling into the Enigma, by connecting the 26 letter terminals on the right-hand side of the plate in a random way to the 26 terminals on the other side of the plate (e.g. A to K, B to X, and so on, with equally random choices for the remaining 24 letters). However, Rejewski had a hunch that the German engineers had simply connected the terminals in order—A to A, B to B, etc. He turned out to be right. The British never did manage to work out the wiring of the entry plate.[15] Perhaps they had a greater respect for German ingenuity. The Enigma's designers were no fools, though, and had probably gambled on the enemy disregarding such a crass choice of wiring.

Only a few weeks before the German armies poured across Poland's frontiers in September 1939, the Polish codebreakers invited two of their British opposite numbers to Warsaw for a highly secret meeting. 'The Poles called for us at 7 a.m.,' recalled Commander Alastair Denniston, 'and we were driven out to a clearing in a forest about 20 kilometres from Warsaw.'[16] There the Poles revealed the wiring of the entry plate and of the wheels. 'At that meeting we told everything we knew and showed everything we had,' Rejewski said.[17] After the meeting Denniston's colleague, Dilly Knox, who was the main player in the British work on Enigma, sang for joy—although his immediate reaction, as he sat listening to Rejewski's triumphs, was undisguised fury that the Poles had pipped him to the post.[18]

Thanks to these and other discoveries by Rejewski, the Poles had been reading German military Enigma from 1933. At the beginning of 1938 about 75 per cent of all intercepted Enigma material was being decoded successfully by the Biuro Szyfrów.[19] This was a tremendous achievement, but unfortunately Rejewski's techniques for breaking the messages all depended on a single weakness in German operating procedures: an unnoticed flaw in the method the sending operator used to tell the receiving operator which positions he had twisted the wheels to before he started enciphering the message. In May 1940 this procedure was abruptly discontinued on most Enigma networks. Perhaps the Germans had discovered the flaw at last. Anyway, that was the end of the loophole that had let Rejewski in. Suddenly the Poles' techniques were useless.

As Chapter 3 mentioned, Turing's own battle with Enigma began several months before the outbreak of war.[20] At that time there were no more than a handful of people in Britain tackling Enigma. Turing worked largely in isolation, which was exactly the way he liked it. He paid occasional visits to Knox at a secret establishment in central London known as 'GC & CS'—the Government Code and Cypher School, as the British government's tiny group of codebreakers was euphemistically named. In 1937, during the Spanish Civil War, the great Knox had broken the type of Enigma used by the Italian navy, but that machine had no plugboard, and Knox was now battling the more secure form of Enigma favoured by the German military. He and the much younger Turing were in many ways evenly matched, both fellows of King's, both brilliant, both deliciously eccentric. Knox, an Old Etonian, was tall like Turing but more of a gangly figure; his narrow face was said to resemble a pang of hunger.[21] He admired Lewis Carroll's *Alice in Wonderland* almost to the point of obsession, and when not breaking codes he devoted himself to translating the work of the ancient Greek poet Herodas. 'They were both strictly loners,' recollected Peter Twinn, an Oxford mathematics graduate who was recruited to assist Knox a few weeks before Turing joined the Enigma fight.[22] 'Turing was the mathematician and Knox relied on flashes of genius,' Twinn said with a touch of irony. As mathematicians, Twinn and Turing were in fact very rare creatures in the pre-war world of British codebreaking. The Poles had understood right from the start that Enigma was fundamentally a mathematical problem, but to the British way of thinking there were, Twinn explained, 'doubts about the wisdom of recruiting a mathematician as they were regarded as strange fellows, notoriously unpractical'.[23] Such abstract thinkers, it was felt, lacked 'appreciation of the real world'.

Knox was an old hand who had been breaking codes since the First World War, and there were many affectionate stories about him in circulation. Eric 'Vinca' Vincent, who worked on Mussolini's codes, recounted that once Knox 'stayed so long in the bathroom that his fellow-lodgers at last forced the door. They found him standing by the bath, a faint smile on his face, his gaze fixed on abstractions, both taps full on and the plug out. What then was passing in his mind could possibly have solved a problem that was to win a battle.'[24] Even Knox, though, found Turing's creative anarchy heavy going. 'Turing is very difficult to anchor down,' he complained.[25] 'He is very clever but quite irresponsible and throws out a mass of suggestions of all degrees of merit.' Knox went on rather pompously, 'I have just, but only just, enough authority and ability to keep him and his ideas in some sort of order and discipline.' 'But he is very nice about it all,' Knox ended sweetly.

When Turing joined GC & CS it was a small organization ill-prepared for war, but at least it would soon have a new home outside London. This was purchased by Admiral Sir Hugh Sinclair, Chief of the Secret Intelligence Service (out of his own pocket, some said). Sinclair made an excellent choice. Bletchley Park, a large, if ugly, Victorian mansion, had ample grounds and within months these would be cluttered by an untidy sprawl of makeshift military buildings. The mansion was located just a few minutes' walk from Bletchley railway station, a major junction linking the main university centres of London, Oxford, and Cambridge. Denniston, who was the head of GC & CS, had been busy recruiting potential codebreakers from these intellectual powerhouses, building up what he described as his 'emergency list' of 'men of the Professor type'.[26] An ill-assorted bunch of such men, plucked suddenly out of everyday life, took up residence at Bletchley Park in early September 1939. Almost overnight the mansion filled up with strangers. 'It was more like the prim first day at a public school,' recollected codebreaker Nigel de Grey.[27] Turing, of course, was among these 'men of the Professor type', and he arrived at Bletchley Park a few hours after Chamberlain declared war on Germany.[28] Winston Churchill summed up the new mood: this was 'war against a monstrous tyranny, never surpassed in the dark, lamentable catalogue of human crime'.[29]

The Bletchley codebreakers, about thirty in number,[30] soon organized themselves into a system of 'huts'—Hut 3, Hut 6, and so on. Originally these were simply the designations of hastily constructed single-storey wooden buildings in the grounds, but the names quickly came to refer to the specialized organizations housed within the huts. Hut 6 dealt with Army and Air Force Enigma, and Hut 3 with translating and analysing the

Figure 9. Codebreakers playing rounders on the front lawn of Bletchley Park mansion. Daphne Bradshaw of Hut 5 has her back to the camera

Credit: Estate of Barbara and Joe Eachus

decrypted messages produced by Hut 6. Hut 8, established a little later, dealt with Naval Enigma. The names remained unchanged throughout the war, despite moves into new premises. On his arrival at Bletchley Park, Turing first joined Knox's Research Section, located in a small row of estate workers' poky cottages at the back of the mansion. Then, early in 1940, Turing established Hut 8 and began an eighteen-month battle with the Atlantic U-boats. It was not until the middle of 1941 that he tasted victory.

In the huts, university dons worked alongside uniformed military personnel. Military discipline never took root among the 'men of the Professor type', and the codebreakers' world had the atmosphere of an Oxbridge college. 'We acknowledged only the discipline we imposed on ourselves,' recalled Peter Hilton, who was a mere eighteen years of age when he joined Hut 8.[31] Hilton, a genial mathematician, loved palindromes—sentences that read the same backwards and forwards, such as STEP ON NO PETS and SEX AT NOON TAXES. He once spent a sleepless night creating the monster palindrome: DOC NOTE, I DISSENT. A FAST NEVER PREVENTS A FATNESS. I DIET ON COD. Catherine Caughey, one of the 'Wrens' (members of the Women's Royal Naval Service) assigned to Bletchley Park, recalled her first impressions as she arrived by military bus: 'The place was WEIRD. There were weedy looking boffin types walking in pairs or on their own. Some were very young.'[32] It was the women's first contact with such alien beings. Rachel Cross, a Wren assigned to Hut 4, also thought them 'strange and weird'. 'They sat in a very smoky atmosphere drinking mugs of black coffee,' she remembered.[33] Another arriving Wren, Eleanor Ireland, recalled a 'lecture about the extreme secrecy of every aspect of the work that was being done at Bletchley Park'.[34] She found the lecture intimidating and walked out of the room feeling subdued and puzzled. 'We were told that we would never be posted anywhere else, because the work was too secret for us to be released,' she said.

During the first months of the war, Bletchley's attempts to break into Germany's Enigma communications were completely unsuccessful. At first, the codebreakers were afraid that the Germans had made some fundamental change to the Enigma machine.[35] Turing went to Paris to confer with the Poles. The French Deuxième Bureau had provided Rejewski and his team with a—temporarily—safe haven just outside the metropolis. Turing quickly discovered why things were going wrong. Crucial details about the Enigma's wheels had got mixed up.[36] During his stay with the Poles they achieved the very first break into wartime Enigma, in mid January 1940.[37] Later Rejewski observed, rather condescendingly, 'We treated [Turing] as a younger colleague who had specialized in mathematical logic and was just starting out in cryptology.'[38] In fact, though, by the time of his Paris visit, Turing was further ahead than Rejewski could ever have imagined. He had already made the conceptual breakthroughs that led to his bombe and to the cracking of U-boat Enigma.

In the early summer of 1940, the British army was pushed into the sea at Dunkirk as the Germans overran northern France. Thousands of small boats set out from the English ports to bring the soldiers home. The threat of a German invasion from French soil was now very real. Turing decided to prepare himself by joining the Home Guard, so that he could learn to fire a rifle accurately. He was required to complete an official form in order to join. 'One of the questions,' recounted Hilton, 'was "Do you understand that, by enrolling in His Majesty's Local Defence Volunteers, you render yourself liable for military discipline?" Turing, who always reasoned from first principles, argued as follows. "I can imagine no set of circumstances under which it would be to my advantage to answer this question yes." So he answered it no.'[39] Evidently the authorities did not examine Turing's application form very closely. 'He was duly enrolled,' Hilton said, 'and soon became a first class shot—he usually did very well the things that he set himself to do.' Once he had learnt to handle a rifle, though, Turing lost interest in attending Home Guard parades, and eventually stopped going altogether. His absence provoked his commanding officer to send him 'nasty notes of increasing irritability', continued Hilton. 'These culminated in a summons to his court-martial, presided over by Colonel Fillingham, Officer Commanding the Buckinghamshire Division of His Majesty's Local Defence Volunteers:

'"Is it true, Private Turing, that you have attended none of the last eight parades?"
'"Yes, sir."

'"Do you realize this is a very serious offence?"

'"No, sir."

'"Private Turing, are you trying to make a fool out of me?"

'"No, sir, but if you look at my application for admission to the Home Guard, you will see that I do not understand I am subject to military discipline."

'The form was produced, Colonel Fillingham read it, and became apoplectic. All he could say was,

'"You were improperly enrolled. Get out of my sight!"'

Turing was always impatient of authority, but in any case he had more important things to do than attend parades. When he had arrived at Bletchley Park, no work at all was being done on German Naval Enigma, since this was widely believed—although not by Turing—to be unbreakable. Naval Enigma had defeated even the Poles. Turing took on this Herculean job because, he said, 'no one else was doing anything about it and I could have it to myself'.[40] As usual, the prospect of working alone appealed to him. It was also perfectly clear to him how serious the situation was. The convoys of merchant ships bringing huge cargoes of food, munitions, and oil to Britain from North America were easy prey to torpedoes, and the Atlantic U-boats threatened to starve Britain into defeat. From the outbreak of war to December 1940, a devastating total of 585 merchant ships were sunk by U-boats, compared with 202 merchant ships sunk by aircraft during the same period.[41] But, if the Enigma network used by the U-boats—called 'Dolphin' at Bletchley Park—could be broken, decoded messages would reveal the positions of the submarines. With the U-boats giving away their positions, the convoys would easily be able to dodge them in the vastness of the Atlantic. Turing seized the challenge.

In 1937 Rejewski's team at the Biuro Szyfrów had taken a good stab at the Germans' naval messages, but in the end the Poles gave up their attempt. One reason why they found Dolphin impossible to break systematically was the tricky method used to tell the receiving operator what positions the sender's wheels were in when he started enciphering the message. The Poles never managed to deduce this method; but where they failed, Turing succeeded. The method depended on the fact that the wheels' positions could be summed up by a triplet of letters, such as MBO, because the 26 letters of the alphabet were marked around the circumference of each wheel (see Fig. 6). Three small windows in the machine's inner lid enabled the operator to see each wheel's uppermost letter. Turing called these the 'window positions' of the wheels. If the sender could say to the receiver, 'When I started to encipher this message, the window positions of my wheels were MBO,' then the receiver could turn his own wheels to MBO and decode the message. The difficult part was to send the information about the window positions to the receiver in a form that eavesdroppers could not read.

The super-secure solution adopted for the Dolphin network involved the sender encrypting MBO *twice*, once using the Enigma machine, and then once again by hand. Other networks used simpler methods, which Bletchley found much easier to break. First, the sender of a Dolphin message rotated the wheels to the day's 'ground' positions (in German, *Grundstellung*), which all the operators in the network knew in advance. For example, the window positions LIC might be the ground positions on a particular day. Next, the sender typed MBO at the Enigma's keyboard and noted down the letters that lit up at the lampboard, e.g. SAM. The first stage of encryption was now complete.

The second stage involved what was called a *bigram* table, issued to all the operators in the network. A bigram table told the operator how to encode pairs of letters (bigrams). The bigram table for a particular day might tell the operator to code WS as IK, AA as PQ, and KM as GO, for example. The sender's next step was to choose another trio of letters, WAK, say, and write beneath it the three letters that the Enigma machine had just produced:

```
W    A    K
S    A    M
```

Using the bigram table, the sender then encoded the vertical columns, producing

```
I    P    G
K    Q    O
```

Turing summed it all up in his usual pithy style: 'The window position is enciphered at the Grundstellung, and the resulting letters replaced by bigramme equivalents.'[42]

When the message's ciphertext was transmitted, the three pairs of letters IKPQGO—called the message's *indicator*—were included at the beginning.[43] The receiving operator then simply reversed the procedure that the sender had followed. He used the bigram tables to decode the indicator and then typed the lower trio of letters, SAM, into his Enigma, after first rotating the wheels to their ground positions, LIC. MBO lit up at the lampboard. He now set his wheels to MBO and deciphered the message. In practice, there were additional bells and whistles designed to achieve even greater security.[44] For instance, the operator was not permitted just to make up a triplet dictating the starting positions of his wheels. This meant that the procedure involved some tiresome extra steps, but their value was that the operator was prevented from selecting obvious triplets that a codebreaker might be able to guess, such as QWE—the first three letters at the top left of the keyboard—or triplets like DOR or CIL forming the first three letters of his girlfriend's name (Dora, Cilla).[45] Own up: how many people use part of a name in their computer password?

Incredibly, Turing was able to work most of this out one winter's night in 1939, starting with a few bygone messages that the Poles had been lucky enough to break in mid 1937.[46] (Turing explains in detail how he did this on pages 279–81 of *The Essential Turing*.) The night of Turing's break, whose exact date was unrecorded and whose discoveries remained shrouded in secrecy for nearly sixty years, was undoubtedly one of the most important nights of the war. Much work remained to be done, though, before the new Hut 8 could decrypt U-boat traffic on a regular basis. Turing needed the bigram tables for the Dolphin network.

Every ship in the network was issued with the same set of sheets of bigram tables, together with a calendar showing which table was in force on any given day. These sheets remained valid for months, so if the codebreakers could get hold of a set, they would be in a strong position to read the daily U-boat traffic. Pirate tactics seemed the best option. The Royal Navy would be co-opted to attack and board a German ship and capture the cipher documents—a 'pinch', in codebreaking slang. The Government Code and Cypher School's 'Cryptographic Dictionary' defined a pinch as the act of obtaining enemy cryptographic materials by 'any available methods'.[47] A seaborne pinch of Enigma material was not an easy proposition, however. All German vessels carrying Enigma were certain to be armed, and in any case the crews were under the strictest of instructions to destroy all secret documents if the enemy were boarding, or in the event of abandoning ship.

So began Hut 8's collaboration with the navy. A story unfolded of derring-do on the high seas—while the men of the professor type waited anxiously on dry land, willing the arrival of precious sheets of paper covered with letters and numbers.

TURING'S U-BOAT BATTLE

Turing began his attack on the U-boat messages—and also messages sent by other types of German vessel—by using what were called *cribs*. A crib is a snatch of plain German that the codebreaker thinks could form part of the message. Because of the stereotyped nature of the German messages, certain phrases were very likely to occur. One crib that Turing used was 'Continuation of previous message' (*Fortsetzung*, abbreviated FORT). Since messages were often sent in several parts, FORT was a very handy crib. Another was WEWA, the Enigma term for a weather station (abbreviating the German *Wetter Warte*). The common group of letters EINS was an ever-reliable crib—there was about a 90 per cent chance that any given message would contain EINS somewhere within it.[1]

Longer and more exotic cribs resulted from the sheer naivety of many of Enigma's users. 'German operators were simple souls with childish habits,' Denniston said drily.[2] The weather stations regularly sent messages containing routine phrases like 'weather for the night' ('WETTER FUER DIE NACHT') and 'situation eastern Channel' ('ZUSTAND OST WAERTIGER KANAL'). One naval station even transmitted the confirmation 'Beacons lit as ordered' ('FEUER BRANNTEN WIE BEFOHLEN') every single evening. This was 'a very excellent crib', said Patrick Mahon, a gifted cribber who in 1944 would take over as head of Hut 8.[3]

The codebreakers could often pinpoint the location of a cribbed phrase within a message by using the basic fact that the Enigma machine never encoded a letter as itself. This was a result of the design of the reflector—the letter that came out of the wheels was bound to be different from the one that went in (see Fig. 7 in the preceding chapter). The cribber would slide a suspected fragment of plaintext, e.g. ZUSTANDOSTWAERTIGERKANAL, along the ciphertext, looking for a location at which no letters matched up. Positions where a letter in the crib stood on top of the very same letter in the ciphertext were called 'crashes' (see Fig. 10). A crash showed that the crib was in the wrong place. If a crib was more than about thirty letters long, there was a reasonable chance that it would 'crash out' everywhere except at its correct location. Or simply everywhere, if the codebreaker's guess was wrong and the crib did not in fact occur anywhere in the message.

Once a potential location had been found for the crib, the cribber would try to extend the break to the left or right. If this proved possible, it tended to confirm that the crib was correct. In his pioneering attack, Turing made use of the fact that FORT—'Continuation of previous message'—was always followed on the right by a number identifying the previous message, such as 2300. The identification number usually referred to the time at which the previous message had been sent. Thanks to the successful interrogation of a captured Enigma operative, Funkmaat (Wirelessman) Meyer, Turing knew that numbers were typed out as words.[4] A 'prisoner told us,' Turing said in a matter-of-fact way, 'that the digits of the numbers were spelt out in full'—ZWEIDREINULNUL, for example (2300).[5] Perhaps Turing himself played a role in the interrogation. Once it was established that only number-words followed FORT, the codebreaker could laboriously try out all the possibilities one after another, looking for a choice that did not crash out. Turing called this the 'Forty Weepy' method, from FORT and a memorable group of letters, YWEEPY that had followed it in a 1937 message.[6]

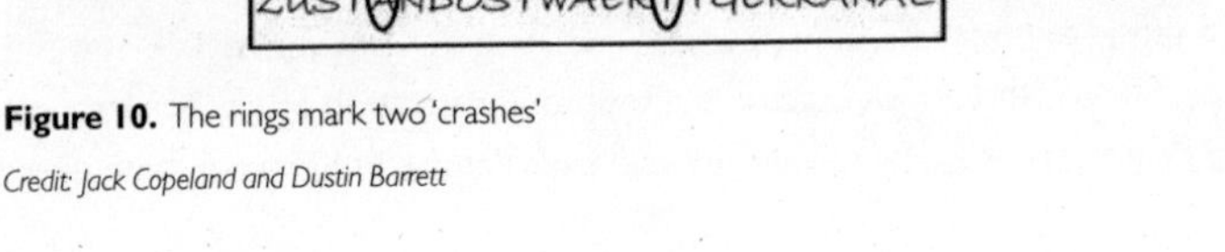

VXZBBKETKCJTRATGVHDXZMQTLCNYMXSVJQXQTYSBDVK
ZUSTANDOSTWAERTIGERKANAL

Figure 10. The rings mark two 'crashes'

Credit: Jack Copeland and Dustin Barrett

The longer the stretch of plain German that the codebreaker managed to reveal, the greater the chance of being able to deduce something about the settings of the plugboard and the wheels. Armed with a good crib and vast patience, it was possible to fiddle with an Enigma machine until the message decoded—a procedure known simply as 'twiddling'.[7] Cribbing developed into a fine art as the war progressed. Expert 'Cribsters', denizens of their own Crib Room, would search continually for new cribs, reading through vast piles of decrypts and keeping meticulous records.[8] The prize was a phrase, or a name, that was likely to be repeated in a later message. It was a standard joke that the crib 'Heil Hitler' broke many a message.

In Hut 8's early days, though, Turing's crib-based attack was not getting very far. As the winter of 1939 passed into the spring of 1940, there was little concrete progress. By now Hut 8 was pinning all its hopes on a pinch. Then, suddenly, the Royal Navy came up trumps. On 26 April, during the Norwegian campaign, a heavily armed German trawler was intercepted while she was sailing for the Norwegian port of Narvik.[9] The trawler, *Schiff 26*, had steamed away from the German harbour town of Wilhelmshaven a few days previously, under the command of twenty-nine-year-old Oberleutnant Heinz Engelien. She was laden with a heavy cargo of munitions for the German forces at Narvik. In fact, the ship was a floating arsenal, loaded to the gunwales with ammunition, high explosives, mines, and depth charges. There was an Enigma machine in the small W/T room close to Engelien's cabin. Engelien had a crew of thirty-eight and so the ship was pretty crowded, but comfortable enough. There was plenty of food, fresh eggs, even beer, although fresh water was in short supply and the crew did not wash. Like pirates they wore unkempt civilian clothes instead of their navy uniforms. Sailors spent the first two days of the voyage disguising the ship. A false name, *Polares*, was painted on the sides and the Dutch flag was hoisted. For good measure they painted crude Dutch flags on the sides as well. In different waters the captain sailed just as happily under the Swedish flag or Danish flag. He only hoisted his German tricolour when close to home. Using fishing nets and baskets, the crew carefully disguised the munitions stacked on deck.

Wooden covers hid the mouths of the two torpedo tubes mounted in the fo'c'sle. They draped the heavy stern gun with a canvas boat-cover, making it look like a lifeboat.

The *Schiff* 26 was a microcosm of the German armed forces. Many of the sailors sympathized with Nazi ideals and saw themselves as fighting the good fight. Engelien believed that Germany had to fight because the masses had insufficient living space in the German homeland.[10] Germans needed *Lebensraum*, space to live and prosper. He was certain that Germany would triumph, and said he wanted 'total war, against men, women and children'. The diary of *Schiff* 26's chief boatswain Karl Reitz makes sober but fascinating reading. '9th April. Thick fog. No wind. About 11 a.m., news…occupation of Denmark and Norway by Germany. Great elation on board—Total war—splendid. 1130 Goebbels's memorandum to Denmark and Norway. Hurrah. March music by Radio increases excitement. German soldiers will prove their worth. One is pleased to be a soldier and we hope this will also bring a change for us.' Then later the same day: 'Bergen occupied. A day of delight.'[11]

At 10.30 on a blowy morning the British destroyer HMS *Griffin* suddenly hove into view. She was steaming towards *Schiff* 26 at a thumping twenty-five knots. So much for the disguise. The Germans were hopelessly outgunned, and in any case they knew their boat would go up like a box of fireworks if shots were fired. Engelien's instructions were to scuttle the ship if capture was imminent. Explosive charges had been laid ready for this purpose in the aft munitions room, but the captain never gave the order to scuttle. He knew lives would be lost in the heavy sea if his ship sank. He had heard a haunting account of a recent sinking from German sailors in port only a few days previously. Reitz had noted down some of the details in his diary: 'It was said to have been awful—screams for mothers, wives and children, help—am drowning…Decks [of rescue ship] full of corpses. Terrible sight. The crew were unable to eat for some time, it affected them so much.'[12] Engelien prepared to be boarded, making sure the Enigma went over the side, and stuffing codebooks and papers into two canvas bags that he hurled into the water. He had hastily weighted one bag with a seashell, but let the other take its chances in the waves and strong wind.

Griffin came close alongside, launching a boarding party in a small boat. The sea tossed them wildly and waves sloshed on board. As a second boat was setting out, someone spotted a half-submerged canvas bag in the heaving waves. The sailors tried reaching it with a grappling hook but the boat was pitching too fiercely. Then one of the gunners, Mr Foord, tied a rope to himself and bravely dived in. Foord succeeded in grabbing the bag but his rope broke and he went under. Hanging grimly onto the bag, he went under for a second time. He came up spluttering and luckily managed to clutch a rope that was thrown. He tied it around himself, and Foord and the bag of secret papers were hauled safely on board.

As the boarding party clambered onto *Schiff* 26, they found Engelien and about fifteen men huddled on the well deck, with the rest below. The men assumed the British would shoot them, and found themselves herded into small boats and carried to the looming bulk of the *Griffin*. But there were no bullets and the men relaxed. 'Perfect treatment,' Reitz wrote in his diary—'One is inclined to say most cordial reception. A treatment which we most certainly did not expect.'[13] He went on: 'Immediately we got on board we were given tea. Shortly afterwards pea soup for supper, two sausages and two fried eggs.' In his diary he wondered, 'Would it have been the same had the boot been on the other foot?'

The documents from *Schiff* 26 turned out to give a precise description of how a message's indicator concealed the window positions of the sender's wheels. This information both confirmed Turing's deductions of the year before and clarified some details.[14] Sadly, the bigram tables themselves must have been in the other canvas bag. However, the haul included the Enigma operator's logbook, which contained the exact plaintexts of a number of transmitted messages—impeccable cribs, from which much could be deduced. There was also a loose scrap of paper that no one at Bletchley bothered to look at for several days, but which by an amazing stroke of good fortune turned out to have the plugboard settings and the wheels' ground positions for April 23–24 scribbled on it.[15]

The Narvik pinch, as it became known, raised hopes and brightened the mood, but in the end only six days' worth of traffic was broken (April 22 to 27). Three of these days were cracked by a new recruit, mathematician

Joan Clarke,[16] a fiercely intelligent woman who in fact got engaged to Turing the following year, though only briefly. The codebreaking bug bit her hard, and in the end she stayed in the business until her retirement in the 1970s. She recollected that when she entered Hut 8's small inner sanctum, where the codebreakers had their desks, one of them said to her, 'Welcome to the sahibs' room'—a reference, almost certainly not ironic, to the strictly male enclaves found across the British Empire.[17] As a female codebreaker, her rate of pay was even lower than the Wrens', scarcely more than £2 a week.[18]

After the excitement of the Narvik pinch, things went very quiet again for Hut 8. Mahon said, 'The next six months produced depressingly few results.'[19] As spring turned into summer, Turing must have felt that Hut 8 was bogged down. To make matters even worse, his hay fever was troubling him. The three-mile bicycle ride through the pollen-drenched Buckinghamshire countryside to and from his lodgings became tiresome. The solution he adopted was characteristically unconventional: Turing donned his government-issue gas mask for the journey.[20] 'For him the logical course was of more account than the conventional,' his mother commented a little stiffly. Turing must have been very determined to avoid the effects of hay fever, because wartime gas masks were notoriously uncomfortable. The wearer felt suffocated, the lower part of the mask quickly filled up with spit, and it was unbearably hot inside the rubber—although in London and the other big cities, many thousands of people gladly pulled their masks over their heads as soon as the air raid sirens screamed out a warning. Masks usually steamed up, making it next to impossible to see anything, but fortunately there was little traffic on Bletchley's country lanes. Perhaps Turing made typically ingenious modifications to his mask and eliminated the worst of the difficulties.

With no sign of a break, tempers wore a little thin. In August the head of the Naval Intelligence section in Hut 4, Frank Birch, wrote to his superiors, complaining bitterly about Turing. Birch, like Knox, was another fellow of King's who had been in the codebreaking game practically since time began—although, unlike Knox, he was also a theatre and movie actor, starring in *Cast up by the Sea* and a number of other pre-war films.

During the pre-war period he had probably had a hand in recruiting Turing into the Enigma fight, although since he was by academic training a historian, he no doubt shared the prejudice that mathematicians had little 'appreciation of the real world'. Birch griped in his August letter that Turing and his assistant Peter Twinn were 'like people waiting for a miracle, without believing in miracles'.[21] He moaned: 'Turing and Twinn are brilliant, but like many brilliant people, they are not practical. They are untidy, they lose things, they can't copy out right, and they dither between theory and cribbing. Nor have they the determination of practical men.' These were harsh words about the people who would soon lay the U-boat's communications wide open. Mahon, on the other hand, thought that Turing's difficulties with those around him arose chiefly because he was 'a lamentable explainer'.[22] The misinterpretations in Birch's letter, Mahon said, demonstrated clearly 'Turing's almost total inability to make himself understood'. Birch's own suggestions for making progress on the code were, Mahon grumbled, 'impossible', and 'simply the result of not understanding the problem'. He added cattily that the defects in Birch's proposals were 'immediately obvious to anyone with actual experience of Hut 8 work'.

Office bitchiness aside, everyone knew that what was desperately needed was another pinch. The Narvik pinch had been sheer luck, but the planners in Naval Intelligence had now begun to consider staging a special operation to capture the Enigma materials that Turing wanted. In September, a gung-ho Naval Intelligence officer, Lieutenant Commander Ian Fleming—later to become the world-famous creator of Special Agent 007, James Bond—proposed a daring Bond-like plan to the Director of Naval Intelligence.[23] Shortly before dawn, in the wake of a night bombing raid on London, one of the RAF's stock of captured German bombers would be flown out into the middle of the Channel by a British air crew wearing German uniforms—'add blood and bandages to suit', wrote Fleming in his stage directions. The pilot would then deliberately crash the plane into the sea near a suitable German vessel. To squash any possibility of suspicion, the plane would be flown with one engine switched off and fake smoke gushing from the fuselage. Fleming's person specification for the pilot was: 'tough, bachelor, able to swim'. Fleming himself would be the group's German speaker. Once aboard the rescue vessel, they would 'shoot German crew, dump overboard' and sail the boat and its 'booty' into an English port. Fleming's plan was appropriately named 'Operation Ruthless'.

Turing awaited the results of Operation Ruthless eagerly. In the middle of October, Fleming and his pirate crew dug in at Dover, hoping for news of a suitably small lone German vessel with Enigma aboard. Luck was not on Fleming's side, however. RAF reconnaissance flights failed to locate a promising target, and eventually the operation was postponed indefinitely.[24] Birch described the effect of this disappointing news on Turing: 'Turing and Twinn came to me like undertakers cheated of a nice corpse two days ago, all in a stew about the cancellation of operation Ruthless.'[25]

Not all the Hut 8 news was bad, though. Earlier that year one very large ray of sunshine had burst through the gloom, in the form of the prototype model of Turing's bombe. In 1938 Rejewski and his colleagues at the Biuro Szyfrów had built a small machine that they called a 'bomba'. Their reasons for choosing this distinctive name, whose literal meaning is bomb or bombshell, were not recorded, although theories abound. One is that Rejewski was eating a bomba—a type of ice-cream desert, *bombe* in French—when the idea for the machine struck him.[26] Rejewski's bomba consisted of six replica Enigma machines. His idea worked well and soon the Poles had half a dozen bomby slogging away at the Enigma traffic. Knox and Denniston saw the Polish machines first-hand: 'we were taken down to an underground room full of electric equipment and introduced to the "bombs",' Denniston recalled.[27]

Like Rejewski's other methods, however, the bomba depended on one crucial weakness in the operating procedures used by the German army and air force (the same weakness mentioned in the preceding chapter). Unlike their counterparts in the navy, Enigma operators in the army and air force produced the message's indicator by setting the Enigma wheels to the day's ground positions and then typing three letters of their choice at the keyboard. These three letters denoted the window positions they were intending to use at the start of the message. In fact, they typed the three letters twice. So if the sender was planning to use the window positions MBO, he typed MBOMBO at the Enigma's keyboard. The six letters that lit at the lampboard were transmitted to the receiver (along with the message), and the receiver reversed the procedure and deciphered the message. Typing the three letters twice was supposed to be a precaution against poor radio reception, and it took the Germans a long time to realize that the repetition was an absolute howler. When this loophole was closed, in May 1940—by the simple fix of typing the three letters only once instead of twice—the bomby method became useless.[28] Fortunately, Turing had by then devised a much more complex form of anti-Enigma machine, working on very different principles.

The engineers began building Turing's bombe in October 1939, and the first, named simply 'Victory', was installed in the spring of 1940.[29] Since space was at a premium, Turing's bulky new machine was housed in the sick bay, Hut 1.[30] It cost approximately £6,500—about one-tenth of

Figure 11. A bombe

Credit: National Archives and Records Administration, Washington DC

the price tag of a Lancaster bomber, and around £100,000 in today's money.[31] In light of what the bombes would achieve, they were one of the most cost-effective pieces of equipment of the war. The bombes were special-purpose electromechanical computers. At superhuman speed, a bombe searched through different possible configurations of the Enigma's wheels, looking for a pattern of keyboard-to-lampboard connections that would turn the coded letters into plain German. At root, though, the machinery depended entirely on human instinct: in order to set the process going, a carefully chosen crib was required. Mahon joked, 'The bombe was rather like the traditional German soldier, highly efficient but totally unintelligent.'[32] Turing's powerful crib-based procedure was unaffected by the May 1940 change to the German system—unlike Rejewski's method, which did not involve cribs—and soon formed the backbone of the whole Bletchley attack on the *Wehrmacht*'s Enigma machines.[33]

Turing's bombe consisted of thirty (later thirty-six) replica Enigma machines. The codebreakers could connect these replica Enigmas together in whatever configuration seemed best for attacking a given message. As increasing numbers of bombes were installed, Bletchley Park became a codebreaking factory. It was cyberwar on a previously unknown scale. Workers arrived in industrial numbers to operate the new machines. They were all Wrens, and by the end of the war there were almost 2,000 women operating the bombes.[34] Turing's boyish good looks were not lost on the Bletchley females, but he was very shy with them. 'I once offered him a cup of tea but he shrank back in fear,' recalled Sarah Norton, an attractive Knightsbridge deb who worked in the index room in Hut 4.[35] 'He seemed terrified of girls,' she said regretfully. Norton remembered him coping with the throngs of young women in the corridors by 'shambling down to the canteen in a curious sideways step, his eyes fixed to the ground'.

At the completion of what were called the 'bombe runs' for the current message, the Wrens would reconfigure the bombe ready for the next message. They replugged the bombe's complex inter-Enigma connections in accordance with a 'menu' drawn up by the codebreaker in charge.

Turing's machines operated 24/7 and the women worked in three shifts. They slept—often in double-tiered bunks—in outlying dormitories with peeling paint, inadequate heating, and terrible food. Turing called them 'slaves'.[36] In those male-dominated times, very few of Bletchley Park's women joined the ranks of the cryptographers, even though a significant percentage had university degrees.[37] One official document noted that 'The cheerful common sense of the Wrens was a great asset'; other, more salient assets tended to go unnoticed by the ruling males.[38] It was a sad waste of talent. However, some of the Wrens did ultimately rise to become 'Controllers'. The controllers oversaw bombe operations, distributing menus among the bombe teams and working in a special Control Room, which was connected by phone lines to Huts 6 and 8, and had a large display on one wall showing all available bombes.[39]

The bombe, housed within a large metal cabinet, was taller than a person and over seven feet long and nearly three feet wide.[40] It contained about ten miles of wire with more than a million soldered connections.[41] Each of the 'drums' that can be seen in Fig. 11 mimicked a single Enigma wheel. Notice the swastikas that someone has doodled along the top of the bombe cabinet and the 'Keep Feet Off' sign at the bottom right. The three special drums on the right, in the middle section, were called the 'indicator drums'. The bombe searched at high speed, its drums spinning, and then would suddenly come to a stop, with three letters showing on the indicator drums—MBO, for example. These were the machine's guess at the positions of the wheels at the start of the message. A panel on the machine's right-hand side (not visible in the photo) recorded the bombe's guess at the plugboard settings. Turing's ingenious method for solving the plugboard was the key to the bombe's power. The Polish bomba, on the other hand, had simply ignored the plugboard.[42] Once the bombe stopped, its guesses were tested by hand on an Enigma machine or a replica. If the message decoded, all was well—and if it didn't, the bombe made another run and searched some more.[43]

In the spring of 1940, however, the newly installed Victory was like a sports car with only a dribble of petrol available. The Narvik pinch in April gave Turing a splash of fuel, just a few weeks after the bombe's delivery from the factory at Letchworth, and he and his team connected up the drums to run a crib from the logbook that the boarding party had captured. After 'a series of misadventures and a fortnight's work the machine triumphantly produced the answer', recalled British chess champion Hugh Alexander.[44] Alexander would in due course replace Turing as head of Hut 8. He had an earthy sense of humour, and colleagues enjoyed quoting his despairing remark, 'We'll have to wait, thumbing our twiddles.'[45] Wait they did. Hut 8 was in a Catch-22 situation. Victory could not be used to read U-boat messages or other naval traffic without a good supply of cribs, and the only way to get the cribs was to be already reading messages. In order to bootstrap the process, the bigram tables were required. In fact, a pinch of at least a month's worth of the paperwork issued to German operators was really what Hut 8 needed to get into operation.[46] If only the navy could deliver the goods, the codebreakers would be able to bludgeon their way into the U-boat traffic, and Victory could be bump-started.

It was a very frustrating period for Hut 8. Just a few yards away, Hut 6 was successfully reading generous quantities of the much easier to break Air Force Enigma—and was producing intelligence that helped Fighter Command in its life-and-death struggle with the *Luftwaffe*.[47] Turing himself had made some early progress in the attack on Air Force Enigma and, back in January, had broken into the *Luftwaffe* traffic known as 'Blue'.[48] Blue turned out to be a special network used for training purposes, but breaking it was a start. Air Ministry staff described Hut 6's decrypts as 'heaven-sent'.[49] A *Luftwaffe* message broken in July 1940 contained an order to the bombers to stop attacking harbour facilities in England's Channel ports, unambiguous warning of an impending German invasion.[50] 'We shall fight on the beaches,' Winston Churchill announced firmly, 'we shall fight on the landing grounds, we shall fight in the fields and in the streets, we shall fight in the hills; we shall never surrender.'[51] Enigma revealed the invasion's codename, *Seelöwe* or Sea Lion, and Hut 6's decrypts provided a wealth of information about Hitler's plans for a massive attack by air and sea.[52] Once the invaders had secured a foothold on British soil, ruthless military subjugation of the rest of the country would follow.

Troop carriers, supply barges, tanks, artillery, heavy machine guns, dive-bombers, paratroops, and thousands of gliders crammed with heavily armed soldiers would pour across the English Channel. Britain would join the rest of Europe under Nazi tyranny.

In August, Hut 6 was given access to the second bombe to be delivered, Agnus, short for Agnus Dei, the Lamb of God. According to the Gospel of St John, the Lamb of God would take away the sins of the world—although those who missed the Biblical allusion tended to hear the name as 'Agnes', and by the end of the war this long-lived machine was known universally as Aggie.[53] Turing now had two bombes to cosset. Agnus, moreover, contained equipment implementing his important new idea for 'simultaneous scanning'. The remodelled bombe was fitted with the dazzlingly ingenious 'diagonal board', an enhancement that mathematician Gordon Welchman had excitedly suggested to an initially incredulous Turing.[54]

Figure 12. Hut 6

Credit: © Bletchley Park Trust/Science & Society Picture Library – All rights reserved

Agnus, though, left a lot to be desired so far as user-friendliness was concerned. In those early days the operators had to push a hand inside the machinery and grope about in order to discover the bombe's guess at the Enigma's plugboard settings.[55]

September brought the start of the Blitz. Massed German bombers pounded British cities, first by day and then night after night. It was the darkest hour. The bombs killed 7,000 people during September alone and another 10,000 were injured.[56] Great swathes of London, Birmingham, Coventry, and Liverpool were smashed to rubble. Familiar landmarks vanished and people's homes and workplaces became no more than memories. So, too, did friends, relatives, parents, children, spouses. London's Joe Loss Orchestra played 'I'll never smile again'. Vera Lynn's tremendous hit, 'There'll always be an England', helped people to deal with uncertainty. Liverpool-born entertainer Arthur Askey sang 'Get in your shelter'. 'Get yourself right underground, when those Nazis fly around,' he chanted cheerily. Hundreds of thousands sheltered each night on the crammed platforms of the London Underground. Babies were born in the relative safety of the deep tunnels, although direct hits on a number of stations brought many deaths. The famous 'Blitz mentality' set in, an enhanced sense of community, coupled with pride at not succumbing, not falling apart. Many of that generation remember the war years as the most fulfilling period of their lives. In another popular song Noel Coward insisted, in his plummy high-society accent, that 'Nothing ever—could override—the pride—of London town.'

Not even the quiet Bletchley countryside was entirely safe from the bombs. One day Turing returned from Cambridge to his 'billet' at the Crown pub in the little village of Shenley Brook End. 'Came back to find great excitement as bombs had dropped 100' away,' he said.[57] The explosions brought down the ceilings of his neighbour's house. Few British lives were not touched in some way by the horrific bombing; but by the late autumn the tide of war, although not turning, was at least slackening off a little. Behind the scenes, and far from the main centres of devastation, Hut 6 had been making a significant contribution to the air battle ever since the bombing began.[58] Enigma messages gave advance warning of the bombers' targets.[59] Guided by Enigma decrypts, the Royal Air Force shot enemy planes out of the sky. Sea Lion itself began to look increasingly risky in light of the RAF's unexpected and continuing strength. Hitler decided to postpone the invasion and turned his attention on Russia. The Battle of Britain was seemingly over. 'Never in the field of human conflict was so much owed by so many to so few,' Churchill famously declared.[60] He was talking about the airmen who held the skies against the *Luftwaffe* during the summer of 1940 but, taking a longer view, his words were also a fair summary of the codebreakers' contributions to the war.

While *Seelöwe* had been averted, the Battle of the Atlantic was still raging. If Britain could not be invaded, then she would have to be starved into defeat. Hut 8 looked on helplessly during the winter of 1940–1 as the U-boats sank appalling numbers of merchant vessels in the freezing Atlantic waters. Hut 8 with its hi-tech machinery was producing no significant intelligence, yet even Knox, with his good old-fashioned paper-and-pencil methods, was reading messages encrypted by the Italian navy's no-plugboard form of Enigma. By now Knox had good-naturedly nicknamed Turing the 'bombe-ish boy'.[61] Perhaps this scholar of ancient Greek poetry found Turing himself just slightly machine-like at times. Knox would ultimately come to feel sidelined by the bombes, but March 1941 brought one of his greatest successes.[62] His 'girl', as he called Mavis Lever, just nineteen years of age, broke the Italian naval messages that gave Admiral Sir Andrew Cunningham, British C-in-C Mediterranean, a decisive victory later that month over a fleet of about twenty Italian vessels at the Battle of Matapan near Crete.[63] 'Give me a Lever,' Knox laughed, 'and I can move the universe.'[64] Churchill trumpeted Matapan as 'the greatest fight since Trafalgar' (Nelson's victory over Napoleon's navy in 1805).[65] The nation's morale lifted a little as cinema newsreel audiences the length and breadth of the country watched the dashing Cunningham directing the action from the bridge of his battleship HMS *Warspite*. A satirical song, 'No lika da war', soon shot to popularity. Sung by propagandist and comedian Stanley Holloway, it was the lament of a disenchanted Italian soldier who missed his macaroni and ice-cream cones, and lived in terror of the 'great big guys from Australia'. On the whole, March was a good month for the codebreakers. At almost exactly the same time that Mavis Lever was brewing trouble for the Italians, Hut 8's luck changed dramatically. The Royal Navy pulled off a pinch that came to be seen as a major landmark in Hut 8's history.[66]

It happened during 'Operation Claymore', a mass seaborne commando raid in the Arctic against various ports in the Lofoten Islands.[67] The Lofotens, along with the rest of Norway, had been in German hands since mid 1940, and the operation's aim was to disable the area's extensive fish-oil industry by destroying factories and storage tanks. Operation Claymore's naval commander, Captain Clifford Caslon, aboard his destroyer HMS *Somali*, was on the lookout for a pinch.[68] Around dawn on the morning of the raid, *Somali* spotted an armed German trawler, *Krebs*. *Somali* opened fire, quickly landing three shells on *Krebs*. The wheelhouse took a direct hit, another shell struck the boiler room, and the third set off one of the *Krebs*'s ammunition stores. Eventually a white flag of surrender was hoisted and a party from *Somali* boarded the shattered trawler. They found the German captain dead by the wheel. Below decks the ship was ablaze, but the captain's cabin was undamaged and the boarding party searched it. The crew had evidently thrown *Krebs*'s Enigma machine into the water but there were Enigma wheels inside a locked box discovered in the cabin. The navy rushed these to Bletchley Park along with technical documents also rescued from the captain's cabin.

There were no bigram tables, unfortunately, but there were sheets giving the plugboard settings and wheel details for the complete month of February. These were in fact even more valuable than the bigram tables themselves.[69] Using documents pinched from *Krebs*, Turing and his team managed to reconstruct the bigram tables entry by entry.[70] Suddenly Hut 8 could look forward to opening for business. The danger, though, was that new bigram tables could come into force at any time (although, in fact, this did not happen until June).[71] Eager to follow up on the *Krebs* success as quickly as possible, Harry Hinsley in Hut 4 had a bright idea. The bespectacled, serious-looking Hinsley, son of a Black Country carter, was still an undergraduate when he joined Birch's Naval Intelligence section.

In later life he would become the Master of St John's College, Cambridge. He was, he admitted, 'scruffy and young, and civilian', but in his opinion the Admiralty would just have to get used to that.[72] Hinsley reasoned that since German weather ships operated alone in solitary surroundings, and yet were only lightly armed, they were ideal targets for a pinch. From decrypts he knew the approximate whereabouts of the weather ship *München*, operating in the deserted Arctic waters north-east of Iceland.[73] He proposed a pinch to the Admiralty and soon *Somali* was sailing north with a posse of destroyers. They sighted the lonely *München* towards the evening of 7 May and *Somali* loosed off a few salvoes of shells.[74] All missed, exploding in the water. The last thing Captain Caslon wanted to do was risk sinking the weathership—his aim was to persuade the terrified German crew to abandon ship. Sure enough, two lifeboats were quickly launched. Caslon drew his vessel alongside *München* and gave the order to board. It was a rerun of the *Krebs* story—the Germans had thrown the Enigma and bigram tables overboard, but the boarding party captured sheets giving the plugboard settings and wheel details for the month of June.[75] These were money in the bank as far as Hut 8 was concerned. Another of Hinsley's raids produced the same information for the month of July, this time from the weather ship *Lauenburg*, situated even further north in the Norwegian Sea.

The most dramatic pinch of all took place just two days after *Somali* fired on *München*. North Atlantic U-boats had been shadowing Convoy OB 318 (Ocean Outward Route B) for at least thirty-six hours, watching nine columns of merchant vessels make their way through the rough waters south of Iceland—thirty-eight merchantmen in all, escorted by about a dozen Royal Navy ships.[76] The night and morning of 9 May had passed peacefully, but a minute or two after noon Kapitän Julius Lemp's *U-110* suddenly torpedoed SS *Bengore Head* and SS *Esmond* within seconds of each other. The Navy corvette *Aubretia* managed to get a fix on the U-boat's position by means of sonar (called 'Asdic' in those days) and dropped ten depth charges overhead. 'It was a classic attack,' said Sub-Lieutenant David Balme of the destroyer *Bulldog*, who would soon be leading the boarding party. 'Depth charges underneath the U-boat blew

Figure 13. U-110 surfaces after the depth charge attack

Credit: Imperial War Museum (Hu 63112)

it to the surface. It was the dream of every escort vessel to see a U-boat blown to the surface. Usually they just sink.'[77] Oil covered the water. The terrified crew leapt from the submarine, 'speeded on their way by small arm fire' an official report said.[78] Eventually the survivors were hauled aboard *Aubretia*.[79] Some of the German submariners saw Lemp with them in the water, but he vanished without trace, perhaps preferring suicide to capture.

Balme launched a small boat from *Bulldog* into the heavy swell and took a party of eight men across.[80] Waves were breaking over the giant bulk of the U-boat and Balme's tiny whaler was swept onto its deck. The whaler smashed to pieces against the U-boat's conning tower. Revolver in hand, Balme peered down through the lower conning tower hatch. He couldn't imagine that the Germans would have abandoned the U-boat without leaving someone on board to sink her. Cautiously he swung down into the Control Room: 'Secondary lighting, dim blue lighting, was on and I couldn't see anybody, just a nasty hissing noise that I didn't like the sound of,' he said.[81] Balme told his men to form a human chain and pass all books and charts up onto deck while he searched the ship. The faded type of his official report gives a glimpse of what life was like for the U-boat men. Below decks he found U-110 a fascinating sight, 'a fine ship', he said, new, well appointed, profoundly foreign. Aubretia's attack had interrupted lunch. A large serving dish of mashed potatoes was sitting in the engine room, and another crammed with shrimps was in the ward-room (the officers' dining room and lounge). The galley—kitchen—was 'magnificent', Balme said. Also in the wardroom he found novels, cards, · dice, pornography, bottles of beer, British Player's brand cigarettes, and luxurious cigars. Elsewhere there were guns stuffed into clothes drawers, sacks of potatoes heaped up beside the submarine's instruments, and great piles of tinned ham and corned beef.

Amazingly, the wireless room contained the U-110's Enigma, 'plugged in and as though it was in actual use when abandoned', Balme said. The current bigram tables, too, were among the papers Balme's men carried away from the submarine.[82] Lemp, a national hero who had been dec-orated by Hitler the previous year, must have been very certain that his ship was going down. Ironically, though, Balme's loot was of no great interest to Hut 8. Turing had already laboriously reconstructed the bigram tables, using the information from the Lofoten pinch.[83] The U-110 pinch does not rate even a mention in the two comprehensive histories of Hut 8 written by Alexander and Mahon at the end of the war.

Thanks to the reconstructed bigram tables, the bombes, and another of Turing's inventions, 'Banburismus'—the three Bs—Hut 8 was now well and truly operational. Turing devised Banburismus on the same pro-ductive night in 1939 that he solved Dolphin's indicator system.[84] 'The terminology was introduced in honour of the famous town of Banbury,' Turing explained ironically.[85] Banbury is a tiny Oxfordshire town where a small workshop produced the special punched paper strips that Turing needed to put his method into practice. Banburismus exploited the fact that if two stretches of Dolphin plaintext are superimposed on one another, the chance of two letters being the same is 1 in 17—whereas if two stretches of *randomly* selected letters are superimposed, the chance of producing an identical letter is only 1 in 26.[86] One user of Turing's method, Jack Good, said wryly: 'The game of Banburismus was enjoyable, not easy enough to be trivial, but not difficult enough to cause a nervous breakdown.'[87] 'I was quite good at this game,' he said, adding modestly: 'but Alexander was the champion.' Good liked using the word 'good'. He titled one of his later books *Good Thinking*. Meeting someone for the first time, he would stick out a hand and announce, in his rather precise way of speaking, 'I am Good.'[88] 'We found Good very entertaining when we got used to him,' said Turing.[89] Good prided himself on his talent for picking the right word; he called Hitler simply 'the megamurderer'.

Hut 8 could not use Banburismus until the bigram tables were known and so Turing's ingenious method sat ready on the shelf for over a year, until March's Lofoten pinch delivered the needed information. Soon after Lofoten, Hut 8's 'Banburists' were using the method to reduce the vast amounts of searching that the bombes had to carry out. Lofoten 'changed the whole position', Alexander said. 'In April we all settled down to an attempt to break the traffic as nearly currently as possible.'[90] During June and July the codebreakers were reading Dolphin messages within a few hours of interception—'almost as quickly as the Germans', said Rolf Noskwith, a German-born mathematics undergraduate who was recruited to Hut 8 that summer from Cambridge.[91]

By this point the 'battle was won', Mahon declared.[92] In fact, Turing had broken into the daily U-boat communications just in the nick of time. At the beginning of June, Churchill's planners were predicting that the U-boat attack would soon tip Britain into starvation.[93] 'The only thing that ever really frightened me during the war was the U-boat peril,' Churchill said later.[94] In the very month that his planners issued this dire prediction, Hut 8's decrypts enabled evasive measures to be taken so successfully that the North Atlantic U-boats did not make a single sighting of a convoy for twenty-three days straight.[95] In July, Turing was summoned to Whitehall, along with Alexander and Welchman, to be thanked officially for what he had done.[96] Each of the three men received a bonus of

£200, a sizeable enough sum in those days—Turing's fellowship at King's paid him less than twice this amount in a year. During the subsequent months, evasive routings continued and the U-boats spent more and more time searching fruitlessly.[97] Tremendous care was exercised to conceal the fact that Bletchley was reading U-boat Enigma. British Intelligence leaked trumped-up information about a revolutionary new type of long-range radar that detected submarines hundreds of miles away, even when they were beneath the surface.[98]

August brought a personal crisis for Turing. He and Joan Clarke decided to snatch a few days hill-walking together at Porthmadog in North Wales.[99] It started badly. On their arrival the Queens Hotel denied any knowledge of a booking, despite Turing's furiously waving the telegram he had received saying ACCOMMODATE FROM 26TH – QUEENS.[100] 'Such barefaced lying is almost unbelievable,' he fulminated.[101] After a tiresome search, the two managed to find a room in the High Street. Something happened during the holiday, something sensitive enough to make Turing's mother Sara blacken out several lines of the letter he wrote to her from Porthmadog. Not long afterwards he abruptly broke off the engagement. 'The coward does it with a kiss,' he told Joan, quoting Oscar Wilde. 'The brave man with a sword!'[102] It was a slightly theatrical way to deliver heartbreaking news. Turing had swerved off a well-trodden path. Homosexual men not infrequently opted for an opposite-sex marriage, children, happy family life. The circumstances of life were coped with, a formula was found for rendering everything consistent. In the end, though, this was not the route that Turing chose for himself.

Meanwhile, Bletchley Park's internal operations were not running as smoothly as they should have. The top administrator, Denniston, a small neat man who had played hockey for Scotland before the First World War, was not shouting loudly enough in Whitehall on behalf of his codebreakers. As chief of the newly formed Government Code and Cypher School in 1919, he had had no more than twenty-four permanent staff—a manageable number.[103] However, the job of heading up the vast organization that the 'School' had now become was just not what he was cut out for. One of his codebreakers commented rather unkindly that he had the talent to 'manage a small sweet shop'.[104] Denniston was at his best when working on a shoestring and his greatest achievement was creating Bletchley Park out of almost nothing in 1939 and 1940.

In 1941 his burgeoning organization was plagued by bottlenecks. He should have been bending ears in Whitehall to get additional staff. As it was, vital *Luftwaffe* 'Light Blue' messages from North Africa were not being decoded for want of about twenty typists. The naval work itself was being delayed for lack of some twenty untrained clerks in the Freebornery (the charmingly named unit headed by Frederic Freeborn). The list went on. Turing and three other senior codebreakers decided to take matters into their own hands. Bypassing Denniston completely, they wrote directly to Winston Churchill. Their letter, dated 21 October 1941, began: 'Dear Prime Minister, Some weeks ago you paid us the honour of a visit, and we believe that you regard our work as important.' Then they cut straight to the chase: 'We think, however, that you ought to know that this work is being held up, and in some cases is not being done at all, principally because we cannot get sufficient staff to deal with it.'[105]

One of Turing's co-signatories, *Times* chess correspondent Stuart Milner-Barry from Hut 6, agreed to deliver the letter by hand. 'I was the most readily expendable,' he joked.[106] He remembered feeling 'a sense of total incredulity (can this really be happening?)' as his taxi carried him towards the prime ministerial residence at 10 Downing Street. Inside No 10, he found himself headed off by Churchill's secretary, Brigadier George Harvie-Watt. The puzzled brigadier agreed to pass the letter on, despite Milner-Barry's inability to identify himself or to explain what the letter concerned.

A few days later Milner-Barry bumped into Denniston in the corridor. Denniston 'made some rather wry remark about our unorthodox behaviour', Milner-Barry said, 'but he was much too nice a man to bear malice'. Immediately upon reading the letter, Churchill sent a memo to his Chief of Staff, General 'Pug' Ismay: 'ACTION THIS DAY Make sure they have all they want on extreme priority and report to me that this has been done.'[107]

1942: BACK TO AMERICA + HITLER'S NEW CODE

1942 was a turning point in the war, both for Turing and for his country. Since the fall of France, Britain had fought on alone. The years 1940 and 1941 were a time of isolation and terrible danger—Britain's 'finest hour', Churchill said. In America the mood had continued to be against getting caught up in someone else's war. Europe seemed far away, and there was no good reason to spill American blood in a fight among foreigners. Churchill hoped that rhetoric might propel America to Britain's aid. If Britain should fail, he warned, 'then the whole world, including the United States, including all that we have known and cared for, will sink into the abyss of a new dark age made more sinister, and perhaps more protracted, by the lights of perverted science'.[1] Then, in December 1941, Japanese aircraft unexpectedly attacked the American fleet at Pearl Harbor and suddenly Britain and the United States were standing shoulder to shoulder in war.

During 1942 hundreds of thousands of US airmen, and later ground troops, arrived on British soil. The mood in Britain swung upwards. 'There's nothing wrong with the Americans,' the English enjoyed complaining, 'apart from them being overpaid, oversexed, and over here.' The dance halls were full, and even if the gaiety was tinged with anxiety and sadness, laughter was still laughter. A hot flood of American music poured into the country. 'I'm trav'lin' light,' sang Billie Holiday. The King of Jazz, Paul 'Pops' Whiteman, belted out 'I've found a new baby,' and many of the new arrivals did exactly that. Glen Miller charmed the entire nation with his cool, hip-wiggling 'Chatanooga Choo Choo'. Incoming Americans soon noticed that wartime Britain's list of entertainment options was pretty much limited to dancing, movies, or bicycle rides in the country. With the Blitz now a memory, cinema audiences no longer left en masse in the middle of a film, although morale-boosting British war movies still formed the staple diet. Hollywood, at first not yet fully adjusted to a wartime role, sent *Bambi* and Mickey Rooney in *A Yank at Eton*. Then, as the Nazis tasted their first major defeat, in North Africa, the classic war romance *Casablanca* began filling cinemas.

The film is set at the beginning of December 1941, less than five days before Pearl Harbor and America's headlong tumble into war. We are told that Humphrey Bogart's Rick, a lone American, fled Paris the previous year to escape Hitler's invading armies. 'They're asleep all over America!' he declares pointedly. Characters from the various warring European nations rub shoulders in the neutral territory of Bogart's Casablanca Café Américain. As Nazi boss Heinrich Strasser enters the café, urbane French chief of police Louis Renault fusses to the waiter, 'Carl, see that Major Strasser gets a good table, one close to the ladies.' The Jewish waiter—now a refugee but formerly a professor—replies, 'I have already given him the best, knowing he is German and would take it anyway.' Hollywood's rhetoric is slicker than Churchill's, but the take-home message is similar: time to make a stand. Bogart, whose catchphrase is 'I stick my neck out for nobody,' ultimately drops his pose of neutrality and joins the French in their struggle against Germany. 'Louis, I think this is the beginning of a beautiful friendship,' he announces to Renault as the film ends. Mysteriously Britain is not mentioned, although Renault—who hardly seems French at all—is played by a very English actor. Maybe it was just myopic casting, or maybe not, but the reality indeed was that America and Britain had bonded against Hitler. For the first time since 1939 victory seemed graspable.

Turing's bombes—there were over 50 by the end of 1942[2]—played their role in the rout in North Africa. On the back of Enigma intelligence, Bernard Montgomery's Eighth Army swept Erwin Rommel's Afrika

Korps out of the deserts of Egypt and Libya. Montgomery's victory at El Alamein, in the autumn of 1942, ended the Nazis' attempt to capture the Suez Canal and open up a route to the vital Middle East oilfields. Shortage of fuel plagued the Nazis for the rest of the war. Before and during the fifteen-day battle of El Alamein, Bletchley's decrypts revealed the routes and cargoes of ships carrying Rommel's supplies across the Mediterranean.[3] The RAF was able to pick and choose the best targets. Rommel's tanks, ammunition, petrol, and food tipped blazing into the Mediterranean. Even bread and pasta were in short supply at El Alamein, let alone tanks and petrol. A single sinking disposed of many tons of ammunition and no fewer than ten tanks—over a quarter of the number that the Afrika Korps had remaining in service by the end of the battle. Other sinkings put paid to thousands of tons of fuel.

Many of these broken messages were sent via the Hagelin C38 cipher machine that the Italians used. The 'Hag' was the brainchild of Swedish engineer Boris Hagelin.[4] Bletchley discovered that, owing to the carelessness of its Italian operators, the Hag was much less secure than Enigma, and the Italian Naval Section, part of Frank Birch's empire, churned out Hagelin decrypts practically by the bucketful.[5] In due course the engineers designed a ten-foot-high machine for breaking the Hag and installed it in GC & CS's London premises, an office above a women's dress shop in Mayfair, close to Berkeley Square.[6] Vera Lynn's hit, 'A Nightingale Sang in Berkeley Square', was playing everywhere at the time, and the machine acquired the name 'Nightingale'. A second Nightingale was soon singing in Vinca Vincent's section at Bletchley. The Swiss company founded by Boris Hagelin, Crypto AG, is alive and well today and is still producing cipher machines. Reports indicate that recent Hagelin users included Colonel Muammar Gaddafi and Saddam Hussein.[7]

Two or three days before Montgomery began his attack at El Alamein, a deciphered message from the Panzer Army HQ revealed that, because of the shortage of fuel, Rommel's tanks had insufficient freedom of movement to fight effectively.[8] Enigma messages gave away crucial details of Rommel's defensive plans.[9] By the tenth day of the battle, the Afrika Korps was in poor shape. A broken message from Rommel to the German High Command confessed that the 'gradual annihilation of the army must be faced'. Hitler's response, eagerly read at Bletchley, told Rommel not to yield 'a step', and said that he must take 'the road leading to death or victory'.[10] Rommel knew that the road leading west to Tunisia was a better bet, but orders were orders. Hitler never was a man to think about saving lives. In 1944, as the Allies liberated France, the Führer ordered that 'Never, or only as a heap of rubble, must Paris fall to the enemy.'[11] Another chilling decrypt, from the end of 1944, instructed General Heinz Guderian—who was occupying the Hungarian capital of Budapest and was surrounded by the Russian army—that evacuation without fighting was 'out of question'. 'Every house to be contested,' Hitler ranted. 'Measures to prevent troops being endangered by the armed mob of the city to be taken ruthlessly.'[12] At El Alamein Rommel held out obediently for another day or so, then sensibly decided to make a run for it, heading towards Tunisia with the remains of his devastated Panzer Army.

Earlier in 1942, Hut 8 had lost Atlantic U-boat Enigma, though not all of Naval Enigma. This happened when the wily U-boat supremo Karl Dönitz introduced the four-wheeled version of the Enigma machine, on 1 February.[13] Except for a few lucky strikes, no more U-boat messages were read until the end of 1942—one of the few decrypts being an 'all staff' message from Dönitz himself, announcing his promotion to admiral.[14] Hut 8 had to wait patiently for a pinch. This did not come until October, when the U-559 was depth-charged and boarded by the HMS *Petard* in the eastern Mediterranean, in an incident resembling the boarding of the U-110 nearly eighteen months previously.[15] This time, though, the boarding party was not so lucky and two British seamen, Anthony Fasson and Colin Grazier, were drowned when the damaged sub suddenly went down. Documents they had managed to pass up to the *Petard* during their last minutes contained a good supply of cribs, and within a few weeks Hut 8 was reading U-boat messages again. At the Admiralty in London, one day in December, decrypted material giving the positions of Atlantic U-boats started to chatter out of the teleprinters again. Once the flow started, the information poured out 'in an unending stream until the early hours of the following morning', said Patrick Beesly, an Admiralty intelligence officer.[16]

As Hut 8 waited to get back into the U-boat traffic, Turing was looking for new horizons. Routine work irked him and he was at his best breaking new ground. Now that he had cracked the fundamental problems posed by Naval Enigma, and had pioneered the methods needed to break the daily traffic, he was left with a more-or-less empty intray so far as Hut 8 went. By this time he had already relinquished his position as head of Hut 8. He loathed administration and always left most of it to Alexander.[17] Then one day he arrived at the gatehouse late for work and duly filled in the late book. He came to a space requiring the name of his head of section and he unexpectedly wrote 'Mr Alexander', explained Donald Michie. 'Nothing was said. But somewhere wheels turned silently. Records were updated. Alexander continued his miracles of inspired and often unorthodox deployment of human and material resources, but now as the official head.'[18] Michie, a cocky schoolboy of eighteen when he joined Bletchley Park, would in later life put some of Turing's ideas about computer intelligence into practice. He also became one of Turing's small circle of close friends. 'When I first met Alan' he said, 'his eccentric manner deceived me into thinking he was all head and no heart. When I knew him better I realized that his emotions were so child-like and fundamentally good as to make him a very vulnerable person in a world so largely populated by self-seekers.'[19]

In November 1942 Turing left Bletchley for the United States to liaise with cryptologists there.[20] He never did any more work in Hut 8, and on his return to Bletchley in March he took up a wider brief as scientific policy advisor.[21] He sailed for New York on a passenger liner during what was one of the most dangerous periods for Atlantic shipping. It must have been a nerve-racking journey. That month the U-boats sank a total of more than a hundred Allied vessels.[22] Turing was the only civilian aboard a floating barracks packed to bursting point with military personnel. At times there were as many as 600 men crammed into the officers' lounge—Turing said he nearly fainted. On the ship's arrival in New York, his papers were determined to be inadequate, placing his entry to the United States in jeopardy.

The US immigration officials debated interning him on Ellis Island. 'That will teach my employers to furnish me with better credentials,' was Turing's laconic comment.[23] It was a private joke at the British government's expense—since becoming a codebreaker in 1939 his employers were none other than His Majesty's Foreign Office. His principal reason for making the trip was to spend time at Manhattan's Bell Labs, but America did not exactly welcome Turing with open arms.[24] The authorities declined to clear him to visit this hive of top-secret projects. General George Marshall, Chief of Staff of the US Army, declared that Bell Labs housed work 'of so secret a nature that Dr. Turing cannot be given access'.[25] In January, after a protracted exchange of letters between General Marshall and Churchill's personal representative in Washington, Sir John Dill, Bell Labs finally opened its imperial-sized gates to the shabby British traveller.[26]

Turing based himself at Bell Labs for the next two months.[27] The imposing thirteen-storey Bell Labs building was on Manhattan's Lower West Side, close to the Hudson waterfront and a short stroll from the gay bars, clubs, and cafeterias of Greenwich Village.[28] New York's relatively open gay community must have seemed a million miles from Bletchley Park, where Turing kept his sexual orientation to himself. During his sojourn at Bell Labs he travelled down to Washington DC from time to time to continue his liaison work with Op. 20 G, the US Navy codebreaking unit. On his first arrival in Washington a couple of months previously, Op. 20 G's Joe Eachus had shown him round the city.[29] Turing was fascinated by Washington's letter-number system of street names—M Street, K Street, 9th Street, 24th Street, and so on. It was reminiscent of Enigma. The number streets run north–south and the letter streets east–west, but because twenty-six letters were not enough, the city planners started the letter names over again at the Capitol, with C Street SW running parallel to C Street NW but a few blocks further south. Turing's first reaction was to ask the key question: 'What do they do in the numbered streets when they get to twenty-six'? He joked that the numbers should go up as high as 26 × 26—corresponding to a potential twenty-six distinguished alphabets of twenty-six letters each—and grinned to hear that actually there were two 1st streets, two 2nd streets, two of everything.

Bell Labs was exploring cryptology's new frontier, the encryption of speech, and Bletchley Park's new head, Edward 'Jumbo' Travis, wanted Turing to get involved. Travis had replaced Denniston less than three months after Turing's devastating letter to Churchill.[30] If speech could be encrypted securely, then top-level secret business could be conducted person to person, by radio or even by telephone. This was a more natural way for military commanders to communicate than by written text, and in addition interactive voice communication was less open to misinterpretation and to the perils of incompleteness. At Bell Labs Turing saw a voice encryption system based on what was called the 'vocoder'. Maybe he even contributed some finishing touches. America and her allies used this system—codenamed SIGSALY—from 1943 to 1946. Today the Bell Labs' vocoder lives on as a musical instrument for transforming the human voice, and if you have listened to performers like T-Pain, Herbie Hancock, Kraftwerk, or Electric Light Orchestra, you will have heard the weird, unearthly sound of the vocoder. Today's vocoders are not much larger than a laptop, while the original military model consisted of many tall cabinets occupying three sides of a room.[31] Once Turing was back in England, he designed a portable voice encryption system consisting of three small boxes each roughly the size of a shoebox. He named his system 'Delilah'...but that is getting ahead of the story.

When he landed in New York, Turing had already been involved in US liaison for at least a year, and in 1941 he had written out a helpful tutorial for Op. 20 G, whose attempts to crack U-boat Enigma were going nowhere.[32] Turing politely made it clear that their methods were utterly impractical. The United States is often portrayed as responsible for breaking Naval Enigma, for example in the Hollywood movie U-571 starring Harvey Keitel and Jon Bon Jovi—but the truth could hardly be more different. Another report of Turing's impressions of the US codebreaking effort survives from his 1942 trip, prosaically entitled 'Visit to National Cash Register Corporation of Dayton, Ohio'.[33] At Dayton, NCR engineer Joseph Desch was heading up a massive bombe-building programme for the US Navy. Turing took the train over to Ohio to give advice. Jack Good described Desch as 'a near genius', but Turing still found a lot to criticize in the American design.[34] 'I suspect that there is some misunderstanding,' he said sharply at one point in his report. He also complained, 'I find that comparatively little interest is taken in the Enigma over here apart from the production of Bombes.' Turing explained how the US bombes would be used: 'The principle of running British made cribs on American Bombes is now taken for granted,' he said. In 1995, Desch's right-hand man on the project, electronics expert Robert Mumma, explained that at NCR, Turing had 'told us what we wanted to do and how to do it'.[35] 'He said, "You've got to do this, you've got to do this,"' Mumma recounted; Turing 'controlled the design more than anyone else did'.

It was not until six months later, in June 1943, that the first Enigma message was broken by an American bombe.[36] Mahon described what he called the 'inexperienced enthusiasm' of the Washington codebreakers at this time.[37] He complained that 'they were content to pour bombe time down the drain'; 'their weakness', he said harshly, was 'a complete absence of judgement'. He added graciously enough, though, that 'doubtless mistakes they made were only the same mistakes as we ourselves had been making 2 years before'. At the end of 1943, Hut 8 condescendingly gave the still inexperienced Washington codebreakers responsibility for breaking the Mediterranean U-boat traffic codenamed Turtle, so that they would have something 'of their own', Mahon said. Turtle traffic, he remarked waspishly, was always dull. Mahon recorded that it was as late as the middle of 1944 before Bletchley thought the Washington codebreakers 'well qualified' enough to be trusted with sole charge of the major U-boat network codenamed Shark. By the end of the war there were about 200 British bombes situated at Bletchley Park and its surrounding outstations, and just over half that number of American bombes at Op. 20 G in Washington.[38] Thanks to excellent transatlantic cable communications, the Washington bombes were absorbed relatively seamlessly into Bletchley's operations. Hut 8 was, Alexander said, 'able to use the Op. 20 G bombes almost as conveniently as if they had been at one of our outstations 20 or 30 miles away'.[39]

Tantalizingly, Turing's Dayton report reveals that he had had a hand in Bletchley's work against the Hagelin cipher machine, and while at Dayton he gave an informal lesson on breaking Hag messages. Even more fascinatingly, the report indicates that he had also had a hand in the attack on the Imperial Japanese Navy's principal code, JN-25 (actually a series of codes that evolved over time, as improvements and modifications came along). During 1942, intelligence from JN-25 decrypts was used in the Battle of the Coral Sea and then, in June, at the fierce Battle of Midway, which saw the United States win a decisive victory over Japan's navy. Decrypts enabled the Americans to ambush and sink four Japanese aircraft carriers at Midway. Turing describes a machine that he says the Letchworth bombe factory built early in 1940. He doesn't specifically mention Japanese codes in his report, but from his description it is evident that the Letchworth machine's function was to help with breaking JN-25 messages.[40] Since Bletchley adhered strictly to the need-to-know principle—don't tell anyone anything that they don't need to know—Turing's knowledge of this machine implies that he played some role in developing the early methods for attacking JN-25. The GC & CS outpost in Singapore put the methods into practice. As much of the story of Turing's involvement with JN-25 as has so far been pieced together will be published by Australian mathematicians Peter Donovan and John Mack.

It was immediately prior to his 1942 trip to the United States, though, that Turing made one of his most spectacular contributions to the war. In the summer of 1942 he was transferred from Hut 8 back to the Research Section, the reverse of the move he had made at the beginning of 1940. His talent for groundbreaking work was needed again. The Research Section was in the early stages of fathoming a new German cipher machine, codenamed 'Tunny'. The Tunny machine was a very different beast from Enigma, technologically more sophisticated and—theoretically—more secure. By the outbreak of war, the Enigma machine was old technology, slow to use and requiring an astounding total of six people to encrypt and decrypt a single message, three at each end of the radio link (typist, assistant, and radio operator). Obviously there was room for improvement; and in 1940 the Lorenz Company, based in Berlin, produced the state-of-the-art Tunny, known to the Germans as Cipher Attachment (*Schlüsselzusatz*) SZ40. The hi-tech Tunny, Hitler's BlackBerry, was created by the Third

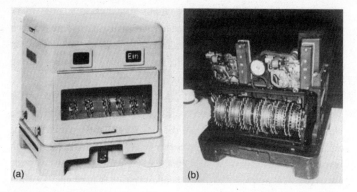

Figure 14. The Tunny machine: (a) in its case and (b) with the workings exposed

Credit: (a) The Turing Archive for the History of Computing – All rights reserved; (b) Imperial War Museum (Hu 56940B)

Reich's scientists specifically for use by the German *Wehrmacht*, and unlike Enigma it carried only the highest grade of intelligence. The story of Tunny and Turing's contributions to breaking it were kept secret for almost sixty years.

Only one operator was required at each end of a Tunny radio link: the sender typed plain German at the keyboard of a teleprinter attached to the SZ40, and the rest was completely automatic. Morse was not used—the encrypted output of the Tunny machine went directly to air. In comparison with Enigma, it is striking how much of the coding and decoding process Lorenz's engineers had managed to automate. Under normal operating conditions, neither the sending nor the receiving operator ever even saw the coded form of the message. As far as they were concerned, German went in and German came out.

The first experimental Tunny radio link went into operation between Berlin and Greece in June 1941.[41] The Germans deemed the experiment a success and soon dozens of Tunny links were sprouting up all over Europe—it was a new phase in communications technology and a distant forerunner of today's mobile phone networks. At Bletchley there was deep concern. Just when things were starting to tick over nicely with Enigma, a new code of unknown nature had suddenly come out of nowhere. The codebreakers gave each Tunny link a piscine name: Berlin–Paris was Jellyfish, Berlin–Rome was Bream, Berlin–Copenhagen Turbot (see Fig. 15). The Germans built a large central exchange at Berlin, and another at Königsberg to handle the eastward links to the Russian front.[42] There were also fixed exchanges at some other important centres, such as Paris, but other than that the links were mobile, moving with the generals and their armies.[43] 'Eventually we were reading lengthy messages almost daily from Hitler's commanders-in-chief, sent from their mobile headquarters on the principal battle fronts,' recalled Jerry Roberts, a tall trim young army captain who joined the struggle against Tunny in July 1942. 'Von Weichs on the Russian front, Kesselring in Italy, von Runstedt on the Western front. They poured their thoughts out to us—battle plans, strategic assessments, details of their troop strengths, tanks and supplies.' 'Going the other way,' Roberts continued, 'were messages containing orders and strategic thinking from the military top brass, such as Wilhelm Keitel, Supreme Commander of the Armed Forces, and the Operational Chief of Staff, Alfred Jodl. And, of course, there were messages signed by Hitler himself. I still remember that shiver of excitement when we got one. ADOLPH9HITLER9FUEHRER was the way his signature looked, once we had decrypted it ('9' was the teleprinter code for 'space'). Elegantly brief, I always thought, in comparison with the overblown titles usually favoured by the German military.'

Each mobile Tunny unit consisted of two trucks, one carrying the radio gear—this had to be kept well away from the teleprinters to avoid interference—and the other containing teleprinter equipment and a pair of Tunny machines, one for sending and one for receiving.[44] Jack Good was among the team to examine a Tunny truck that was captured during the last days of the war. Undamaged, it contained two Tunnies accompanied by their two operators, now prisoners yet seemingly quite content about it, Good recalled.[45] In the truck was some dried tree bark that the men were smoking in place of tobacco—it brought home vividly to Good just how bad economic conditions had become in Germany. This was actually Good's first sight of a Tunny machine, even though he had been breaking Tunny messages since the spring of 1943. No Tunny had been

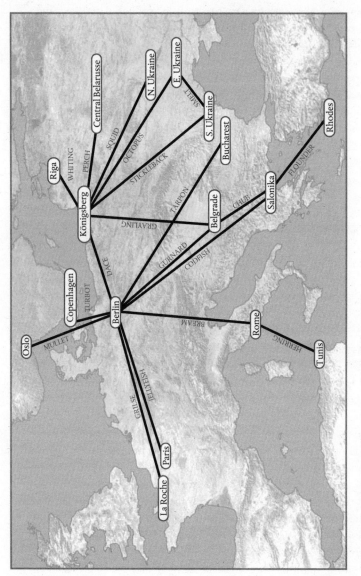

Figure 15. Tunny radio network, German army (March 1943–July 1944)

Credit Dustin Barrett and Jack Copeland – All rights reserved

captured before, at first because of lack of opportunity and then, once the codebreakers were reading Hitler's orders to his generals, because it was feared that a pinch might lead the Germans to modify the machine.

As soon as the experimental Berlin–Greece link went on the air, watchful British wireless operators intercepted messages from the unknown machine. At first nothing at all could be read, but then Colonel John Tiltman scored a tremendous success, managing to break a message about 4,000 letters long. In 1920 the army had lent Tiltman to the Government Code and Cypher School for a fortnight. He didn't leave until his retirement over thirty years later. He was supposed to be helping with the translation of a backlog of Russian messages, but he had tried his hand at breaking a few ciphers and was an instant star.[46] One of codebreaking's legends, Tiltman made a series of major breakthroughs against Japanese military ciphers, including JN-25, before tackling Tunny. Every inch a soldier, he would work in uniform while standing at a specially made wooden desk; a wound inflicted at the Somme made sitting uncomfortable. Like a holy relic, Tiltman's desk now has pride of place in Britain's modern codebreaking headquarters in Cheltenham, a palpable link with codebreaking's glory days.

Tiltman had very little to go on. It was reasonably clear, though, that the plaintexts encrypted by Tunny were expressed in international binary teleprinter code. Teleprinter code was in widespread commercial use and there was nothing secret about it. Each character on the teleprinter keyboard was automatically converted into a string of five os and 1s: A is 11000, B is 10011, and so forth. Tiltman also knew that Tunny messages were transmitted with an indicator, just like Dolphin messages—except that Tunny indicators consisted of a list of twelve names, Anton for A, Berta for B, Caspar for C, Dora for D, and so on (see Fig. 16). It wasn't too difficult to guess that the Tunny machine might have twelve wheels and that the initial letters of the twelve names indicated the positions of the wheels at the start of the message. On top of that, Tiltman had a hunch—like most of his hunches, perfectly correct—that Tunny was what was called an *additive* cipher machine. An additive machine contained a mechanism for generating a stream of random-looking letters, called 'key' at Bletchley, and these were automatically *added* to the plaintext in order to

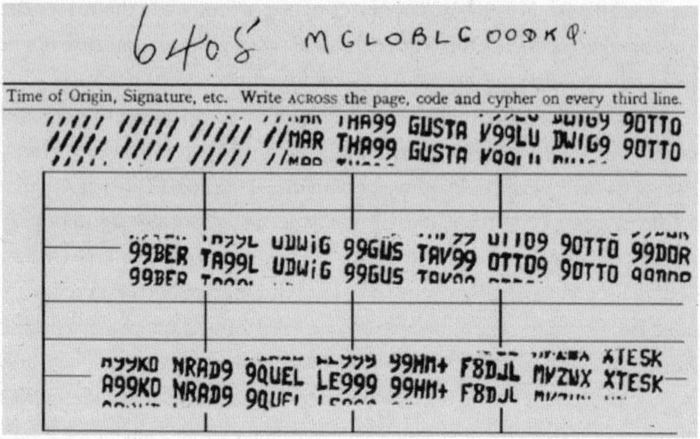

Figure 16. The start of a Tunny message

Credit: Bletchley Park Trust (and thanks to F. Bauer)

obscure it (see Fig. 17). The job of the Tunny's twelve wheels was to generate this stream of random-looking letters or key. The principle was completely different from Enigma.

Sometimes the sending Tunny operator would foolishly use the same wheel positions for two messages. At Bletchley this was called a *depth* and depths usually came about through things going wrong during transmission. The recipient would say something like 'You faded, please repeat' and the sender would start again from the beginning of the message, lazily or stupidly using the same wheel settings rather than picking new ones. If the repeated message was identical to the original, the codebreakers were no better off—instead of one copy of something unintelligible, they had two. But if the sender made a few typos the second time around, or used different punctuation, the depth consisted of two not-quite-identical plaintexts, each encrypted with exactly the same stream of obscuring letters—a codebreaker's dream.

Depths were easy to spot because the two transmissions each had the same indicator (Gustav Ludwig Otto Martha, etc.). Tiltman decrypted a monster depth of 4,000 characters in the late summer of 1941, giving the codebreakers their first entry into Tunny. His success had a whiff of the uncanny about it. On the basis of his prior knowledge of additive cipher machines, he guessed that if he added the two messages together, the key would cancel out, leaving a long and seemingly patternless sequence of keyboard characters in which the two plaintexts were blended together like the butter and sugar in a cake mix. Somewhat against the odds, Tiltman chose to do this addition in a way that turned out to be exactly the way the Tunny machine added teleprint letters: 0 and 0 make 0, and 0 and 1 make 1, but 1 and 1 make 0. Two sames make 0, two differents make 1. For example, adding A, or 11000, to B, or 10011, produces 01011, which is the teleprint code for G. Peter Hilton, the palindrome king, had an unusually powerful visual imagination and could perform these additions in his mind's eye, inwardly watching two long streams of letters merge themselves into one single stream in accordance with the rules of Tunny addition.

Tiltman managed to prise the two plaintexts apart. It took him ten days. He had to guess at words of each message, but Tiltman was a very good guesser. Each time he guessed a word from one message, he added it—at the point where he guessed it belonged—to letters in the cake-mix sequence that he had obtained by adding the two ciphertexts. If his guess was correct, then as if by magic an intelligible fragment of the second message would pop out. For example, adding the word *'geheim'* (secret) at a particular place caused the plausible fragment *'eratta'* to pop out.[47] This short break could then be extended to the left and right by guessing that *'eratta'* is part of *'militaerattache'* (military attache); and then if these new letters are added to their counterparts in the cake-mix sequence, further letters of the first message pop out. Eventually Tiltman achieved enough of these local breaks to realize that long stretches of each message were the same, and so was able to decrypt the whole thing. To top it all off, he added one of the resulting plaintexts to its ciphertext, revealing the 4,000 or so characters of key that had been used to encrypt the message.

Breaking one message was a far cry from knowing how the Tunny machine worked, though. In the case of Enigma, the codebreakers at least had the commercial form of the machine as a starting point, and the operating manuals that Schmidt had photographed told them a lot about the German military version.[48] There was nothing like that with Tunny—pure thought would have to suffice. Incredibly, suffice it did. Tiltman's 4,000 characters of key found their way into the hands of a very humble man, Bill Tutte. 'See what you can do with this,' Tutte's section head told him.[49] Roberts shared an office with Tutte and found him rather like Turing in some ways. 'Both were taciturn and abstracted,' said Roberts. 'Tutte would sit blankly for very long periods, deep in thought and staring into the middle distance.' A shy and unassuming person, Tutte's speech—on the relatively rare occasions when he did speak—was strongly flavoured with his native Suffolk. The son of a gardener and a cook, he grew up at a famous Newmarket racing stable, but a scholarship to Trinity College Cambridge ported him into a different world, and there he started to stretch his young mathematical wings.[50] A few years later, in January 1942, Tutte managed to deduce the workings of the Tunny machine from Tiltman's key. It was one of the most astonishing pieces of cryptanalysis of the war. 'While I sat across the office watching him for all those weeks, I often wondered whether he was doing anything useful at all,' Roberts told me, smiling.

Tutte worked out that the machine produced the key by adding together two separate streams of letters, each produced by the wheels as they turned. One group of five wheels—Tutte named them the 'chi-wheels', after the Greek letter *chi*—generated one of the streams of letters (with each wheel producing a single one of the five bits that made up a letter). Another group of five—the 'psi-wheels'—generated the other letter stream (see Fig. 17). The remaining two wheels of the twelve, called the motor wheels, regulated the movement of the other wheels. It was much more complicated than Enigma, but thanks to Tutte the new machine was naked. His secret deductions saved untold lives. Yet Tutte—who died in 2002—has never been given the credit he deserves. Because of the need-to-know principle, even the people at Bletchley who went on to break the daily Tunny messages were unaware of Tutte's seminal role. 'No one told us,' said Roberts. 'Tutte's fantastic achievement just dropped into oblivion. There should be a statue of Tutte on London's Embankment,

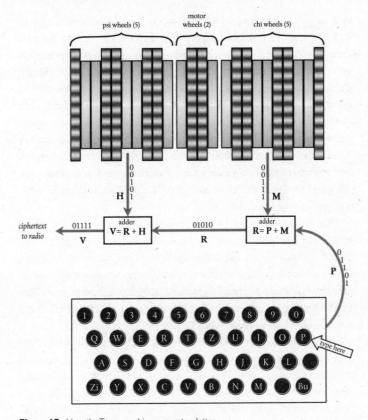

Figure 17. How the Tunny machine encrypts a letter

Credit: Dustin Barrett and Jack Copeland – All rights reserved

alongside Britain's other great war heroes. There should be a statue of Turing too.'

It was after Tutte denuded the machine that Turing entered the Tunny picture. Knowing how the machine worked was one thing; being able to read the daily messages was quite another. Turing shifted over from Hut 8 to tackle the problem, and within a few weeks he had come up with a paper, pencil, and eraser method for breaking the daily messages. In the terse jargon of Bletchley Park, his invention became known simply as *Turingery*. Like the methods Turing invented for use against Enigma, Turingery delivered the wheel details that the codebreakers needed in order to crack the messages. Turingery was the way into Tunny. 'Turing did not look like a superstar,' Roberts said, 'although he was already well known as someone who had done brilliant work.' Turing dressed rather scruffily for the times, and had no qualms about turning up unshaven and with his hair wild. 'He dressed in a somewhat untidy sports jacket and nondescript grey trousers,' Roberts remembered. 'I can clearly recall him walking along with his eyes turned away sideways from other people, gazing towards the lower part of the corridor wall and flicking the wall with his fingers.'

Tutte described Turingery a bit sniffily as 'more artistic than mathematical'.[51] The method depended on insight—on what you 'felt in your bones', Tutte said. Tutte himself would soon create a method that could be carried out at fantastic speed by a dumb machine—Colossus—but to do so he borrowed the central trick of Turingery. This was a procedure invented by Turing called 'delta-ing' (again from a Greek letter). Delta-ing is a process of 'sideways' addition. To delta the four characters ABCD, you add A to B, B to C, and C to D (producing three characters). One could be excused for thinking that adding the letters of an encrypted message together in this way would only scramble it further, but Turing showed that delta-ing in fact *revealed* information that was otherwise hidden.[52]

Soon Roberts and his fellow codebreakers were putting Turingery to work in earnest, and during July to October they read nearly every message intercepted from the experimental Tunny link. Using Turingery, they could work out the positions of the many adjustable pins that were situated around the circumference of each of the Tunny's wheels (each pin produced an individual bit, 0 or 1). The only other information they required were the positions of the twelve wheels at the start of the message. Obligingly, the German operators themselves gave these away via the twelve-name indicator. Unlike indicators in Dolphin, Tunny indicators were transmitted unencrypted—an incredible blunder on the Germans' part.

By the time this stupid practice was discontinued, in October 1942, the damage had been done. Roberts and company had been reading Tunny for long enough to be able to keep on going, armed with Turingery. Engineers from the British Post Office built replica Tunny machines, following Tutte's schematics, and letters of German plaintext came chattering out by the million. 'In those early days (mid 1942 to mid 1943) Turingery was our only weapon,' Roberts said. 'We used it to break thousands of ultra-secret messages. Nothing like this had ever happened before, not even with Enigma. Thanks to Turing, Tutte, and Tiltman we knew from day to day what Hitler and the top brass were thinking, what they were saying to each other over breakfast as it were. It changed the nature of the war fundamentally.'

One of the Tunny-breakers' greatest successes, in the summer of 1943, was the Battle of Kursk, often described as the mightiest tank battle of all time. Hitler was smarting from his overwhelming defeat at Stalingrad, where 300,000 or more German soldiers had perished, and he decided to try to regain the initiative on the Eastern Front by launching a pincer movement near the Russian city of Kursk. Preparations took months as the Germans moved huge numbers of tanks and men into the area. All the time, messages from Generalfeldmarschall von Weichs back to the German High Command in Berlin were bleeding information, and the British passed on a detailed account of von Weichs's planned pincer movement to the Russians.[53] 'We found out everything,' Roberts said, 'even down to the individual divisions and tank units that were going into battle.' The Germans threw practically every tank division on the Russian Front into the battle, but it was hopeless.[54] Hitler called off the attack after only ten days. Kursk was the beginning of the end. The powerful Russian counterattack developed into an advance that moved steadily westwards, finally reaching Berlin in April 1945.

As the Russians advanced towards Berlin they built up a stock of captured Tunny machines. It seems that after the war they reconditioned these and used them to protect their own military communications. Bad move. Although any documentary evidence remains classified, it seems very likely that during the Cold War Bletchley Park's successor, GCHQ,

Figure 18. The Battle of Kursk

Credit: © ITAR-TASS Photo Agency/Alamy

continued to read Tunny messages, now written in Russian instead of German. The British, too, put reconditioned Tunny machines to use. Ugandan dictator Idi Amin, who ruled from 1971 to 1979, was supplied with a Tunny system by British intelligence. Naturally, the British did not mention to Amin that they would be reading his secret messages.

By the end of 1942 the German military had stopped making life so easy for the Tunny breakers. Turingery required depths, but, as the Tunny network expanded, security became tighter and depths became scarcer. Fortunately, Tutte had another brainwave before the year was out. Combining Turing's idea of delta-ing with some fundamental insights of his own, he came up with a method that made no use of depths.[55] Turingery and occasional depths would now keep the codebreakers abreast of the wheels' pin patterns (which were changed only every once in a while) and Tutte's method would expose the positions of the wheels at the start of each individual message. There was only one snag. His method involved such a vast amount of calculation that breaking a single message might take a human being as long as a hundred years![56] Tutte shyly explained his method to Max Newman who, in mid 1942, had abandoned his Cambridge teaching for the challenges of Bletchley Park and was focusing his considerable energy on Tunny. Newman suggested using high-speed *electronic* counters to mechanize the necessary calculations.

It was a brilliant idea. In a flash of inspiration Newman had realized that some pioneering electronic technology he had seen in use before the war in Cambridge—where scientists in the Cavendish Laboratory were using electronic circuits to count radioactive emissions—could be applied to the very different problem of breaking Tunny messages. The codebreakers were about to witness the birth of the electronic computer.

COLOSSUS, DELILAH, VICTORY

Quiet and boyish, with a hesitant manner and his hair perpetually shiny with Brilliantine, Tommy Flowers did not look much like a man who was about to transform warfare. Flowers, an exceptionally talented engineer, was always something of an outsider at Bletchley Park, where 'NQOC' meant 'not quite our class'. In class-conscious England, Flowers was from a working-class background, and unlike Tutte did not have the passport of an Oxbridge education. He gained his training in engineering not at a university but as an apprentice at Woolwich Arsenal, in the docklands of East London.

Grandma Flowers had been a char and Grandpa Flowers a poacher. By fleeing to London from the Cambridgeshire countryside, Grandpa narrowly forestalled a spell in prison for his illegal meat gathering. Flowers's father, also Tom, was born in Whitechapel within the sound of Bow Bells, the traditional criterion of cockneyhood, and Flowers grew up in a cockney-speaking world. 'He is not here' would be pronounced ' 'e ain't 'ere,' Flowers said with a twinkle in his ultra-intelligent eyes. He retained a residual cockney accent, not broad, but cockney nevertheless. 'It must have been a handicap to me,' he told his grandchildren.

Whitechapel, he recounted, was 'the poorest part of the city of London'. When young, his father would sometimes have to 'sleep on a coke heap with rats running round and over him,' Flowers said. Flowers himself was born in 1905, in rented rooms in the East London district of Poplar, a short walk from Whitechapel. While he was a youngster the family lived not far above subsistence level, although things did get better later. 'We were taught to be frugal in everything.' He could remember barefooted children in the streets. Houses rarely had bathrooms, and a latrine usually lurked at the bottom of a small backyard. Tuberculosis was rife, made worse by the overcrowded dwellings. Yet there were also brightly polished door knockers and carefully whitened doorsteps.

Even as a small child, Flowers was serious about engineering. Told at the age of nine that he was going to have a new baby sister, he responded that he would rather have a new Meccano set. Once his apprenticeship at Woolwich Arsenal was over he obtained a job in the engineering department of the General Post Office. He taught himself electronics, picking up a night-school degree in engineering along the way, and quickly became an expert in the new art of using electronic components as high-speed digital switches. On or off, 1 or 0. It was the way of the future, but back in those days Flowers was one of the very few engineers who appreciated the potential. By the late 1930s he was building a jumbo-sized digital electronic memory for use with telephone equipment. The Post Office was responsible for Britain's entire telephone system and Flowers dreamed of replacing the slow, wear-prone relay-based equipment of the day with racks of digital electronics. He was years ahead of his time. Electronic telephone exchanges finally became a reality, thanks to Flowers and others, in the 1960s. By 1939 he had been working at the forefront of digital engineering for nearly a decade, and he told me that when war arrived he was possibly the only person in Britain who realized that electronic valves could be used for large-scale high-speed digital processing. ('Valve' is the term that British engineers use for what is called a 'vacuum tube' in America.)

Flowers's first major assignment during the war concerned Fighter Command's radar systems. During the Battle of Britain, in the summer of 1940, he perfected the communications circuits for displaying German aircraft positions to the top brass at Fighter Command's headquarters.[1] 'I was there in Fighter Command on September the fifteenth,' Flowers recounted, 'and I was amongst all the excitement.'[2] He looked on

Figure 19. Tommy Flowers

Credit: © With kind permission of Kenneth Flowers. Photo restoration by Dustin Barrett and Jack Copeland

fascinated as the RAF's heavily outnumbered fighters broke up massed attacks by German aircraft. Shortly after this work for Fighter Command, he was summoned to Bletchley Park, where he again turned out to be the right man in the right place at the right time. His giant electronic digital computer, Colossus, was soon cracking Tunny messages at speeds that no one else would have believed possible.

Flowers was sent to Bletchley Park to assist Turing, and at first he explored machines for use not against Tunny but against Enigma. These included an early form of electronic bombe—Flowers knew that electronics offered the speed necessary for breaking the four-wheeled version of Enigma—and also a relay-based apparatus for attempting to decode stretches of an Enigma message once the bombe had produced settings worth trying out. Flowers's machine mimicked an Enigma, taking in ciphertext and outputting plain German—or simply garbage, if the bombe's guess at the settings was wrong. Even though Turing himself had requisitioned this machine, it never went into regular use, because the codebreakers' needs had changed by the time it was manufactured.

Turing's brush with Flowers's Colossus changed his life. As soon as the war ended he plunged into creating an electronic computer of his own, initially with Flowers assisting. At Bletchley, Flowers impressed Turing and Turing impressed Flowers. He was one of the fortunate few who found Turing easy to work with. In Flowers's gruff assessment, Turing was 'a very nice bloke'. 'A loner,' he added. Probably with a helping hand from Turing, Flowers was awarded the MBE (Member of the Order of the British Empire) in 1943 for his work on Enigma.[3] With another helping hand from Turing he entered the attack on Tunny in 1942. When Newman was experiencing problems with some experimental equipment, Turing said: 'Flowers.'

With Turing's expert assistance, Newman had succeeded in selling his idea of an electronic Tunny-breaking machine to Jumbo Travis, head of codebreaking operations.[4] However, the project had now run into difficulties over the design of the machine's logic unit. Flowers did a redesign and got the logic unit working, but he didn't like the look of Newman's machine one bit. Newman was planning to use no more than a couple of dozen electronic valves, and the rest of the machine consisted of the very same slow, wear-prone mechanical devices that Flowers was longing to banish from telephone exchanges. He could see that Newman's machine would never give the codebreakers the necessary speed and reliability, so he made a daring counterproposal: an all-electronic machine, containing between one and two thousand valves.

Newman took advice on Flowers's proposal, but was told that a hookup of so many valves would never work reliably. According to conventional wisdom, valves were just too flaky to be used in large numbers. Each one contained a hot glowing filament, and the delicacy of this filament meant that valves were prone to sudden death. The more valves there were in the equipment, the greater the chance that one or two would fizzle out in the middle of a job. Plagued by continually blowing valves, a big installation would be completely impractical, or so most engineers believed. It was a belief based on experience with radio receivers and the like, which were switched on and off frequently. But Flowers had discovered that so long as valves were left running continuously, they were in fact very reliable. He also discovered ways of boosting the reliability even further, such as using lower-than-normal electric currents. As early as 1934, he had successfully wired together an experimental installation containing three or four thousand valves (the equipment was for controlling connections between telephone exchanges by means of tones, like today's touch-tones). Outside Flowers's small group, though, few knew that electronic valves could be used reliably in such large numbers. Bletchley Park declined to support Flowers's proposal. The proposal was met with 'incredulity', he said.[5]

Flowers knew he was right. He went back to his laboratory in London and quietly got on with the job of building his all-electronic computer. He kept in close touch with Newman, who personally believed that Flowers's machine would work, despite what he called its 'ambitious' nature.[6] 'If you think you can make it, you go ahead,' Newman told Flowers.[7] Newman himself pressed on to finish the other cranky machine as quickly as possible. This was soon dubbed 'Heath Robinson' after the cartoonist William Heath Robinson, who drew absurd devices. Installed in June 1943, Heath Robinson was always breaking down.[8] As if a harbinger, smoke rose from its innards the first time it was switched on.[9] By the end of September, Heath Robinson had managed to assist with the elucidation of fewer than twenty intercepts (although later Jack Good and Donald Michie did manage to improve its performance).[10] Meanwhile, in utmost secrecy, Flowers and his team of engineers worked day and night for ten months to build Colossus—worked until their 'eyes dropped out', Flowers said. They 'did in ten months what in normal peace time conditions would have taken three to five years', he underlined. All this was 'without the concurrence of BP' (Bletchley Park), and was done 'in the face of scepticism'. 'BP weren't interested until they saw it [Colossus] working,' he recalled with wry amusement. Fortunately, Flowers's boss at the Post Office engineering research laboratories, Gordon Radley, had greater faith in Flowers and his ideas, and gave him whatever he needed.[11]

In January 1944 Flowers's lads took Colossus—the world's first large-scale electronic digital computer—to Bletchley Park on the back of a lorry. It caused quite a stir. 'I don't think they understood very clearly what I was proposing until they actually had the machine,' Flowers said.[12] 'They just couldn't believe it!' The codebreakers were astonished by the speed of Colossus—and also by the fact that, unlike Heath Robinson, it would always produce the same result if set the same problem again! About a fortnight after its delivery, Colossus began real work on the German messages, notching up its first success on Saturday 5 February. Flowers noted laconically in his diary, 'Colossus did its first job. Car broke down on way home.'

Colossus's very existence was so far against the odds as to be almost a fluke. If Radley hadn't elected to back Flowers, the idea would never have become a reality. If Turing hadn't mentioned Flowers to Newman, Flowers might have passed the rest of his life without ever hearing of Tunny. If the Post Office had sent someone else along to assist Turing, he might never have heard of Bletchley Park either. In fact, Flowers was nearly trapped in Germany at the beginning of the war, and that this didn't happen was another lucky pebble in the little heap of long shots on which Colossus balanced. At the end of August 1939, just a few days before war was declared, some bright spark in the Post Office had sent Flowers to Berlin on engineering business. 'Your people must be mad to send you here,' he was told when he arrived, but the authorities politely gave him a driver and a large black Mercedes with a swastika fluttering on its flagstick. Next morning there was an urgent phone call from the British Embassy telling him to get out of Germany as quickly as possible. He threw his belongings into his suitcase and got on a train bound for the coast, making his escape into Holland only hours before the frontier closed. Things might have gone very differently if Flowers had missed that call. There was no one else in the picture who could have built his computer—no one 'with sufficient knowledge of the new technology,' he said—and so the war might have toiled on. 'Those chance events changed the course of the Second World War,' Flowers believed. 'If they had not, history would now record the devastation of a large part of Europe and a death toll much greater than actually occurred.'[13]

The name Colossus was apt. Flowers's computer was the size of a room and weighed about a ton. Input was via punched paper tape. The tape span around in a giant loop supported on numerous aluminium wheels (see Fig. 20). The wheels were mounted inside a metal frame that resembled an old-fashioned iron bed standing on end, although a bed big enough for Goliath. Naturally enough, this frame was called the 'bedstead'. Flowers could remember tapes snapping and disintegrating at high speed, festooning everyone and everything with dangling shreds.

Output was via the grandfather of computer printers, a manual typewriter that the engineers had modified by fitting short, electrically driven rods to the keys.[14] The rods depressed the keys automatically. Jack Good, whose initials were 'I. J.', watched fascinated during one decoding run

Figure 20. Colossus with two operators, Dorothy Du Boisson (left) and Elsie Booker

Credit: © Bletchley Park Trust/Science & Society Picture Library – All rights reserved while the typewriter wrote, as if possessed, I J G O O. He laughed that if the next letter had been D, he would have assumed—unless someone were playing a practical joke, which they weren't—that a miracle was happening.[15] Later versions of Colossus processed five different input streams simultaneously, in parallel, at a breathtaking rate of 25,000 letters per second. Colossus's performance was creditable even against the first Intel microprocessor chip, which was introduced three decades later. 'The speed of Colossus actually compares well with the first home computer kits running the Intel 4004 CPU chip at 108 KHz,' says computer historian Pete Wells.[16] 'Colossus bore about as much resemblance to a modern computer as Stephenson's Rocket locomotive did to the Royal Scot,' Flowers explained, 'but it embodied all the basic features of a modern computer.' Each of the cascade of inventions that Colossus pioneered is now bread and butter to modern computer scientists: clock pulses, bitstream generators, control circuits, loops, counters, shift registers, interrupts, parallel processing.[17] The list goes on.

Colossus's banks of valves, with their glowing filaments, produced more heat than a hundred electric fires. When the computer's Wren operators got too hot, they would slip outside the building and splash themselves with water from the emergency fire tank.[18] The heat was a blessing in winter, though, when the chronic fuel shortages meant that Flowers's engineers had to cover themselves with sheets of newspaper to keep warm in bed—occasionally they even chopped up furniture to feed a feeble fire.[19] Catherine Caughey, one of the first Wrens to operate Colossus, remembered the computer curing the painful chilblains that covered her hands and feet.[20] Caughey was scathing about the living conditions of the women who so faithfully tended Colossus: 'We suffered from exhaustion and malnutrition. The Wrens at Quarters gave us very poor food. I shared one of the servants' poky little rooms under the roof with three others. It was freezing cold, with dreary brown wallpaper and an unstained floor. The unaccustomedly large number of residents was too much for the plumbing and all water was contaminated.'[21]

No sooner was Colossus in action than the number of Tunny decodes doubled, and then trebled, quadrupled, and quintupled.[22]

The codebreakers were witnessing the earliest manifestation of the massive power of electronic computing—a glimpse of the future. Even so, Colossus did not incorporate Turing's all-important stored-program concept. While Flowers was designing Colossus, Newman showed him Turing's 1936 paper about the universal machine, with its key idea of storing programs in memory, but Flowers, not being a mathematical logician, said he 'didn't really understand much of it'. Colossus was programmed by hand, by means of large panels of plugs and switches that Flowers had incorporated for this purpose. The Wrens used these to quite literally rewire parts of the computer each time it was required to follow a new set of instructions. This laborious process seems unbearably primitive from today's perspective, when we take Turing's glorious stored-program world for granted. Colossus was not even an all-purpose computer. Schoolroom-type long multiplication—unnecessary for Tunny breaking—was found to be just beyond its scope, Good told me. Nevertheless, Flowers had succeeded in giving the codebreakers everything they needed for the job in hand.

Colossus is often said to have been Turing's baby, but this wasn't so. A leading historian of computing described Colossus, quite inaccurately, as 'the cryptanalytical machine designed by Alan Turing and others'.[23] *Time Magazine* confused everyone by saying that 'Alan Turing built a succession of vacuum-tube machines called Colossus that made mincemeat of Hitler's Enigma codes.'[24] Colossus had nothing to do with Enigma, and Turing was in any case away in the United States when Flowers worked out the design for his all-electronic machine. Colossus was entirely Flowers's idea.[25] He told me that Turing 'made no contribution' to the design of Colossus. 'I invented the Colossus,' he said. 'No one else was capable of doing it.'

Turing's key contribution was not to the computer itself, but to what it *did*. The central ingredient of his 'Turingery' method—delta-ing—was the basis for every main algorithm used in Colossus. The entire computer-based attack on Tunny flowed from Turing's fundamental discovery, developed further by Tutte, that delta-ing revealed hidden information. Turingery itself, though, was purely a hand method, and was not used by any electronic machine.[26] Another of Turing's inventions was also indispensable to the mathematicians using Colossus—although, unlike delta-ing, it never showed up in the computer's actual algorithms.[27] This was Turing's technique for scoring pieces of evidence, originally part and parcel of his anti-Enigma method Banburismus. The technique enabled the codebreakers to add up the weights of various individual pieces of evidence in favour of a hypothesis. Michie, echoing Newman, described this technique as Turing's 'greatest intellectual contribution during the war'.[28] The emphasis here is on *intellectual*—Turingery, the bombe, and the cracking of Naval Enigma, while outstanding contributions to the war, were not contributions to the discipline of mathematics itself. Michie emphasized that Turing's weight-of-evidence technique is essentially the statistical tool now known as sequential analysis. The Hungarian mathematician Abraham Wald rediscovered the method, coined the term 'sequential analysis', and published an influential book with that title in America in 1947. In Michie's judgement, though, Turing's 'weight-of-evidence approach to rational belief-revision was more general and far-reaching than Wald's'.[29] There is a strong connection between Banburismus and what statisticians call 'Bayes theorem'. Bayes was an 18th-century Presbyterian minister who did pioneering work in mathematics in his spare time. Turing recognized this connection, but wrote as though he had devised his 'factor principle', as he called it, independently of Bayes's work. He said: 'Nearly all applications of probability to cryptography depend on the "factor principle" (or Bayes' theorem).'[30]

Jerry Roberts and the other codebreakers who had been breaking Tunny by hand since 1942 quickly integrated Colossus into their operations. 'Among ourselves we used to have a quiet smile at Newman's bizarre contraptions,' Roberts told me, 'but when we saw Colossus, we knew that Flowers had changed everything.' From that time on, the work was shared between human brain and computer. Newman's section—called simply the Newmanry—would use Colossus to strip away the layer of encryption that the Tunny machine's five chi-wheels had added to the message. The resulting 'de-chi', which contained only the layer of encryption contributed by the five psi-wheels, was passed on to Roberts and the others in Ralph Tester's section, known universally as the Testery. Tester, a balding forty-something Army major, was venerated by his youthful crew. Michie remembered Tester's 'mesmeric impact on female spectators in the lunch break as he leapt, daemonic and glowing, about the tennis court—with an animality that I had only ever envisaged as radiating from the great god Pan'.[31] Tester's boys would break the de-chi by hand, using cribs that they added to the coded letters Tiltman-style. The process became so ingrained in Roberts's brain that even today he catches himself idly adding standard Testery cribs—such as EINS (one) and FEIND (enemy)—to car number plates. Sometimes enciphered operator chat was broken first, before the message proper. Hilton never forgot the evocative breaks 'Ich bin so einsam,' (I am so lonely) from an operator on the Leningrad front, and 'Mörderische Hitze,' (murderous heat) from the Italian front.[32]

Meanwhile, Turing set up an electronics project of his own. He established a small lab in a Nissen hut at Hanslope Park, another Buckinghamshire country pile a few miles away from Bletchley Park.[33] Now that Tunny was essentially solved, Jumbo Travis wanted Turing to continue pushing the frontiers of cryptography, and told him to pursue the speech-encryption work he had begun in New York.[34] It was like his move from Enigma to Tunny in 1942: now that the pioneering work on Tunny was done, Turing's battering-ram mind was needed elsewhere to break more fresh ground. Flowers too had a hand in this new, highly secret project at Hanslope.[35] He and Turing spoke each other's language. 'Turing had the reputation of being practically incoherent in explanation,' Flowers said in an amused way, yet he himself never had any trouble at all understanding Turing.[36] 'The rapport was really quite remarkable,' Flowers said. Turing set about designing a portable speech system of roughly the same size as a Tunny machine—the Bell Labs' SIGSALY secure speech system he had been involved with earlier in the year was as big as Colossus. Turing's talent for electronic circuit design blossomed in his Hanslope lab. His surviving blueprints, each the size of a desk and still, after all these years, bright powder-blue in colour, depict the complex speech system called 'Delilah'.[37]

Delilah's method of encrypting speech was analogous to the way the Tunny machine encrypted typed text. Tunny added obscuring key to written words; Delilah added obscuring key to spoken words. In Delilah's case, the key was a stream of random-seeming numbers. The first step in the encryption process was to 'discretize' the speech, turning it into a series of individual numbers (each number corresponded to the speech signal's voltage at that particular moment in time).[38] Delilah then added key to these numbers, creating the enciphered form of the spoken message. This was then automatically transmitted to another Delilah at the receiving end of the link.

As with Tunny, the receiver's Delilah had to be synchronized with the sender's, so that both the transmitting and receiving machine produced identical key. The receiving machine stripped the key from the enciphered message, and the resulting decrypted numbers (specifying voltages) were used to reproduce the original speech. The result was a bit crackly, but generally quite intelligible—although if the machine made a mistake, there would be 'a sudden crack like a rifle shot', Turing said.[39] It must have been hard on the receiving operator's straining ears. In designing Delilah, Turing ingeniously adapted existing cryptographic technology. At the heart of Delilah's mechanism for producing the key was a five-wheeled text-enciphering machine modelled on Enigma (see Fig. 22 on page 122).

At Hanslope, Turing lived in an old cottage and took his meals in the army mess.[40] 'In spite of having to live in a mess and with soldiers,' the commanding officer recollected, 'Turing soon settled down and became "one of us" in every sense; always rather quiet but ever ready to discuss his work even with an ignoramus like myself.'[41] After a few months, the army sent several recent university graduates to Hanslope and Turing made two firm friendships. Robin Gandy shared Turing's Nissen hut, working on improvements to equipment used in intercepting German messages.[42] At first Gandy thought Turing a bit austere, but later was 'enchanted to find how human he could be, discussing mutual friends, arranging a dinner-party, being a little vain of his clothes and his appearance'.[43] The second new friendship sprouted when Don Bayley came to Hanslope, in March 1944, to assist with Delilah.[44] The three of them would take long walks together in the Buckinghamshire countryside. One day Turing entered his name for the mile race in the regimental sports. Some of the soldiers thought it must be a leg-pull, but when the race was run, Turing 'came in a very easy first', the CO remembered.[45] It was the beginning of Turing's career as an Olympic-standard runner. Soon after the war ended he began to train seriously and was to be seen 'with hair flying', his Cambridge friend Arthur Pigou said, as he raced home at the end of a '10, 15 or 17 miles solitary "scamper"'.[46]

Back at Bletchley Park, the official scepticism about Colossus had very rapidly disappeared. By March 1944 the authorities were demanding four more computers, and by April they were demanding twelve.[47] Flowers found himself under tremendous pressure to deliver. His instructions came from the very top, Churchill and the War Cabinet. Churchill's Chief of Staff, Pug Ismay, did not mince his words when he minuted the Post Office's chief of engineering, Sir Stanley Angwin, telling him politely but very firmly that production of additional Colossi was of 'overriding importance' and must be given 'the very highest priority, both as regards labour and material'.[48] Flowers, never a man to be pushed around, caused consternation when he said flatly that no more than one new Colossus could be wired together by June.[49] He knew that he had only managed to build the first one because his men 'did nothing but work, eat, and sleep for weeks and months on end'; and now they were doing it all over again.[50] Flowers remembered that one day some Bletchley people came to inspect the work, thinking that he might be 'dilly-dallying'; he told me they returned 'staggered at the scale of the effort'.

In May, Colossus II was shipped partly finished from Flowers's London laboratory to the Newmanry. He had agreed to get the new computer into operation by 1 June, but it was plagued by a mysterious fault and was still not working properly as the final hours of May ticked past.[51] Exhausted, Flowers and his team threw in the towel at one o'clock on the morning of the first, heading home to snatch a few hours' sleep.[52] He left one of his right-hand men, Bill Chandler, to continue searching for the fault, since the problem appeared to be with a part of the computer that Chandler had designed. It was a tough night—around three a.m. Chandler noticed

Figure 21. Allied D-Day landings on the heavily defended beaches of Normandy
Credit © Illustrated London News Ltd/Mary Evans

his feet getting wet, and saw that a radiator pipe along the wall had sprung a leak, sending a dangerous flood of water towards the computer's high-voltage equipment.[53] But he finally managed to track down the fault in Colossus and made a few quick adjustments with his soldering iron. Flowers returned to find the computer running perfectly. The puddle remained, though, and the Wren operators had to wear gumboots to insulate themselves.[54] Bill Tutte and Gerry Morgan looked in. With his quiet chuckle, Tutte remembered Morgan eyeing the wet floor and joking that the new machine had not been house-trained yet.[55]

Flowers and his 'band of brothers'[56] had met the deadline, and less than a week later the Allied invasion of France began. It was the start of the European war's final act. A massive fleet of some 6,000 vessels crammed with men and equipment headed from the English south coast toward the beaches of Normandy, travelling under the cover of darkness in con-voys five miles long.[57] The landings, code-named Operation Overlord, began on the morning of 6 June, D-Day. For months, Turing's bombes and the first Colossus had been providing an unparalleled window on the German counter-preparations. The fundamental breakthroughs by Tur-ing and Tutte had enabled a massive cyber-attack, resulting in 'an all but totally accurate assessment of the German order of battle in the Overlord area on D-day', Harry Hinsley explained.[58] One useful message, decoded by the Testery–Newmanry team in May, contained the itinerary for Gen-eral Guderian's grand tour of inspection of the Panzer troops.[59] This very helpfully revealed the positions of many of the Panzer divisions in north-ern France.

Preparations for Overlord included Operation Fortitude, an elaborate deception aimed at tricking the Germans into believing that the main invasion would come further north, close to the French port of Calais, which lies a mere twenty or so miles from its English counterpart of Dover.[60] America's General George Patton presided over a vast but entirely fictitious army located opposite Calais and equipped with ply-wood artillery batteries and inflatable rubber tanks. A telegram from the Japanese ambassador in Berlin (decoded on 1 June) reported Hitler as say-ing that the Allies would soon establish a bridgehead in Normandy, or perhaps in neighbouring Brittany a little further to the west, but would then shortly afterwards launch the real invasion at Calais.[61] Fortitude was working.

This information fitted hand and glove with a Tunny message from General Jodl, decoded a little earlier, revealing that a huge Panzer force would be held in reserve and moved only on Hitler's orders.[62] The reserve force included the massive 12th SS Panzer Division, known as *Hitlerjugend*, or Hitler Youth. Thanks to Guderian's itinerary, the codebreakers knew *Hitlerjugend* was based at Evreux, a small town nearer to Paris than to the Normandy beaches. Decrypts showed that *Hitlerjugend* possessed about 150 tanks and armoured guns, and over 22,000 men—an enormous force, more than twice the size of an average infantry division.[63] Also in Hitler's personal reserve was the Panzer *Lehr* Division, known from decrypts to be in Chartres, even further from Normandy than *Hitlerjugend*.[64] *Lehr* was one of the top divisions of the German army and had required no less than eighty-four trains to carry its troops from Hungary in its recent move to France.[65] The name *Lehr* came from '*Lehrer*', meaning 'teacher'—a crack division to teach the others how to fight. Poised to deploy to Calais if necessary, the combined fighting force of *Hitlerjugend* and *Lehr* was as much as twenty-four hours away from the Normandy beaches[66]—essential information for the Overlord commanders, who now knew that they would have a crucial breathing space before the German defences were at full strength.

The first airborne landings in Normandy began just after midnight. For several hours Field Marshal Gerd von Runstedt, the German Commander-in-Chief West—customarily denoted in Bletchley's reports by the not very dignified title Charlie-in-Charlie—remained in the grip of disinformation. He 'still believed they were faced only with a diversionary operation preceding an invasion in the Pas de Calais,' Hinsley said,[67] and von Rundstedt reported that he did 'not consider this to be a major operation'.[68] Eventually he realized that what was happening was on too large a scale to be a mere diversion, and around four a.m. he asked for the assistance of *Hitlerjugend* and *Lehr*. The servile Jodl would not issue the orders without Hitler's say-so—and that day the Führer slept in until lunchtime.[69] Maybe he was comfortably dreaming of pushing the British dogs back into the sea at Calais. It was afternoon before he agreed to commit *Hitlerjugend* and *Lehr*, a vital delay that enabled the Allied troops to establish themselves in their beachheads.[70] Hitler blamed his subordinates. His attitude showed 'a violent stiffening from Normandy on', according to a Hut 3 analysis of his messages to his generals: 'One has the impression of a growing despair (whether or no he owned it to himself), a growing distrust of his generals, as either knaves or fools who would let him down whenever he gave them a chance.'[71]

The Allies fought slowly but surely towards Germany. 'We kept the Allied troops very well informed as they pressed on into France and then Germany,' Roberts said with pride. 'New Colossi were arriving monthly and we were breaking a torrent of messages,' he recalled. Decryption was so much faster by this time, although still nowhere near the speeds that were being achieved with Enigma. From late 1943 Turing's bombes were deciphering Enigma messages at the incredible rate of roughly two messages every minute, night and day—84,000 broken messages each month.[72] On the other hand, the process of breaking a Tunny message, from receipt at Bletchley through to printing out the German plaintext, took on average a bit more than a day.[73] 'The last four months of the war were our busiest period,' Roberts said, 'and we produced almost as many decodes then as we did during the whole of the previous year.'[74]

Around the beginning of February 1945, Bletchley decrypted a message from Dönitz, now Commander-in-Chief of the German navy, declaring, 'The genius of the Fuehrer will know how to secure what is best.'[75] Famous last words. Within weeks Hitler was dead, and Germany's capitulation followed on 8 May 1945. 'I was with Donald Michie at the cinema in Fenny Stratford when the programme was stopped to announce the end of hostilities in Europe,' remembered Helen Currie.[76] Her job was to operate the Testery machines that turned Tunny ciphertexts into plain German once Roberts, or one of his colleagues, had broken a few words of the de-chi. While Currie and Michie were in the cinema, Catherine Caughey was on night shift in the Newmanry. She saw the chattering teleprinters that brought in the intercepted Tunny messages suddenly cease their activity.

Hitler's last words to be decrypted—a final desperate cry transmitted the evening before he shot himself—were 'Where is Wenck's spearhead? When is he advancing? Where is 9 Army? Where is *Gruppe* Holste? When is he advancing?'[77] The last remnants of the Nazi elite used heavy crates of yet-to-be awarded Iron Cross medals to barricade the windows of Berlin's Reich Chancellery as Russian troops entered the city.[78]

A few hours after the teleprinters fell silent, Michie and Currie jumped aboard a packed train to London. They danced wildly in Trafalgar Square, hugging and kissing complete strangers amid the euphoric crowds. Turing celebrated victory more quietly, ambling through the countryside with Bayley and Gandy.[79] 'Well, the war's over now,' Bayley said to Turing as they rested in a clearing in the woods, 'it's peacetime so you can tell us all.' 'Don't be so bloody silly,' Turing answered. 'That was the end of that conversation!' Bayley recollected sixty-seven years later. The five years of war had, in a way, been time out. 'We lived totally in the present, greedy for life and with no thought for the future,' Currie remembered. 'There were some passionate romances,' she added with emphasis. But, with Hitler defeated, the time had now arrived to consider the future.

By the war's end, Newman had nine Colossi working round the clock in the Newmanry and another stood in the factory almost ready for delivery. The computers were housed in two vast steel-framed buildings. It was the world's first electronic computing facility, with job queues, teams of operators working in shifts, specialized tape-punching crews, and engineers continually on hand to keep the machinery running smoothly. Not until the 1960s was anything like it seen again, when the first modern large-scale computing centres began to emerge. Newman was well aware that he had created something utterly new. Around the summer of 1944, when the first few Colossi were in action, he decided that his peacetime future lay with computers.[80] The post-war years would see his collaboration with Turing continuing, as he founded the Royal Society Computing Machine Laboratory in Manchester and oversaw the construction of an electronic stored-program computer. It was the first universal Turing machine in hardware, and Turing would spend most of the rest of his life programming it.

Newman was in fact the ideal person to direct a scientific computing laboratory, even though he was not always the easiest of men to get along with. 'Supremely confident of his judgement, even when wrong,' Michie observed. 'Obstinate as a mule.' There was a hard edge to Newman. 'He did not suffer fools gladly,' recalled Michie with an impish smile.[81] No less a warrior than Wittgenstein, who was hardened by years of the cut and thrust of logical argument, was pricked by something Newman said, and muttered that he 'should have been drowned at birth'.[82] Yet the staff of the futuristic Newmanry revered their chief, even if he did orbit well above their heads. Decades ahead of his time in management practices, Newman encouraged them to call each other—although never himself—by their first names. 'This was a marvellous idea—at once we were a team,' recollected Colossus operator Dorothy Du Boisson.[83] The informality must have perplexed and perhaps even irritated Bletchley's military blimps and crusty Civil Service administrators. Another of Newman's innovations was a democratic forum going by the strange name 'tea party'. 'These "tea parties",' Jack Good explained, 'were free-for-all informal meetings where many decisions were made'; 'but,' he added, 'there was no tea.'[84] In his other life, as one of Britain's leading mathematicians, Newman pioneered topology, the abstract study of shape; and reflecting on the problems of management, he observed 'It's wonderful how many shapes the neck of a bottle can take.'[85] He was in fact every inch the professor, despite his flair for far-sighted administration. Catherine Caughey once spotted him on Bletchley station, swinging a dead hare by its hind legs (a tasty meal for several people in those days of meat rationing) while anxiously searching the platform for something he had dropped. With a distressed look he said to her, 'Until I find my ticket I cannot remember whether I am going to Oxford or Cambridge.'[86]

Newman's incredible factory of giant computers did not outlast the war, however. Shortly after the victory in Europe a high-level meeting decided the fate of the Colossi. Churchill himself might have been present. The codebreaking capacity at Bletchley was obviously excessive for peacetime. German teleprinter cipher machines would continue to be used for years to come, since these were some of the most advanced encryption equipment in existence; toward the end of 1945 the RAF itself considered adopting German machines to protect its teleprinter communications.[87] It was a reasonable assumption that the Russians, and perhaps even the French, would also start to use captured Tunny machines. Even so, Britain had no need for all ten Colossi. The codebreakers could already see the potential for building a new generation of Tunny-breaking machines combining the best features of Colossus and the 'Super-Robinson', a multi-tape machine descended from Newman's prototype Heath Robinson.[88] All in all, it was decided that two Colossi would be enough. Surplus equipment was destroyed. In fact, outgoing Bletchley staff were told that all ten Colossi had been destroyed—upon Churchill's orders broken into pieces no larger than a man's fist.

Two Colossi were quietly transferred to Eastcote, the codebreakers' new headquarters in suburban London, and the rest were dismantled. 'Suddenly the Colossi were gone,' Du Boisson recounted, 'broken up on the orders of Churchill, we were told at the time. All that was left were the deep holes in the floor where the machines had stood.'[89] (Du Boisson, by the way, is the Wren standing with her back to the camera in Fig. 20.) 'Our instructions ruled that no element remaining should be sufficient to give any indication of its possible use,' recollected Norman Thurlow, one of the Newmanry engineers who now found himself ordered to smash up the Colossi, after many months of devoting his life to keeping them in action.[90] 'A final memo to staff reminded us of the continued need for secrecy,' Thurlow recalled, 'but noted that many years in the future it might be possible to tell our grandchildren of "the tapes that span on silver wheels".'

Bletchley's electronic computers, the most sophisticated machines in Europe, were smashed to pieces. The fact that this brutal reversal of scientific progress was unknown to the outside world hardly lessens the magnitude of the blow. The Colossi might have become part of public science. Turing, Newman, and Flowers would quickly have adapted them for new applications, and they could have become the heart of a scientific research facility. With eight massive electronic computers in the public arena from mid 1945, the story of modern computing would have begun very differently. Who can say what changes this different start would have brought? With clones of the Bletchley computing centre popping into existence elsewhere, the Internet—and even the personal computer—might have been developed a decade or more earlier. Even before the new millennium began, social networking might have changed the political map of the world.

The secret of Tunny and Colossus was a long time coming out—much longer than Enigma. Ex-staff of the Testery and Newmanry rigidly followed their orders to relate nothing of what they knew. Caughey even feared going to the dentist, in case she talked while under anaesthetic.[91] Her greatest regret was that she could never tell her husband about her extraordinary job as operator of the first large-scale electronic computer. Roberts, too, regretted that his parents died knowing nothing of his war work in the Testery—work of such importance that, in different circumstances, he might reasonably have expected a knighthood from the British Crown. Currie spoke of the immense burden of being unable to share her memories with her family. During the 'years of silence', she said, her wartime experiences 'took on a dream-like quality, almost as if I had imagined them'.[92] Turing's mother wrote ruefully of the 'enforced silence concerning his work'.[93] 'No hint was ever given of the nature of his secret work,' she said, complaining that the necessary secrecy 'ruined' their communication. Newman's son, William, himself a leading light in the computer graphics industry, said that his father spoke to him only obliquely about his war work and died 'having told little'.[94] In June 2000, though, and thanks largely to Michie's tireless campaigning, the British government at last declassified an ultra-secret 500-page official history of the whole Tunny operation, written in 1945 by Michie, Good, and their fellow codebreaker Geoffrey Timms.[95] Finally the secrecy ended. This 1945 history laid bare the incredible story of Colossus and the assault on Tunny.

Unexpectedly, Turing and Flowers had another encounter with Tunny just after the war, when the two travelled together to Germany. Turing's brief was to investigate German cryptological systems, while Flowers was to look at the communications side of things. They were there when the atomic bombs fell on Japan. Flowers was surprised to learn that Turing knew how the bomb worked. Then one day a talkative German engineer told them about a twelve-wheeled cipher machine used by the army—and showed them a Tunny machine. They couldn't let on, Flowers chuckled. It required a supreme effort to betray no trace of familiarity with Tunny. The engineer told them that major changes were to have been made to the Tunny machine, but the plans were put on hold because of the heavy Allied bombing of German factories from 1944. It was a narrow squeak—enhancements to the machine could have put the codebreakers back to square one. Yet if Germany's cipher experts had been more alert, they would have recommended continual changes to the machine.

Nazi Germany did have its own codebreaking organizations, but nothing on the incredible scale of Bletchley Park. The German Navy's *B-Dienst* (*Beobachtungsdienst*, or Surveillance Service) succeeded in reading various British naval ciphers from 1940 to 1945, and *B-Dienst* was able to keep the U-boats supplied with the positions of North Atlantic convoys.[96] But this was an isolated success; on the whole, Nazi codebreaking was a feeble affair. In fact, it is doubtful whether anything like Denniston's Bletchley Park, brilliant but eccentric organization that it was, could ever have flourished in the rigid and fundamentally anti-intellectual world of the Nazis. Besides, many of Bletchley's star players were unemployable by the Nazis' warped standards—homosexuals like Turing, people of Jewish blood like Good, Hilton, and Newman. Good was born Isadore Jacob Gudak, while Newman's father, Herman Neumann, had emigrated to London from the German town of Bromberg.[97] The Hilton family changed their name from Erdberg after traumatic encounters with British anti-Semitism during the era of Oswald Mosley's British Union of Fascists.

This filtering away of unacceptable talent cannot be the whole explanation for the desultory state of Nazi codebreaking, however; the same ideological filters were imposed on German engineering, yet there is no doubt that the German engineers performed spectacularly. A whole new generation of advanced weaponry was coming on stream as the war ended: jet fighters and bombers, a jet-propelled precursor to the Cruise missile, rocket-powered ballistic missiles, and super-submarines capable of remaining submerged for their entire mission—not to mention Germany's nascent atomic bomb programme. Most probably the underlying explanation for the weakness of German codebreaking was ultimately the Nazis' faith in the unbreakability of their own and other people's ciphers. It had been the same in the early days at Bletchley Park with Naval Enigma—no one bothered to work on it because of the defeatist belief that it was unbreakable. 'You know, the Germans don't mean you to read their stuff, and I don't suppose you ever will,' Denniston had told Frank Birch.[98] It was the turbocharged confidence of people like Turing and Flowers—who did not know the meaning of the word 'defeatism'—that made Bletchley Park possible; and it was their machines, the bombes and the Colossi, that were responsible for the vast scale of the British codebreaking operation.

In his quiet way, Flowers influenced Turing profoundly. With Colossus, Flowers had established decisively, and for the first time, that large-scale electronic computing was a practical proposition. From then on, he said, it was just a matter of Turing's waiting to see what opportunities might come along for putting the idea of the universal computing machine into practice. Turing didn't have to wait all that long. In June 1945, a man from the National Physical Laboratory paid Turing a surprise visit.

Figure 22. Turing's Delilah

Credit: National Archives Image Library, Kew

8

ACE, A MONTH'S WORK IN A MINUTE

John Womersley, an affable Yorkshireman on his way up the career ladder, was a new man in a new job. He was enjoying his success. His think-big attitude and refreshing good-natured enthusiasm made him the ideal person to be building up a new scientific organization. As the war came to a close, he had adroitly grasped the opportunity to head a new mathematical research division on the leafy campus of the National Physical Laboratory.[1] The NPL, as everyone called it, was a pillar of British science, located a few miles upriver from central London, in the genteel suburb of Teddington. Established in the Victorian era, the NPL had initially been managed by the Royal Society of London, but it now resembled a small university—although one with no students.[2] Womersley's official title was Superintendent of the Mathematics Division. He saw himself as a disciple of Babbage, even naming one of his new buildings after the great man. In Womersley's vision of the future, scientific computing would no longer be done by armies of human clerks but by automatic machinery. As he put it, the new machines would 'do much of the work of the lower staff classes'.[3]

Womersley had a knack for understanding the potential of new developments.[4] It was something that went hand in hand with his powerful sense of adventure. A long-time admirer of Turing's ideas, he had read 'On Computable Numbers' not long after its publication. Turing's paper opened his eyes. Straight away he began drawing up rough schematics for a Turing machine made from automatic telephone equipment—the very equipment that Flowers was eager to replace with electronics.[5] Womersley quickly decided that if the machine was built in this way, it 'would be too slow to be effective'.[6] A year or two later the war swept him into work on ballistics and statistics, but he never forgot the idea of building a Turing machine, and one day in 1944 he had a pregnant conversation about large-scale calculating machinery with physicist Douglas Hartree.[7] Hartree, a high flier in British scientific circles—and before long a member of the NPL's governing body—knew about Flowers's creation at Bletchley Park.[8] The Official Secrets Act limited what he could say, but nothing could prevent him from conveying a sense of the fabulous potential of electronic computing. Womersley was very soon talking about applying electronics 'to computations of all kinds'.[9] He coined the apt phrase 'Turing in hardware',[10] and the idea formed in his mind of inviting Turing to join his new Mathematics Division to build an all-electronic Turing machine.

Simply locating Turing, who was still engaged in secret work, was a challenge in itself. A few weeks after Germany fell, Womersley paid a visit to Newman. Hartree probably opened some doors for him. Womersley explained that he wished to meet Turing, and Newman brought the two together the same day.[11] Turing had been delving deeply into electronics since 1943, even giving a series of lectures on electronic theory at Hanslope,[12] and was probably itching to start work on an electronic Turing machine. Womersley invited him to his home and offered him the opportunity to create the first all-purpose electronic computer. It was the luckiest of lucky breaks, dropping into Turing's lap as if by divine predestination. Back at Hanslope, he told Don Bayley that he was going to 'make a brain'.[13]

Meanwhile, news was leaking out about an electronic computer being built in America. The ENIAC (Electronic Numerical Integrator and Computer) was classified, but Womersley had managed to see it a few weeks prior to his meeting with Newman and Turing, again with Hartree's help.[14] It was the brainchild of John Mauchly and Presper Eckert, two engineering visionaries who had been commissioned by the United

States army to build a high-speed calculator.[15] The army wanted this for the mammoth job of preparing complex tables that gunners needed to aim artillery. Construction got under way in Philadelphia at the University of Pennsylvania, and ENIAC eventually went into operation at the end of 1945, almost two years after the first Colossus. While Colossus remained cloaked in secrecy, ENIAC was made public in 1946 and was trumpeted as the first electronic computer. John von Neumann—wholly unaware of Colossus—told the world, in charismatic public addresses and his prominent scientific writings, that ENIAC was 'the first electronic computing machine'.[16]

Flowers saw ENIAC just after the war. He told me that in his opinion Colossus was 'much more of a computer than ENIAC'. He had included elaborate facilities for logical operations in Colossus, whereas ENIAC was just a 'number cruncher', he said. Neither of these two pioneering machines incorporated Turing's stored-program idea, however.

Figure 23. ENIAC

Credit: © 2000 Topham Picturepoint/TopFoto.co.uk

Colossus and the larger ENIAC were both programmed by rerouting cables and setting switches.[17] It could take ENIAC's operators as long as three weeks to set up and debug a program.[18] The process was a nightmare.

As far as Womersley was concerned, ENIAC's most useful feature was its propaganda value. A master of the art of winning support, he skilfully brought in references to ENIAC as he expounded his own proposals to develop an electronic computer. 'The possibilities,' Womersley told the NPL's director, Sir Charles Darwin—who spent his life in the shadow of his grandfather, *the* Charles Darwin—'are so tremendous that it is difficult to state a practical case to those who are not au fait with the American developments without it sounding completely fantastic.'[19] Turing, who did not like Womersley, might have been quietly amused by the fact that Womersley himself was not au fait with the rather more fantastic Bletchley developments.

During the remainder of 1945, Turing drew up detailed designs for his stored-program electronic computer. Womersley had already dubbed the unborn machine the Automatic Computing Engine, a reference to his hero Babbage's Analytical Engine, and everyone called it simply 'the ACE'.[20] Turing penned the first more-or-less complete design that the world had seen for an electronic stored-program digital computer, finishing his forty-eight pages of typescript and fifty-two diagrams and tables by the end of the year.[21] It was titled 'Proposed Electronic Calculator'. Turing even included a detailed estimate of the cost of the machine's components—£11,200, about £400,000 in today's money.[22] He specified a high-speed memory with roughly the same capacity as an early Apple Macintosh—enormous by the standards of his day. Turing understood that memory capacity and speed were the keys to computing. He was 'obsessed with the idea of speed', his assistant, Jim Wilkinson, remembered.[23] The ACE's clock speed was a very respectable 1 MHz, only 1600 times slower than my current laptop.

As Turing worked out the technical details, Womersley oiled the tracks. Unless Womersley could persuade Darwin to persuade the British government to cough up the cash, Turing's design would be of academic interest only. Womersley suggested to Darwin that Turing's computer was going to 'alter the whole tempo' of scientific research—and, moreover, would be 'one of the best bargains' that the British government had ever sunk money into. Womersley knew his onions, and he fed Darwin a steady stream of simple but potent messages for use in his meetings in Whitehall. 'Speeds hitherto unattainable' was one of Womersley's stodgy yet effective phrases. Darwin became a zealous convert, and was soon explaining to his government bosses that Turing's computer 'would suffice to solve all the problems that are demanded of it from the whole country'—Britain's one and only computer, controlled by Darwin.[24] There was also the question of who was going to take care of the engineering side, but as far as Turing was concerned, the answer was obvious: Tommy Flowers. Womersley explained to Darwin that Flowers 'had wartime experience in the right field'.[25] It was a crashing understatement, but neither Womersley nor Darwin had any way of knowing that.

Once Turing had completed his design paper, Womersley's job was to shepherd the proposal through the NPL's governing body, the doughty Executive Committee. He wrote a workmanlike summary of Turing's paper, in language that the scientists and captains of industry on the committee would be able to follow, and in March 1946 he and Turing were summoned to be grilled about their plans. This meeting, one of the significant moments in the history of computing, was held in a large formal room in the ornate 17th-century mansion on Piccadilly housing the offices of the Royal Society. Darwin, who was chairing the meeting, motioned Womersley to speak.

Tall and heavily built, Womersley rose imposingly to address the committee, immediately setting proceedings off on the right foot. He spoke of the computers currently in existence in the United States—ENIAC, and two relay-based machines, neither capable of running a stored program—and then he pointed out dramatically that 'Dr Turing's machine, when fully completed, would have a potential output of work greater than the three of them put together.'[26] Once he had warmed up the committee, Womersley introduced Turing. Turing straightaway plunged into a detailed discussion that inevitably went over the heads of many of those present. Before he could finish his overview of what we now call computer programming, Darwin cut him short, calling for a discussion of the entire proposal. Hartree helpfully chipped in that the ACE would have 'a "memory" capacity of 6000 numbers compared with the 20 numbers of the ENIAC'—and 'at no greater cost', he added. Darwin tediously asked Turing a series of clever-clever questions. What would happen, he wanted to know, if the computer were set a mathematical problem that had several different solutions? Turing patiently replied that the programmer 'would have to take all these possibilities into account, so that the construction of instruction tables might be a somewhat "finicky" business'.

The minutes of the meeting record that once the discussion came to an end the committee pledged its unanimous and enthusiastic support. That was the first hurdle cleared. Darwin's next stop was Whitehall, and he managed to extract a promise of £100,000 over three years for the project. The ACE's future seemed assured. Turing's plans soon caught the interest of the newspapers, with headlines like '"ACE" Superior to U.S. Model—Bigger Memory Store', '"ACE" Will Speed Jet Flying—Solving Problems in Aerodynamics', '"ACE" May Be Fastest Brain', and 'Month's Work in a Minute'. The US model was ENIAC, of course, and although the newspaper article was right about the ACE's bigger memory, it failed to mention the most important difference, namely that unlike the ACE, ENIAC had been designed with no thought for running stored programs.

Now that we know of Newman's magnificent computing facility at Bletchley Park, some of Womersley's well-intentioned statements about ENIAC seem ridiculous. For instance, he gingered Darwin and the Executive Committee with the observation that 'we are now in a position to reap handsome benefits from the pioneer work done in the United States'.[27] It was the pioneer work done at Bletchley that was being reaped, however. Secrecy about Flowers's achievement still bedevils the history of computing even today. The myth that ENIAC was the first became set in stone soon after the war, and for the rest of the 20th century, book after book—not to mention magazines and newspapers—told readers that ENIAC was the first electronic computer. An influential textbook for computer science students gave this woefully inaccurate historical summary: 'The early story has often been told, starting with Babbage [and] up to the birth of electronic machines with ENIAC.'[28] Flowers was simply left out of the picture. It was monstrously unfair, although inevitable given the secrecy. In later life, Flowers became tinged with bitterness. 'When after the war ended I was told that the secret of Colossus was to be kept indefinitely I was naturally disappointed,' he said.[29] 'I was in no doubt, once it was a proven success, that Colossus was an historic breakthrough, and that publication would have made my name in scientific and engineering circles—a conviction confirmed by the reception accorded to ENIAC,' he added sourly. He went on: 'I had to endure all the acclaim given to that enterprise without being able to disclose that I had anticipated it.' Worse still, his views on electronic engineering carried little weight with his colleagues, who had no idea what he had done, and he gained a reputation for 'pretentiousness', he said. 'Matters would have been different, I am sure, both for myself and for British industry, if Colossus had been revealed even ten years after the war ended.'

ENIAC changed the life of another of Turing's circle, the mathematical logician turned atomic bomb scientist, von Neumann. At Los Alamos, roomfuls of 'lower staff classes' armed with desk calculating machines were struggling to carry out the massive calculations required by the physicists. When he heard about ENIAC during a chance encounter with a stranger on a railway station during the summer of 1944, von Neumann saw the future. Herman Goldstine, an army ordnance officer who had attended some of his lectures and recognized him on the platform, let it slip that he was involved in the construction of a machine designed to compute at electronic speeds.[30] Von Neumann leapt. As one of America's leading scientists, he had no difficulty getting himself appointed as consultant to the ENIAC project. It would have been obvious to him as soon as he saw the plans that Eckert and Mauchly had left the most important thing out of the design—Turing's stored-program idea. It was too late by then to make any big changes, since ENIAC's design was fixed and construction was under way; but von Neumann, Eckert, and Mauchly went on to hold a series of weekly meetings during the winter of 1944 and spring of 1945, working out how to design a stored-program electronic computer.[31] They called their proposed computer EDVAC (Electronic Discrete Variable Arithmetic Computer). Von Neumann wrote up their ideas, in what would become one of the most infamous documents of computing history.[32]

The trouble was that Goldstine circulated a draft version of von Neumann's report before Eckert's and Mauchly's names had been added to the title page. This draft was supposed to go only to members of the EDVAC group, but some outsiders were favoured with copies, including Womersley.[33] People quickly showed the fascinating report to their friends and neighbours, and soon anybody who was anybody in the world of mechanized computing knew about it. Eckert and Mauchly were horrified. They feared that von Neumann would now get credit for everything in the report, their ideas as well as his. Von Neumann was unrepentant. 'My personal opinion,' he said defiantly in 1947, 'was at all times, and is now, that this [the distribution of the report] was perfectly proper and in the best interests of the United States.'[34] Distribution had, he said, furthered 'the development of the art of building high speed computers'; and as far as he was concerned, that was all that mattered. It's a pity that someone equally committed to computer development, and equally hard-nosed, did not publish a description of Colossus—and Bletchley's spectacular electronic computing facility—in 1945.

So it was not only Flowers but, ironically, also Eckert and Mauchly who tasted the bitter pill of seeing their achievements attributed to others. Had Turing lived he too might have seen cause to feel bitter. Computer science textbooks, and books and articles describing the history of the computer, often attribute Turing's stored-program concept to von Neumann. It was von Neumann, with his high profile in American science, who made the concept widely known, but he certainly never claimed it as his own. On the contrary, von Neumann said that Turing's 'great positive contribution' was to show that 'one, definite mechanism can be "universal"'.[35] 'The importance of Turing's research,' he emphasized, lay in its demonstration that an appropriately designed machine 'can, when given suitable instructions, do anything that can be done by automata at all.'[36] 'Many people have acclaimed von Neumann as the "father of the computer"', von Neumann's friend Stanley Frankel observed, 'but I am sure that he would never have made that mistake himself'.[37] Frankel, one of the physicists working at Los Alamos, continued: 'In my view von Neumann's essential role was in making the world aware of these fundamental concepts introduced by Turing and of the development work carried out in the Moore school and elsewhere.' Von Neumann 'firmly emphasized to me, and to others I am sure, that the fundamental conception is owing to Turing', Frankel said. Von Neumann's great contribution was to tell America's electronic engineers about Turing's universal machine.

The EDVAC group broke up in the fracas following the circulation of von Neumann's report. Von Neumann decided to set up his own computer group at Princeton. Eckert and Mauchly turned their backs on EDVAC and started a computer company in Philadelphia, hoping that this would afford their ideas some legal protection. Others finally turned the EDVAC design into hardware, but it did not run a program until 1952, well behind the first wave of pioneering stored-program computers.[38] With the disintegration of the EDVAC group, the number of horses in the race was multiplying—Turing in London, Newman in Manchester, Eckert and Mauchly in Philadelphia, and now von Neumann in Princeton. Von Neumann gathered a group of engineers around him at the Institute for Advanced Study, priming them for their new work by giving them Turing's 'On Computable Numbers' to read.[39] Ideas were flowing from America to Britain too. Womersley showed von Neumann's EDVAC report to Turing during their first meeting.[40] Turing studied the report but went on to design a very different type of computer. He focused on squeezing as much speed as possible out of the hardware.[41]

The design proposals that Turing set out in his 'Proposed Electronic Calculator' were much more concrete than those in von Neumann's report, which described the EDVAC at a very high level of abstraction. Von Neumann hardly mentioned electronics at all. Harry Huskey—the engineer whose job it was to draw up the first detailed hardware designs for the EDVAC—said he found von Neumann's report to be of 'no help'.[42] Turing's design paper, on the other hand, gave detailed specifications of the hardware, and also included sample programs in machine code.

Turing was quite happy to borrow from the more elementary material in von Neumann's report, though. For example, his diagram of an adder is essentially the same as von Neumann's diagram.[43] This borrowing is probably what Turing was referring to when he told a newspaper reporter in 1946 that he gave 'credit for the donkey work on the A.C.E. to Americans'.[44] Yet the similarities between Turing's design and the von Neumann–Eckert–Mauchly proposals are relatively minor in comparison to the striking differences.

Turing's philosophy of computer design was to use as little hardware as possible, and to compensate for the leanness of the resulting physical machine by writing complex programs. So instead of building special- ized hardware for long multiplication, long division, or floating-point arithmetic, Turing believed that complex processes like these should be carried out by software. In his desire to keep the physical machine as sim- ple as possible, he anticipated the modern approach to computer design known as 'RISC' (Reduced Instruction Set Computer).[45] It was a sensible policy, especially at a time when building complicated electronic hard- ware was beset with engineering problems. Turing had, after all, been writing computer programs since 1936—he knew, in what were comput- ing's rugged pioneering days, that programming was the easier part of the struggle. His opinion of designers who didn't subscribe to his phil- osophy is recorded in his 1946 memo to Womersley concerning Maurice Wilkes, an ex-radar man with plans to build a computer of the EDVAC type in Cambridge.[46] Wilkes's design ideas, Turing said impishly, were 'very contrary' to his own, and 'much more in the American tradition of solving one's difficulties by means of much equipment rather than thought'.[47]

Turing disliked Wilkes, saying that he looked like a beetle.[48] His atti- tude to Womersley—whom he called a 'salesman'—was also extremely negative.[49] Womersley was Turing's line manager, but Turing made no effort at all to get on with him, usually simply ignoring him. Their bad relationship hung over the ACE project, poisoning the atmosphere. Turing's mother, Sara, pointed out insightfully that in Turing's view, the only acceptable ground for being in charge was 'that you had a better grasp of the subject involved than anyone else'.[50] Many put up graciously with a superior who knows less than they do, but Turing could not. He was simply 'intolerant of authority not justified by ability', Sara said.[51] Actually, Womersley was a capable mathematician. He had published with Hartree on equation-solving methods, and had also made important contributions to the mathematics of textiles, inventing a system of equations for calculating the stresses and strains in a piece of cloth that is being pulled at its edges.[52] Nevertheless, he was many light years distant from Turing's league.

Turing's lack of respect for Womersley rubbed off on some of the other Mathematics Division staff. A clandestine competition—a silly one, in view of Womersley's past work—involved offering a prize to the first person to encounter him making use of a mathematical equation. 'The competition closed after three months for lack of entries,' Robin Gandy recollected with a wicked smile on his face.[53] He did not know Womersley well: it was a case of his friend's enemy being his enemy. He pronounced the name 'Wormsley', with scathing emphasis on 'worm'. Gandy explained that both Womersley and Wilkes were what Turing sarcastically called 'magnates'—'high-up front-office people with enormous desks'. Womersley even kept a copy of *How to Win Friends and Influence People* in his office. Magnates were exactly the kind of people that the irreverent Turing loved to despise.

Gandy, Donald Michie and I were drinking wine and eating pasta. The cheery seventy-seven year old mathematician was hard to keep on track, and he veered off into an account of how he had recently capsized his bicycle in the heavy Oxford traffic. This in turn put him in mind of once driving his sports car through the front window of a fish-and-chip shop. Gandy explained radiantly that although his passenger was unharmed, one lens of the man's spectacles, which were still perched on his nose, had cracked through from top to bottom. The improbability of this delighted Gandy. Michie drained his glass and raised one eyebrow comically. 'Womersley was basically a credit grabber,' he volunteered, returning the conversation to its previous topic. Yet all Womersley had done was make use of his managerial expertise to try to turn Turing's dream into a reality. He certainly never gave the impression of taking credit for Turing's ideas. Turing's refusal to get on with him was a mistake, and it put the whole ACE project into jeopardy.

Of his friends from the secret war, Gandy and Michie were the two that Turing was seeing most during his new life in London. One escapade he shared with Michie had its origins in the early days of the war. Turing realized that if the Nazis were to invade Britain there would be financial chaos, and he sensibly sank his savings into two silver ingots.[54] He transported the heavy metal bars in an old-fashioned baby carriage and buried them in the countryside at two different spots. Now the war was over, the time had come to retrieve the bullion. Turing asked for Michie's help, offering to split the proceeds once the ingots were retrieved. Michie, a canny Scot, offered his labour for a fixed fee. They set off carrying spades and Turing's home-made metal detector, as well as his cryptic map of the hiding places. Unfortunately they were unable to locate the ingots' graves, and after two fruitless expeditions the search was abandoned.

Another presence from his wartime days was Turing's ancient bicycle, the brunt of many jokes at Bletchley Park. By now its chain had been faulty for more than five years. 'Rather than repair it,' Henry Norton related, 'he had found that by counting the number of rotations of the pedals, he could get off and walk a few paces and then remount and ride without the chain jumping off the sprocket.'[55] Norton joined Turing's team at the NPL in the autumn of 1947. 'My main memory of him is his irascibility,' he said with a grin. There is no doubt that life at the NPL ground Turing down.

A tinier memento of his war effort, less useful than a bicycle, was the OBE that arrived by post in 1946. Turing kept the shiny medal with its red ribbon in a tin box full of screws, nails, and other odds and ends.[56] The OBE is regularly awarded for services to local government, business, and sport. It was hardly adequate recognition for Turing's war work—Newman described it, mildly enough, as 'ludicrous'.[57] Yet elsewhere in the state machinery's fragmented consciousness there were no mistakes concerning the value of what Turing had done. Hugh Alexander, now a big cheese at GCHQ, offered him the astronomical sum of £5,000 to break post-war codes—a figure more than six times his starting salary at the NPL.[58]

Turing was not just a commuter cyclist. He enjoyed serious bike tours in France and Switzerland, peddling through the Grand Massif and the Swiss Alps.[59] With his cycling, mountain walking, tennis, hockey, rowing, sailing, and running, the muscular Turing was not just a mental athlete. Running came to the fore while he was working on the ACE. 'Once in London a cross-country team, finding itself a man short, asked him to make up the number,' Arthur Pigou recollected; he 'came in, I believe, at the head of the field'.[60] Suddenly, in his mid-thirties, Turing emerged as a runner of first-rate potential. He 'began to train seriously with a view to Marathon racing', Pigou said. Turing joined the Walton Athletic Club, located less than three miles distant from his lodgings in picturesque Hampton-on-Thames. You 'heard him rather than saw him', recollected the then secretary of the club.[61] 'He made a terrible grunting noise when he was running, but before we could say anything to him, he was past us like a shot out of a gun.' Eventually Turing was elected to the club's committee.[62]

When he needed to visit Tommy Flowers's North London laboratory, which was in Dollis Hill, Turing put on old clothes and ran the fifteen or so miles from the NPL. His running garb included a pair of ancient flannel trousers that he tied at the top with a piece of rope.[63] Always careful about his timing when running, he was seen pounding along with an alarm clock knotted round his middle.[64] Purple juice had covered his running clothes with liberal stains when he climbed a mulberry tree in Hampton to gather the ripe fruit.[65] A fifteen-mile run to Dollis Hill was nothing to Turing—and infinitely preferable to the tedious journey by bus and Underground. He would even run the eighteen miles from Hampton to his mother's house in Guildford for lunch.[66] He was fast and had terrific stamina. One wet afternoon, while on holiday with the Newmans in Wales, he changed into blue shorts and slipped out for a short while; when asked later where he had gone, he pointed out over Cardigan Bay to a promontory so distant as to be almost invisible.[67]

Turing's races for Walton AC were soon being written up in the papers. His mother kept some of the cuttings. An article in the *Evening News* in December 1946 began: 'Antithesis of the popular notion of a scientist is tall, modest, 34-year-old bachelor Alan M. Turing.' 'Turing is the club's star distance runner,' the reporter said, 'although this is his first season in competitive events.' Later the same month Turing was hero of a three-mile race at Walton. The race was won by a competitor from Surrey AC who 'started from the 10-yards mark', yet even so managed to beat Turing only 'by one foot in the last stride', a sports correspondent wrote.[68] 'A very exciting race indeed' Turing said enthusiastically.[69] At a Motspur Park race, the reporter 'was agreeably surprised to see Turing regain the lead and finish so strongly that he had 20 yards to spare'. 'That was the meeting at which all the stars were trying to break records,' Turing said self-effacingly, 'but in fact were all pulling muscles instead.'[70] He came fifth in the national marathon championship at the 1947 Amateur Athletic Association meeting, a qualifying event for the 1948 London Olympics, and he decided to enter the coming Olympic trials.[71] When he developed a problem with his hip, however, his Olympic hopes came to an end, although he remained a very serious recreational runner for the rest of his life.

At first, the Turing–Flowers computer-building partnership seemed to be going very well. Flowers planned to have a 'minimal ACE' ready by about mid 1946.[72] But he came under tremendous pressure from his boss, Gordon Radley, to devote himself to the restoration of Britain's war-ravaged telephone system. Despite his desire to collaborate with Turing, he rapidly became 'too busy to do other people's work', he said.[73] He could spare only two engineers for the ACE, Allen 'Doc' Coombs and Bill Chandler, his right-hand men from the Colossus days. Weeks and months dragged by with little or nothing to show. As Turing waited impatiently for the engineers, he spent his days pioneering computer programming, and he prepared a large software library for the not-yet-existent machine. It was the availability of this stock of ready-made programs that accounted for the success, once the prototype ACE was finally working, of the NPL's Scientific Computing Service. The computing service, the first in the world, took on commissions from government, industry, and universities.

Coombs and Chandler had got bogged down in the messy details of engineering the ACE's high-speed memory. Memory was the leading problem facing computer designers at that time. Both Colossus and ENIAC had used electronic valves for their high-speed memory, but the cost of these was so high that it limited the practical size of the memory. ENIAC wastefully tied up around five hundred valves to store a single ten-digit number.[74] New technology was needed before a fast, relatively inexpensive, high-capacity memory could become a reality. Eckert had the idea of using a component called a 'delay line', originally developed for use in radar. This was a five-foot-long pipe through which beeps of sound travelled. Turing seized on Eckert's idea as a means of storing '1000 binary digits at a cost of a few pounds'.[75] It was no USB flash drive. Turing considered improving the delay line's performance by filling it with a mixture of alcohol and water, referred to by some as gin.[76] Eventually he chose mercury rather than alcohol. Zeroes and ones—bits—arrived at one end of the pipe from elsewhere in the computer, in the form of electrical pulses. The pulses were converted into blips of sound that travelled relatively slowly through the mercury to the other end of the pipe. There they were converted back into electrical pulses, and these were amplified to make up for any degradation suffered by the signal while it was travelling along the pipe. The refreshed pulses were then routed back to the pipe's entry, where the process was repeated ad infinitum. In theory, thousands of zeroes and ones could be stored forever in this way, circulating round and round in the mercury memory medium. The ACE's memory would be built from approximately five hundred mercury delay lines, Turing decided.[77]

In practice, though, mercury delay lines proved ticklishly difficult to develop. For one thing, the pipe and the various mechanical parts had to be machined very accurately. Moreover, errors occurred unless the memory was kept at a constant temperature. Coombs and Chandler, ready to try anything that might work, used a thick covering of hay to protect their prototype memory from temperature changes.[78] Screening the memory from electrical interference was even more difficult. They discovered early on that motorcycles and cars passing the laboratory filled the memory with random bits. The engineers' progress towards a working delay line was so infuriatingly slow that a frustrated Turing began his own experiments, using a length of drainpipe.[79] He told Don Bayley that he wanted to build the ACE himself.[80] It wasn't until as late as the spring of 1947 that Coombs and Chandler succeeded in producing a 'tolerably satisfactory mercury line'.[81] But worse delays lay ahead, thanks to Darwin's mismanagement.

As 1946 dragged to a close, the ACE was not the only thing that was frozen solid. The country was suffering from one of the coldest winters on record. Snow lay for what seemed like months, everyone's pipes iced up, and in postwar-austerity Britain there was not enough coal to go around. As the New Year came in, Harry Huskey arrived at the icy NPL, a breath of fresh air from across the Atlantic. With his rimless glasses, brushed-back hair, and checkerboard jacket, he looked every inch the bright young American. Previously he had worked with Eckert and Mauchly on the ENIAC, writing operation and maintenance manuals.[82] When von Neumann, Eckert, and Mauchly abandoned the EDVAC, the University of Pennsylvania offered him the job of directing the project. Unfortunately he was under contract as a lowly instructor in the university's mathematics department, and the head of mathematics politicked to get the offer withdrawn, Huskey explained ruefully. He was so irate that he left Philadelphia altogether and went back to Ohio, but was luckily pursued by a job offer from the NPL. Hartree had pulled a few strings to get him a twelve-month contract in London. Smelling adventure, Huskey sold his car to pay for the boat tickets and arrived with his wife at the port of Southampton, carrying a copy of *How To Like an Englishman* in his luggage.

Despite the ice and snow, Womersley sent him out on a motorcycle to visit Newman in Manchester and Wilkes in Cambridge. His hardy wife travelled in the sidecar. Huskey and Turing got on well enough. Once they raced each other from the NPL to Dollis Hill—Turing ran and Huskey went by train, carrying Turing's clothes in a satchel. The American won but only by a minute or two. On another occasion, he accompanied Turing to a lecture he was going to give; they travelled by train and soon fell into a discussion about computing. The discussion grew heated. 'Turing became so upset that he could hardly give his lecture,' Huskey reminisced.[83] It didn't take Huskey long to weigh up the situation at the NPL. They had Turing's design, but there was nobody to build it. This was something that the energetic, independent-minded Huskey felt he could help them with.

It was becoming obvious to Turing, too, that his computer was never going to exist unless the NPL itself built it. He told Darwin: 'It is clear that we must have an engineering section at the ACE site eventually, the sooner the better, I would say.'[84] He could not possibly have foreseen the fiasco that was going to ensue from his sensible suggestion. Darwin mulled the idea over—nothing ever happened quickly in his organization. Meanwhile, Huskey was pawing the ground with impatience. Building a computer seemed a reasonably straightforward proposition to him. Why weren't these strange Englishmen getting on with it? He told Womersley that he intended to build a 'pilot model' of the ACE, and by sheer force of personality recruited Turing's two young assistants, Mike Woodger and Jim Wilkinson, to help him.[85] They were soon calling their nascent computer the Test Assembly.

Turing should have seized this opportunity to start building the ACE. He didn't, owing to differences in outlook between himself and Huskey. Huskey wanted to start the ball rolling by wiring together a relatively small computer, whereas Turing wanted to focus on building a much larger computer, the ACE as he had designed it. In the abstract, Turing was right, but in the circumstances that actually prevailed—there were no engineers on hand to build a large machine—Huskey's plan was more pragmatic. Unfortunately, though, Turing would have nothing to do with it. He 'tended to ignore the Test Assembly', Wilkinson said.[86] Woodger remembers there being 'a scene' when Turing discovered him writing a program for the Test Assembly.[87] Mostly, however, Turing simply stood to one side and acted as though Huskey's project did not exist.[88] It was a mistake, like his refusal to cooperate with Womersley. But Turing was a loner, not a team player. He may even have thought that he was just letting the others get on with what they thought best. His failure to give active support to Huskey cost him the race with Manchester.

By the middle of the year, Huskey finished his paper design, known colloquially as 'Version H' of the ACE, and began to put the computer together in—appropriately enough—the Babbage Building. The NPL workshops were making a mercury delay line to his specifications, and his first goal was to run a very simple stored program using a single delay line and a minimum of electronics.[89] Then he planned to construct a small but substantial computer containing about thirteen delay lines and capable of doing serious mathematical work.[90] Womersley, ever the optimist, was expecting the first program to run by November.[91] The Test Assembly, it seemed, was well on its way to becoming the world's first stored-program computer.

Meanwhile, Darwin eventually came round to Turing's idea of an in-house electronics group, and he appointed Horace Augustus Thomas to head it. Thomas, Darwin thought, was just the man to build a prototype of Turing's computer.[92] In fact, Thomas was a disastrous choice. He specialized in a quite different field of electronics and had vanishingly little interest in digital computers, but he sensed the opportunity to build a small empire within the NPL. As empire builders do, he acted swiftly to stamp out his rivals—in this case Huskey's group—and petitioned Darwin to rule that the Test Assembly be discontinued. The bumbling Darwin went along with Thomas and forbade further work on Huskey's budding computer. It was one of the worst administrative decisions in the history of computing. The NPL's hopes of building the first stored-program computer turned to dust. Morale fell through the floor. If Turing had been behind the Test Assembly, though, it might all have worked out differently. Thomas, not content with the damage he had already done, dealt another crushing blow to the ACE less than six months later, abandoning his fragile new electronics group for a job with the manufacturers of Sunlight soap.[93]

Huskey, who was naturally disgusted with Darwin's handling of the situation, left the NPL and returned to America at the end of 1947. Turing left too. Very fed up, he asked Darwin for a spell of sabbatical leave, and in the autumn went back to Cambridge to spend twelve months doing research.[94] Darwin explained to his superiors in the ministry that Turing would be investigating whether a computer 'could learn by experience'.[95] 'This will be theoretical work, and better done away from here,' he said, putting a brave face on losing the best scientist in his organization. He added that he was granting Turing leave only on 'the condition that he is under a gentleman's agreement to return here for at least two years after the year's absence'. Turing dropped in on the NPL the following spring to compete at the annual Sports Day, winning the three-mile race.[96] The ACE was no further forward than when he had left. Womersley reported gloomily that hardware development was 'probably as far advanced 18 months ago'.[97] Turing had had enough, and he accepted Newman's timely offer of a position at his Computing Machine Laboratory in Manchester. When Darwin was given the news, he retaliated by sacking Turing on the spot—a pointless and vindictive action that nevertheless gave Turing a terrible shock.[98] He escaped the NPL, leaving his colleagues to build the ACE if they could.

The story of Newman's Computing Machine Laboratory is told in the next chapter. Manchester won the race to build the first electronic universal Turing machine, in June 1948, about nine months after Darwin scuppered Huskey's small ACE. At the NPL, responsibility for the ACE now fell onto Jim Wilkinson's shoulders. Wilkinson was a gentle, soft-spoken man who liked to grow his own tomatoes on the roof of the mathematicians' building. He had the right touch to make things flourish, and did everything that Thomas ought to have done twelve months previously. It was obvious to him that the way forward was to resuscitate the Test Assembly. Politician enough to realize that he needed to mask the true state of affairs from Darwin, the Test Assembly became the Pilot Model ACE.[99]

Wilkinson built bridges with Thomas's replacement, Morley Colebrook, and as the tomatoes ripened, a sunny relationship developed between the mathematicians and the engineers. With Colebrook's encouragement, the mathematicians even got their hands dirty. 'Each of us had a soldering iron,' Mike Woodger told me.[100] It was unheard of. The two groups worked together harmoniously in a kind of production line, churning out the computer circuit by circuit. 'Oh, it was tremendous fun,' Woodger remembered wistfully. On 10 May 1950, the Pilot Model ACE ran its first program. There were a small number of other stored-program computers functioning by that time, but Turing's 1 MHz design left them all in the dust.

Womersley, always restless, quit the NPL not long after the Pilot Model ACE came to life. He jumped ship to work on another electronic computer project, started up by the same company that had manufactured

Figure 24. The Pilot Model ACE

Credit: National Physical Laboratory – © Crown copyright

Turing's bombes (the British Tabulating Machine Company in Letch-worth).[101] When restlessness next overcame him, he moved to St Bartholomew's Hospital in London. There he did some of his most significant mathematical work, on the flow of blood in the arteries.[102] He outlived Turing, but not by very long. In 1955, his roving habits took him to a job in America, and there he died at the age of only 50, less than four years after Turing.

Turing never worked with the Pilot Model ACE, but at least he had the satisfaction of seeing a small family of different computers start to sprout from his ACE design. The NPL called in the English Electric Company to produce a marketable version of the Pilot Model ACE. The result, the DEUCE, was an immensely successful computer—one of the foundation stones of Britain's developing computer industry. DEUCEs remained in use until about 1970. Flowers's men Coombs and Chandler eventually completed their version of the ACE, an ultra-secret computer called

MOSAIC that played an important role in Britain's air defences during the Cold War.[103] Packard-Bell, EMI, and Bendix Corporation all built ACE-type computers. Ultimately the NPL constructed an early supercomputer based on Turing's ACE design.[104] There is a photo of it in Chapter 2 (Fig. 4).[105]

The driving force behind the Bendix computer—named simply the G15—was Harry Huskey.[106] A few years ago, Huskey took a cruise ship to New Zealand. I met him on the harbour wharf, with the gigantic P&O liner he had sailed in towering above us. We set out in my four-wheel drive to visit a Maori marae (village), enjoying the sunshine and some precipitous views over the blue South Pacific. Soon we were talking about the G15. 'You've got to be careful what you mean by the term "personal computer",' he said. Nowadays this term tends to be used for a very specific product range, but in its generic sense, a personal computer is simply one that's cheap enough and user-friendly enough for a single person, perhaps an engineer or accountant, to have in their office for their own personal use. The G15 was a personal computer in that sense, Huskey said with pride—in fact, the very first personal computer. It was larger than the machines we adore today, approximately as large as a jumbo-size kitchen refrigerator. Huskey followed Turing's philosophy of substituting programming for hardware, and the result was a cheap, compact computer requiring no air conditioning and plugging into a normal 115-volt electric supply. It cost one-tenth of the price of the closest competitor from IBM—a multi-user mainframe requiring a team of operators and engineers to cosset it. To increase the G15's processing speed, Huskey had included a number of Turing's tricks with time and his computer was blazingly fast for its size. During the 1950s and 1960s his mighty midget was marketed very successfully as a single-user desk-side computer by the Detroit-based Bendix Corp.

Old-fashioned histories of the computer did not even mention Turing. Yet Turing is at the root of it. There is a direct line from the universal Turing machine of 1936 that leads not only to the influential EDVAC blueprint, on which generations of computers are based, but also—via Colossus—to the very first modern computer, in Newman's Manchester laboratory, and onwards to the first personal computer.

Figure 25. The first personal computer

Credit: With kind permission of Harry Huskey

9

MANCHESTER'S 'ELECTRONIC BRAIN'

The chief engineer of the Manchester 'Electronic Brain', Freddie—later Sir Freddie—Williams, was, like Flowers, one of Britain's electronics superstars. The son of a railway engine designer, Williams was a plain-talking man from Stockport, the grimy industrial town a stone's throw to the south of Manchester.[1] He talked fast and fluently, usually gesticulating energetically with a lighted cigarette between his fingers. F.C., as people called him, was often to be seen sitting deep in thought at his desk, pen in one hand and cigarette in the other—he insisted on this characteristic pose for his official portrait when elected a Fellow of the Royal Society in 1950. As he sat working, he would from time to time park his lighted cigarette vertically in a curious tube-like holder that sprouted up from the front of the desk. If not smoking, gesticulating, or writing, he would usually be gripping a hot soldering iron in one hand and a strip of lead solder in the other, leaning forward with an expression of intense concentration on his face as he added yet more complexities to a tangle of wire and valves (the ever-present cigarette jutting out of his mouth at a determined angle). Often the tangle of components would grow so large and stretchy that it drooped over the edges of his workbench.[2] Williams could look serious to the point of grimness, but his irreverent sense of humour was never far away.

During the war he was a leading light in the development of airborne radar. Incongruously, he did this maximum-priority work in a small cricket pavilion at Malvern College, a top-notch private school for boys nestled in the hills of rural Worcestershire. The Air Ministry had requisitioned the school's buildings to house its secret radar group, known as the Telecommunications Research Establishment (TRE for short). The name was a front; TRE's research had little to do with telecommunications. Williams's main interest was the use of radar to identify and track enemy aircraft. He'd designed and built his first radio in a cigar box at the age of ten, and from his tiny pavilion at TRE he churned out invention after invention. He enjoyed giving these bizarre names, such as the 'Phantastron' and the 'Sanaphant',[3] and his peers regarded him as a brilliant and creative engineer. Although never a shrinking violet when it came to mentioning his own achievements, Williams was also the master of British understatement. Reminiscing not long before he died in 1977, he said in a matter-of-fact way, 'I was rather—let's admit it—well-known as a circuit engineering type.'[4] 'No one can teach you how to invent,' he said, adding, 'I think really good inventors are about as rare as good painters or good musicians.'[5]

As one of the top men at TRE and the leader of a problem-solving group, Williams was free to tackle any project he thought might be useful.[6] With the end of the war in sight, he began to realize that (as he put it) 'nobody was going to care a toss about radar' once the German armies had collapsed.[7] 'People like me were going to be in the soup unless we found something else to do,' he said. The new line of research that he eventually selected was building a digital computer. Computers were 'in the air', he remembered. 'Knowing absolutely nothing about them I latched onto the problem of storage and tackled that.'[8] It was a good call—his electronic computer, built around the new type of memory he invented, was the greatest success of his career.

Williams thought up a form of computer memory later called simply the 'Williams tube'. Basically this consisted of an ordinary television tube (a cathode ray tube) with some clever circuitry attached. Because cathode ray tubes were a widely used component, they were available off the shelf at a low cost—unlike Turing's delay lines, which had to be specially made by a highly skilled machinist. Cheapness and ready availability were

Figure 26. Freddie Williams (right) and Tom Kilburn standing in front of the 'Baby' computer

Credit: With kind permission of the University of Manchester School of Computer Science

immediate pluses for the Williams tube. The American pioneer of computing Herman Goldstine was not exaggerating when he said that Williams's new type of memory made a 'whole generation of electronic computers possible'.[9] The high-speed memory of many first- and also second-generation computers consisted of a huge bank of what were effectively TV screens, extraordinary though this now sounds.

A big problem with Turing's delay-line memory was that it stored data in a queue. Each piece of data had to wait its turn to pop out of the memory. It was like waiting for a passenger to get off a bus—the further back in the bus they are, the longer they take to emerge from the front exit. If the piece of data that the computer needed at a particular moment was right at the far end of the sausage-like delay line, it would take longer to pop out than if already positioned close to the exit. So delay lines kept the computer waiting at nearly every step of the computation. This form of memory was a terrible brake on the potential speed of the machine, and Williams was certain he could do better. He knew that in principle he could store computer data—zeroes and ones—on a TV screen. The memory would look like a black-and-white television picture consisting of nothing but rows of blips across the screen. A zero was stored in the form of a bright dot, and a 1 as a bright dash. No matter whether the computer needed to access the data stored in the top row of dots and dashes or in the bottom row, the access time was always the same. The back-of-the-bus phenomenon was eliminated. Nowadays it's called 'random access memory', or RAM, and most of us have a few chunks of it somewhere or other in our homes—but at the end of the Second World War it was a very new idea just waiting for someone to put it into practice.

Turing was as usual way out in front. Six months or more before Williams even heard of the problem of computer memory, Turing had rather uncannily noted down a description of what was in effect the Williams tube. 'It seems probable,' Turing wrote in his design paper, 'Proposed Electronic Calculator', 'that a suitable storage system can be developed without involving any new types of tube, using in fact an ordinary cathode ray tube with tin-foil over the screen to act as a signal plate.'[10] But Williams knew nothing about Turing's ideas at that time. It was in America that he came face to face with the problem of computer memory, while he was paying a visit to Presper Eckert's lab in Philadelphia during the summer of 1946.[11] Under Eckert's direction, a young engineer by the name of Kite Sharpless was attempting to store data on the screen of a cathode ray tube.[12] They were even using a sheet of metal foil over the front of the screen, exactly as Turing had envisioned in his mind's eye. But Sharpless was thwarted by the discovery that the bits would decay and vanish as quickly as he put them onto the screen. It was almost like trying to write in water: the tube would remember the data for only the briefest of moments before forgetting it again. Later Williams summed up the difficulty like this: 'You could put your signal on, and provided you went and looked for it again within half a second or so, there it was—but if you hoped to find it the next day, there it was gone.'[13]

Just a few weeks after getting back to TRE from the United States, Williams threw himself at the problem of how to fix the data in memory.[14] His breakthrough came quite quickly,[15] and he called his invention the 'anticipation pulse'. It was one of those things that seems obvious once you know how. Consider the brain teaser 'How do you use rapidly fading ink to draw a permanent dash?' The solution is to keep re-inking the dash before it has time to disappear, and that is exactly how Williams solved the memory problem. In a black-and-white TV tube there is a beam that 'paints' the picture on the screen, and Williams wired the tube up so that the beam would keep redrawing a dash. This lone dash was his first experimental piece of data, a single bit. His 'anticipation pulse' told the tube very precisely when to operate the beam, so that the dash stayed in exactly the same place for as long as he wished. Modern RAM effortlessly stores gazillions of bits, but in the autumn of 1946 Williams was overjoyed to see one single bit sitting unwaveringly on the screen. He knew that with some fiddling it should be possible to store a couple of thousand bits per TV tube—a whopping quarter of a kilobyte!—and rushed to patent his invention. If Turing's achievement in 1936, namely the invention of the universal stored-program machine, was like thinking up the wheel, then Williams's achievement in 1946 was like designing the first working axle. Soon he would progress to building the first functioning cart. His electronic stored-program computer was the first on the planet.

Eckert always believed that Williams had stolen his idea. A few years after Williams got his memory working, Christopher Strachey—in later life one of Britain's leading experts on programming theory—dropped in on Eckert. He learned that Eckert was outraged at Williams. 'Eckert said that Williams visited,' Strachey related, 'and then returned to England and subsequently patented some of the work he saw.'[16] Williams, on the other hand, thought Eckert was the one doing the stealing. Under his own name, Eckert published details of a cathode ray tube memory that was to all intents and purposes identical to the one Williams had patented in Britain. He didn't want Williams deriving patent royalties in the United States for what he considered to be his own idea. The fact of the matter, though, is that the experimental memory seen by Williams in Eckert's lab could not store information for more than a fraction of a second. It was Williams who made the crucial breakthrough that led to the first working device.

Meanwhile the engineering world forgot, if it ever knew, that Turing had outlined the design of a cathode ray tube memory in 1945. The National Physical Laboratory had mailed Williams a copy of Turing's 'Proposed Electronic Calculator' in October 1946, the month before Williams lodged a draft application for a patent on the Williams tube. It isn't recorded whether Williams read 'Proposed Electronic Calculator' at that time, but there is no reason to think that he didn't. He need only have opened the envelope and glanced at the table of contents to see the irresistible chapter title, 'Alternative Forms of Storage', the very field he himself was pioneering. Racing to the chapter, he would have found Turing's pithy description of the Williams tube—enough to make his cigarette pop out of his mouth with surprise. He might have objected, though, to Turing's airy statement that turning the basic ideas into engineering reality would not involve 'any fundamental difficulty'. Turing did not know about the anticipation pulse, and he gave a high-level logical description of an approach that was more general than the one Williams had discovered. Williams quickly dropped the anticipation-pulse method in favour of more general arrangements, similar to those outlined by Turing.[17] There is, now, no way of knowing for sure whether or not Williams learned this lesson from Turing's 'Proposed Electronic Calculator'. But, in any case, Turing's involvement with Williams's project began in earnest a few weeks later, in November, when Williams's assistant Tom Kilburn walked into a lecture room in London and sat down to listen to Turing explaining how to build a computer.[18]

Kilburn had joined Williams's group at TRE in 1942, fresh from Cambridge University.[19] Williams had earned his doctorate at Oxford, where he was a keen rowing cox,[20] but no inter-varsity rivalry got in the way of the blossoming of a lifelong friendship. The two men worked together on radar and by the end of the fighting there wasn't much that, between them, they didn't know about the state of the art in electronics. Kilburn, a young Yorkshireman with a determined chin, shared Williams's taste for plain, blunt speaking. But there most of the similarity ended. Williams was the funny guy—and he was quite a charmer—while Kilburn was the straight man. He could be brusque, impatient, and even insensitive.

A man of strong opinions, Kilburn was hungry for success and not averse to treading on a few toes to achieve it. Succeed he did. He is remembered as one of Britain's greatest computer scientists (he died in 2001). Kilburn's big break came in October 1946, when Williams invited him to help with the development of the new computer memory.[21]

As Williams admitted with his usual disarming frankness, 'neither Tom Kilburn nor I knew the first thing about computers'.[22] They heard that Turing was giving a course of lectures on computer design in London. It was a golden opportunity to plug the gaps in their understanding. Kilburn attended as one of two representatives from TRE.[23] The nine weekly lectures, arranged by Womersley, were held on Thursday afternoons, starting in December 1946 and continuing through into the following February. Turing's audience assembled in a dingy function room in the basement of the Adelphi Hotel in London's Strand. Dr Watson, narrator of the Sherlock Holmes stories, related that once he lived 'at a private hotel in the Strand, leading a comfortless, meaningless existence'.[24] London in Sherlock Holmes's day was probably much more amusing than in grim 1946, though, with food rationing, a lack of basic comforts, and a squeeze on space brought about by the many square miles of bombed-out buildings. But probably the dismal venue for the lectures didn't bother Turing. In the first couple of sessions he went over the basics of the new art (binary numbers, high-speed memory, logical operations, circuits for arithmetic) and then he dived into the details of the ACE. Wilkinson gave some of the lectures too, probably from notes supplied by Turing. Kilburn was a good pupil. He quickly progressed from not knowing the first thing about computers to the point where he could start designing one for himself.

In fact, Kilburn's initial design for what would eventually be the Manchester Baby computer followed Turing's principles closely.[25] Unlike von Neumann and his group in the United States, Turing advocated a *decentralized* computer with no central processing unit, or CPU—no one central place where all the logical and arithmetical operations were carried out. The term 'decentralized', and its opposite 'centralized', were due to Jack Good, for whom Newman had created a special lectureship in mathematics and electronic computing in his Manchester department.[26] Kilburn designed a decentralized computer very much along the lines that Turing set out in his lectures. When explaining his design in a report to his superiors at TRE, Kilburn employed the same distinctive vocabulary that Turing used in the lectures ('table of instructions', 'universal machine', 'source', 'destination', 'temporary store', 'staticiser', 'dynamiciser', and so on).[27] It was all very different from the centralized type of design that von Neumann was proposing. When asked, in later life, where he got his basic knowledge of the computer from, Kilburn usually said rather irritably that he couldn't remember.[28] In an interview, he commented vaguely, 'Between early 1945 and early 1947, in that period, somehow or other I knew what a digital computer was,' adding, 'Where I got this knowledge from I've no idea.'[29] But it is not a mystery where Kilburn got his knowledge from—Turing taught him!

Meanwhile, Williams got himself a new job at the University of Manchester, where Newman had spent the last eighteen months digging himself in as the new Fielden Professor of Mathematics. Newman had progressed as far as establishing a Computing Machine Laboratory at the university, funded by the Royal Society of London, and he was on the lookout for the right engineer to bring into the project.[30] What he needed, as he had explained in his funding application to the Royal Society, was a 'circuit-designing engineer' who, although 'he would not be expected to provide the main ideas', would 'need a rare combination of wide practical experience in circuit design, with a thorough understanding of the abstract ideas involved'.[31] As his language indicates, Newman was in no doubt that, so far as designing computers was concerned, it was the mathematicians and not the engineers who were in charge. However, his Computing Machine Laboratory was little more than an empty room. Williams, who poked fun at the room's 'fine sounding' title, recollected that the 'walls were of brown glazed brick and the door was labelled "Magnetism Room"'.[32] It was, he suggested with blunt good-natured humour, 'lavatorial'. But Newman the dynamo was planning to found a new Newmanry, this time containing a true universal Turing machine in hardware—a stored-program electronic computer that would revolutionize peacetime mathematics and science, just as Colossus had revolutionized warfare.

Williams did his undergraduate work at Manchester and then followed through with some postgraduate research before making the shift to Oxford.[33] Although really a bit too young to enter the crusty upper echelon of the university hierarchy, he decided to chance his arm and apply for Manchester's recently vacated Edward Stocks Massey Chair of Electro-Technics. Newman was on the interview panel and when Williams began explaining the virtues of the new form of computer memory he was perfecting at TRE, the prospect of joining forces must have started to look like a marriage conceived in heaven.[34] Williams, only thirty-five, suddenly acquired 'Professor' in front of his name—the most coveted title in British academia. He left sleepy picture-postcard Malvern for gritty Manchester in December 1946, taking Kilburn with him.[35] The Manchester weather was terrible, but the pubs sold Boddingtons bitter beer, and in any case the North of England was God's own country.

Newman spent the autumn and winter of 1946 in Princeton[36] hobnobbing with John von Neumann, and by the time he returned to Manchester he had decided to adopt von Neumann's design principles for his own computer. At the start of 1947, when Harry Huskey dropped in to visit the Newman–Williams project (as he called it) he learned that the Manchester plan was 'to more or less copy the von Neumann scheme'.[37] Newman had originally had in mind copying the NPL design, and assumed that Flowers and his team in London would be involved in building his computer,[38] but he gradually went off this scheme. When he and Jack Good travelled down together to the NPL to learn about Turing's plans for the ACE, he grew so irritated by Turing's inability to make himself clear that he excused himself and returned to Manchester, leaving Good to hold the fort.[39] Good explained later to Michie that 'Turing plunged into some arbitrary point in the thicket, and insisted on defining and describing every leaf and branch at that particular spot, fanning out from there.'[40] The ACE was not for Newman. He found von Neumann's design principles simple and straightforward by contrast. When he discovered that Williams's bright young assistant was full of ideas for an ACE-like computer, he may not have been too impressed.

Not long after Williams and Kilburn arrived in Manchester, Newman himself gave them a few lectures on how to design a computer.[41] Naturally his lectures laid emphasis on the von Neumann centralized design.[42] 'Newman explained the whole business of how a computer works to us,' Williams recollected.[43] At this point, Williams left it to Kilburn to fathom out the details of what they going to build—apart from being preoccupied with perfecting the new memory, Williams now had his Department of Electro-Technics to run.[44] Kilburn gladly put his ideas for an ACE-like design behind him and now consulted Good, asking him to suggest the basic instruction set for the computer.[45] The basic instruction set is the logical heart of any computer; it details the computer's 'atomic' operations, the elementary building blocks for all its activity. Good suggested a set of twelve basic instructions. It seems he did not mention to Kilburn that he distilled these from a design paper by von Neumann and his collaborators (titled 'Preliminary Discussion of the Logical Design of an Electronic Computing Instrument').[46] Kilburn simplified the twelve instructions that Good gave him[47]—dropping a number that seemed to him unnecessary—and then he and Williams built the centralized computer that Good's instruction set described.[48]

By the start of summer 1948, the machinery was wired together and ready to try out. Painstakingly, Kilburn and Williams entered the first program by hand, literally bit by bit, using a panel of switches to plant each bit in memory. Every time they made a mistake they had to wipe the memory and start again right from the beginning.[49] The program's function was to find the highest factor of a given number, a task that many people can carry out rather easily on the back of an envelope. Eventually the program, only seventeen instructions long, was stored successfully on the screen of a single Williams tube. Gingerly, the two pioneers pressed the start switch. 'Immediately the spots on the display tube entered a mad dance,' Williams related.[50] This turned out to be a 'dance of death', he said, a hiding to nowhere that was repeated again and again during the following week. 'But one day,' he recounted, 'there, shining brightly in the expected place, was the expected answer.'

Figure 27. The Baby gets bigger

Credit: © Science Museum/Science & Society Picture Library – All rights reserved

It was Monday 21 June 1948, the first day of the modern computer age—never before had electronic hardware run a stored program. Manchester had won the race. Williams said drily, 'We doubled our effort immediately by taking on a second technician.'[51] The next year, when delivering an invited lecture at IBM's headquarters in the United States, he was asked how come he had succeeded with only a small team. The giant corporation's motto, 'Think', was emblazoned everywhere in the building. Williams answered impertinently, 'It's very simple—we pressed on regardless without stopping to think too much.'[52] At NPL, they took defeat in their stride: the news that a tiny machine in Manchester had run a program, just seventeen instructions long, for a mathematically trivial task was, Mike Woodger told me, 'greeted with hilarity' by Turing's group.[53] Nevertheless, the Baby soon led to the first purchasable computer, built to Kilburn's and Williams's design by the

Figure 28. The Ferranti computer

Credit: With kind permission of the University Librarian and Director, The University of Manchester Library/
The Centre for Heritage Imaging and Collection Care (CHICC)

Manchester engineering firm Ferranti. The first was delivered in February 1951, a few weeks before the earliest American-built commercial machine became available, the Eckert-Mauchly UNIVAC I.[54] Only five years later, Kilburn began designing his Atlas, an early supercomputer.[55]

The Manchester Baby owed everything to Turing's 1936 idea of storing programs in memory, and also stood on the shoulders of Flowers's Colossus. In fact, the Baby even contained components salvaged from the Newmanry. Newman had shipped a dismantled Colossus to Manchester—after every indication of its original purpose had been eradicated[56]—and one of the bedsteads, the giant iron frame that supported part of the machinery, was used in the Baby.[57] 'It reminds me of Adam's rib,' Good said—a wonderfully apt simile.[58] Williams and Kilburn themselves knew nothing of Bletchley Park and its secret computers, but for those who did know, the new Baby computer was simply the next stage of what Flowers had set in motion at Bletchley.

Actually Williams and Kilburn had quite a restricted view of the origins of the machine they had built. Not only was Colossus invisible, but they had probably never even looked at Turing's 1936 paper. There was also the connection, invisible to them, with von Neumann and his group at Princeton. The Baby is regarded as a British triumph, a world first for British computing. Yet one of computing's greatest ironies is that, thanks to Good and his Princeton instruction set, the logical design of the Baby was virtually identical to a 1946 American design, thought up but not built by von Neumann and his group in the United States[59]—seemingly without Kilburn or Williams ever realizing that this was so. However, the Baby's memory at least was British (despite Eckert's complaints) and Williams tubes soon powered the first stored-program computers to spark into life in the United States. These included a large computer eventually built by von Neumann's group at Princeton and which used a bank of forty Williams tubes as its main memory.[60]

As the previous chapter related, when Newman offered Turing a job at Manchester in 1948, he unceremoniously dumped the NPL. Darwin was furious, but ineffectual. Turing's new position was Deputy Director of the Manchester Computing Machine Laboratory. There was no director—effectively he would run the lab, and Newman intended him to orchestrate the computer's application to serious mathematics.[61] Turing used Bletchley technology to get the computer working properly. The Baby had no input mechanism apart from the switches that Kilburn and Williams had used to enter the first program.[62] These switches inserted bits into memory one at a time—not much use for real computing. Nor did the Baby have any output facilities. All the user could do was to try to read the patterns of dots as they appeared on the screen.[63] Turing designed an input–output system based on the same teleprinter tape that ran through Colossus.[64] He also designed a programming system for the computer and wrote the world's first programming manual.[65] Thanks to Turing, the computer became ready for work. His tape reader, which converted the patterns of holes punched across the tape into electrical pulses and fed these pulses to the computer, incorporated a row of light-sensitive cells. The cells read the holes in the moving tape—exactly the same technology that Colossus used. But even cranked to their fastest operating speed, the Manchester computer's electronic circuits were able to suck in input at no more than 4 per cent of the normal input rate of Flowers's first Colossus.[66] If only Flowers and Turing had stuck together, they might have built a computer that was in a different league.

Sadly, Turing and also Newman have been pretty much written out of the official Manchester version of Manchester computer history. At the Baby computer's 'Golden Anniversary' festival, held fifty years after the first program ran—a vast civic event lasting several days, with Kilburn as guest of honour—neither Newman nor Turing received so much as a mention. Although in his first papers on the Manchester computer, Kilburn gave credit to both Turing and Newman, in later years he was at pains to assert the independence of his and Williams's work from outside influence. He presented the history of the Baby in a way that assigned no role to Turing or to Newman. Kilburn emphasized to me[67] that Newman 'contributed nothing to the first machine' (the Baby). He continued: 'What I'm saying is that the origin is not Newman in any way whatsoever. I know it has been described by others as such—but it wasn't.' Williams, on the other hand, was candid: in the days when he and Kilburn knew nothing about computers, Turing and Newman 'took us by the hand', he said.[68] Kilburn assured me that Turing's only contribution came *after* the Baby was working, and consisted chiefly of preparing what he described as a 'completely useless' programming manual.

'Kilburn couldn't make head nor tail of Turing,' Michie said with a grin.[69] On a personal level the two barely got on at all. Turing's words, 'The mechanic who has constructed the machine', perhaps give a glimpse of his attitude toward Kilburn.[70] Unfortunately Turing's position as de facto head of the Computing Machine Lab brought the two into constant contact, and Turing had no idea how to handle a man like Tom Kilburn. 'Kilburn was making Turing's life hell,' Michie told me. Kilburn didn't want Turing interfering with what he regarded as his computer, and he even attempted to restrict Turing's access to the machine. Eventually it was agreed that Turing would have sole use of the computer for two nights a week. Spending the whole night sitting alone at the control panel suited him well enough, and during these nocturnal sessions Turing pioneered the field now called Artificial Life.

His relationship with Kilburn aside, things at the university could have been worse. In 1951 he was elected a Fellow of the Royal Society of London, following in the footsteps of such great scientists and mathematicians as Newton, Einstein, Gauss, Bessel, Boole, and Hardy. 'I sincerely trust that all your valves are glowing with satisfaction,' a Manchester colleague congratulated him.[71] Then, in 1953, the university gave him a specially created readership in the theory of computing. It was an accolade.

At Manchester, Turing decided to give up his home-is-wherever-you-hang-your-hat lifestyle and bought a house of his own, picking a plain but large Victorian red-brick semi. It went by the rather twee name of Hollymeade. Located in Wilmslow, an affluent and deeply respectable suburb some ten miles distant from central Manchester and the computer, Hollymeade was a curiously conventional choice. Its appeal may have lain in the opportunity for a daily twenty-mile run to the university and back, as well as forays into the nearby Peak District National Park—hill country attracted Turing. The inconvenience of arriving at the university in sweat-soaked running gear was nothing to him compared with the satisfaction of getting there under his own steam. If working all night on the computer, he often travelled by bicycle, easily tolerating the drenching rain for which Manchester is famous.[72] Eventually he succumbed to the dubious luxury of attaching a small motor to one of his bike's wheels.[73]

Turing kept his house sparsely furnished, and even then much of the furniture was shabby.[74] Mike Woodger remembered visiting. He and Turing spent the evening sitting in a large spartan room trying to make conversation.[75] Smalltalk was never much to Turing's liking and he could be heavy going, although if in the right mood he was a lively and amiable conversationalist.[76] Hollymeade was a bit too big for one person, and with its conventional appearance it made an odd match for his bohemian-spartan-intellectual way of life. But his surroundings may not have mattered terribly much to him. 'I think I shall be very happy here,' he wrote to his mother. He gardened, cooked, made friends with his neighbours, enjoyed having people to stay.[77] With guests in the house he was fussy about the temperature of the wine, and put careful thought into the menu. A Mrs Clayton came in to clean and sometimes cook for him, serving mutton chops and other good plain British fare. It was the house he would die in—Mrs Clayton discovered his body—but that was a while in the future yet.[78]

Turing's visits to the Newman household, in the village-like suburb of Bowdon, exposed him to a more comfortable way of life. Lyn, Newman's wife, was a good friend. 'He always appreciated finding himself warm and well-fed,' she remembered.[79] 'But he was at least half a Spartan,' she joked, 'and did not believe in expending much trouble and expense on physical comforts.' Lyn took his education in hand, gently pressing reading upon him. She failed to inspire any interest in poetry, and found him, she said, 'not particularly sensitive to literature or any of the arts', although she did score a hit with Tolstoy's *War and Peace*. As a boy, Turing maintained that there was *one* line he liked in Shakespeare's *Hamlet*. It was the last one: 'Exeunt, bearing off the dead bodies'.

Lyn obviously admired Turing's appearance: his 'chin like a ship's prow', and what she described as his 'oddly-contoured head, handsome and even imposing'. Her few words capture his physical presence particularly vividly. 'He never looked right in his clothes,' she said. 'An Alchemist's robe, or chain mail would have suited him.' Warming to her theme, she continued: 'The chain mail would have gone with his eyes too, blue to the brightness and richness of stained glass.' It was easy, though, to miss the colour and intensity of his eyes, since he had a tendency to avoid direct gaze. Lyn described his 'strange way of not meeting the eye, of sidling out of the door with a brusque and off-hand word of thanks'. But when eye contact finally came, she said, you saw 'candour and comprehension...something so civilised that one hardly dared to breathe'. Once Turing had looked 'directly and earnestly at his companion, in the confidence of friendly talk, his eyes could never again be missed'.

Although Lyn knew him better than most, her assessment that he was 'totally uninterested' in poetry was not completely accurate. Turing composed a number of short, almost haiku-like, verses.[80] He sent these to Robin Gandy, calling them 'messages from the unseen world'. One said simply 'The Universe is the interior of the Light Cone of the Creation.' Turing signed this 'Arthur Stanley', a playful reference to Arthur Stanley Eddington, the famous physicist who had worked with Einstein and written on the relationship between science and religion. Another message ran:

> Hyperboloids of wondrous Light
> Rolling for aye through Space and Time
> Harbour those Waves which somehow Might
> Play out God's holy pantomime.

There was a short story too. Written in Turing's scratchy and sometimes impenetrable handwriting, and full of inky crossings out and rewordings, this makes fascinating reading.[81] Although only a few pages long, it offers an intimate glimpse of its author. The central character, a scientist by the name of Alec Pryce who works at Manchester University, is a thinly disguised Turing. Pryce, like Turing himself, always wore 'an old sports coat and rather unpressed worsted trousers'. Turing called this Pryce's 'undergraduate uniform', saying it 'encouraged him to believe he was still an attractive youth'. At just the wrong side of forty, Turing must have been feeling his age. Pryce, whose work related to interplanetary travel, had made an important discovery in his twenties which came to be called 'Pryce's buoy'. The nature of the discovery is left unexplained and Pryce's buoy is obviously a proxy for the universal Turing machine. 'Alec always felt a glow of pride when this phrase was used,' Turing wrote revealingly.

'The rather obvious double-entendre rather pleased him too,' he continued. 'He always liked to parade his homosexuality, and in suitable company Alec would pretend that the word was spelt without the "u".' Pryce, we are told, has not had a sexual relationship since 'that soldier in Paris last summer'. Walking through Manchester, he passes a youth lounging on a bench, Ron Miller. Ron, who is out of work and keeps company with petty criminals, makes a small income from male prostitution.

He responds to a glance Alec gives him as he passes, calling out uncouthly, 'Got a fag?' Shyly, Alec joins him on the bench and the two sit together awkwardly. Eventually Alec plucks up courage to invite the boy to have lunch at a nearby restaurant. Beggars can't be choosers, Ron thinks meanly. He isn't impressed by Alec's brusque approach and 'lah-di-dah' way of speaking, but says to himself philosophically, 'Bed's bed whatever way you get into it.'

Lyn was Turing's confidante. She worried about him, calling him a 'guileless homo'.[82] Even his psychotherapy sessions were fair game for discussion between them.[83] Sometimes he would run the twelve miles from his house to hers. He didn't always arrive at the most sociable of hours; the Newmans' son, William, remembers hearing a noise in the early hours of the morning and opening the front door to find Turing in running gear. 'He wanted to invite us to dinner and, thinking us all asleep but having nothing on which to write, was posting through our letter box an invitation scratched on a rhododendron leaf with a stick,' William recalled with an amused expression.[84] He also remembers Turing holidaying with the family in a rented house on the Welsh Riviera.[85] The philosopher Bertrand Russell and other intellectual heavyweights would drop by and sit in the homely seaside living room, engaging in freewheeling debate with Turing and Newman.

Turing and the young William became good friends. They played Monopoly and chess, and Turing earned high marks for his choice of birthday presents—one year a model steam engine, a toolkit another.[86] Alec Price admitted to usually choosing presents that he liked himself. Turing was good with children. He befriended his neighbours' little boy, Rob, and once when they were sitting together on the garage roof they were overheard debating whether God would catch a cold if He sat on damp grass.[87] When a friend's seven-year-old broke her right arm, Turing gave her a biscuit tin crammed with chocolate and sweets, explaining to her that it was a 'left-handed tin' she could open with her good arm.[88]

While Lyn and Turing sat talking, Max would often go upstairs and play his piano, filling the house with music.[89] Every day that he lived in Manchester he sat down at his Bechstein grand and delivered a concert to whoever might be listening. Bach, Beethoven, Brahms, Debussy—his technique was formidable. At Princeton he played sonatas with Einstein, who was an avid violinist. Lyn wrote to her parents about these musical soirees, saying that Einstein was 'so naively pleased with the music which he & Max made'.[90] Turing was not much of a musician himself, yet ultimately he made a far greater mark on music than did either Einstein or Newman. One of his contributions to the digital age that has largely been overlooked is his pioneering work on transforming the computer into a musical instrument.

Turing was the first to write a computer program for playing musical notes. It's no news to users of NoteWorthy or MasterWorks that computers can play music; but if the computer is thought of as simply a high-speed calculating machine—the default view in those early days—then it takes an almost impossible leap of imagination to regard computers as musical instruments. Yet if you think of the computer as a universal machine, it is perfectly natural to regard its potential behaviour as including playing music. The only question is how to create a computer program that will make the universal machine behave as a musical instrument.

Figure 29. Max Newman

Credit: With kind permission of the Master and Fellows of St John's College, Cambridge

The engineers had wired a loudspeaker into the Manchester computer—the 'hooter', they called it—and this served as an alarm when the machine needed attention.[91] It produced a loud, raw beep of electronic sound. Turing realized that, with some clever programming, this unpromisingly simple source of sound could be made to emit the notes of the musical scale. The computer's 'hoot instruction' (which he named /V, pronounced 'slash vee') worked like this. There was an electronic clock in the computer that synchronized all the operations. This clock beat steadily, like a silent metronome, at a rate of over 4,000 noiseless ticks per second. Executing the hoot instruction a single time made one of these ticks come alive with sound (emitted at the loudspeaker), but the sound lasted only for as long as the tick, a tiny fraction of a second. Turing described the sound as 'something between a tap, a click, and a thump'.[92] Executing the hoot instruction over and over again resulted in this brief sound being produced repeatedly, on every fourth tick: tick tick tick click, tick tick tick click, and so on.[93] When repeated thousands of times a second, these regular clicks delude the human ear into hearing a steady note. Turing figured out that if the hoot instruction is repeated not simply over and over again, but in different patterns, then the ear hears different musical notes. For example, if the pattern tick tick tick click, tick tick tick tick, tick tick tick click, tick tick tick tick is repeated, the note of C_5 is heard (an octave above middle C). Repeating the different pattern tick tick tick click, tick tick tick click, tick tick tick tick, tick tick tick click, tick tick tick click, tick tick tick tick produces the note of F_4, a fifth lower than C_5—and so on.[94] It was a wonderful discovery.

One of the music world's well entrenched urban myths is that the first-ever computer-generated musical notes were heard in 1957, at Bell Labs in America.[95] In fact, computer-generated notes were first heard in the Manchester Computing Machine Laboratory, and Turing's programming manual—written around the end of 1950—contained the first tutorial on how to make a computer make music. Turing himself seems not to have been particularly interested in programming the machine to play conventional pieces of music. He used the different musical notes that he created as indicators of the computer's inner life—one note for 'job finished', others for 'error when transferring data from the magnetic drum', 'digits overflowing in memory', and so on.[96] Running one of Turing's programs must have been a noisy business, with different musical notes and rhythms enabling the user to 'listen in' (as Turing put it) to what the program was doing.[97] He left it to someone else, though, to program the first complete piece of music.

One day Christopher Strachey turned up at the Computing Machine Laboratory. He had known Turing at King's before the war.[98] A solidly upper-middle-class figure, with a curious voice that swung from high-pitched to low and back again as he spoke,[99] Strachey had some gold-standard relatives: his uncle was the famous author Lytton Strachey, and his father, Oliver, who was one of Dilly Knox's cronies, had worked on Enigma at Bletchley Park. Growing up in London's Bloomsbury, Strachey inhabited the world of the famous Bloomsbury group—a loose-knit clan of writers and intellectuals such as Virginia Woolf, E. M. Forster and John Maynard Keynes, as well as Uncle Lytton. Strachey's war, like Williams's and Kilburn's, was spent in radar development, but by the time he strode into the Manchester Computing Machine Laboratory he was a mathematics and physics master at Harrow School—one of Britain's spiffiest, founded in 1572 by charter of Queen Elizabeth I. Strachey never completely lost his schoolmasterly manner, and once he had left schoolteaching behind and entered the wonderful new world of computer science, his lord-of-the-classroom demeanour sometimes grated on the nerves of his high-powered colleagues.[100]

Strachey felt drawn to digital computers as soon as he heard about them. His first hands-on experience was with the ACE: Mike Woodger knew a budding programmer when he saw one, and got him access to the computer. When Woodger mentioned the new machine at Manchester, Strachey was keen as mustard to try his hand at programming it. Taking the bull by the horns, he wrote to Turing.[101] Both were King's College homosexuals coping in a largely straight world, and they had a lot in common. This turned out to include a life-dominating passion for programming. Although the term 'hacker', meaning a programming addict, was not coined until later, Turing was undoubtedly the first hacker, with

Strachey hard on his heels. Hackers, Steven Levy wrote in his 1984 classic of the same name, are 'computer programmers and designers who regard computing as the most important thing in the world'.[102] Nowadays the term is generally used for programmers who break into other people's computer systems, but real hackers know the true meaning of the word. When Strachey showed up in Manchester, Turing decided to drop him in at the deep end, and suggested he try writing a program to make the computer simulate itself. At that time this was a devilishly difficult task—a bit like running the four-minute mile, as Roger Bannister would soon do for the first time in recorded history. When Strachey left the laboratory, Turing turned to Robin Gandy and said impishly, 'That will keep *him* busy!'[103]

It did keep him busy. Strachey read Turing's programming manual assiduously. This was 'famed in those days for its incomprehensibility', Strachey said.[104] An ardent pianist, he appreciated the potential of Turing's terse directions on how to program musical notes. Eventually he returned to Manchester with twenty or so pages covered in lines of programming code; previously the longest program to run on the computer had amounted to no more than about half a page of code.[105] 'Turing came in and gave me a typical high-speed, high-pitched description of how to use the machine,' Strachey recollected.[106] Then he was left alone at the computer's console until the following morning. It was the first of a lifetime of all-night programming sessions. 'I sat in front of this enormous machine,' he said, 'with four or five rows of twenty switches and things, in a room that felt like the control room of a battle-ship.'[107] Turing came back in the morning to find Strachey's simulator program running like a top—and then, without warning, the computer raucously hooted out the British National Anthem, 'God save the King'. Turing was his customary monosyllabic self. 'Good show,' he said in an enthusiastic way.[108]

Strachey had started a craze and more programs were soon written. The BBC heard about the musical computer and a *Children's Hour* radio presenter known as Auntie was despatched with a recording team to cover the story.[109] Besides 'God save the King', the BBC recorded a version of Glen Miller's swinging 'In the Mood'. The American superstar's hair might have curled up with horror if he had been able to hear the computer's reedy and wooden performance of his famous hit. But there was also an endearing, if rather brash, rendition of the nursery-rhyme tune 'Baa Baa Black Sheep'. The simplicity of the music and the goofy electronic tone worked well together. The computer was full of glitches, though—it had only recently been delivered from the Ferranti factory—and it managed to crash in the middle of its Glen Miller party piece. 'The machine's obviously not in the mood,' Auntie gushed.

The unedited BBC recording of the session conveys a sense of people interacting with something entirely new. 'The machine *resented* that,' Auntie observed at one point. The idea of a thinking machine, an electronic brain, was in the air at Manchester. Turing merrily fanned the flames. Not long after joining the Computing Machine Laboratory, he told a reporter from *The Times* that he saw no reason why the computer should not 'enter any one of the fields normally covered by the human intellect, and eventually compete on equal terms'.[110] The diplomatic Newman fielded the barrage of telephone calls triggered by Turing's provocative statement, which *The Times* had printed in a centre-page article titled 'The Mechanical Brain'. As usual, Turing was ahead of the pack in his thinking. The rest of the world was just starting to wake up to the idea that computers were the new way to do high-speed arithmetic, while Turing was talking very seriously about 'programming a computer to behave like a brain'.[111]

Strachey added further to the computer's mystique by creating a program that wrote love letters. The steamy notes were signed 'Manchester University Computer' (M. U. C.). He used programming tricks that he described as 'almost childishly simple' (and to him they probably were).[112] He made up a couple of recipes for building sentences and stored these in the computer's memory, together with lists of words and expressions that he culled from Roget's *Thesaurus*. The program would follow one or another recipe step by step, including steps like 'Here choose a word from list so-and-so'. The program made its selections using a random-number generator that Turing had designed, a kind of electronic roulette wheel.[113] It was a bit like deciding whether to say 'I think I love you' or 'You can kiss me if you like' by tossing a coin. Turing even toyed with the idea that his randomizer was a way of giving a machine something like free will.[114] He joked that unpredictable results could lead the computer's owner to say proudly, 'My machine'—instead of 'My little boy'—'said such a funny thing this morning.'[115]

The computer's letters were eerily alien:

DARLING SWEETHEART
YOU ARE MY AVID FELLOW FEELING. MY AFFECTION CURIOUSLY CLINGS TO YOUR PASSIONATE WISH. MY LIKING YEARNS FOR YOUR HEART. YOU ARE MY WISTFUL SYMPATHY: MY TENDER LIKING.
YOURS BEAUTIFULLY
M. U. C.

HONEY DEAR
MY SYMPATHETIC AFFECTION BEAUTIFULLY ATTRACTS YOUR AFFEC-TIONATE ENTHUSIASM. YOU ARE MY LOVING ADORATION: MY BREATHLESS ADORATION. MY FELLOW FEELING BREATHLESSLY HOPES FOR YOUR DEAR EAGERNESS. MY LOVESICK ADORATION CHERISHES YOUR AVID ARDOUR.
YOURS WISTFULLY
M. U. C.[116]

Rather more practically, Turing typed his own letters at the computer keyboard, making use of the slash symbol to produce punctuation and crude formatting. He printed these out and dropped them into the post. One was to Robin Gandy concerning his PhD viva.[117] It began:

DEAR/ROBIN//////////////SORRY////IT/REALLY/ISNT/POSSIBLE/TO/MAKE/ YOUR/ORAL/ANY/EARLIER////

Trust Turing to be the first person on earth to deal with his correspond-ence by word processor.

Strachey's next tour de force was to create the world's first computer game. As a young child, he used to lie in his mother's bed in the mornings playing imaginary three-dimensional noughts and crosses.[118] He decided, though, that noughts and crosses is too easy a game to be worth pro-gramming. (It was later done on a DEUCE; see Fig. 30.) Strachey picked something mathematically harder, but not too hard—the game of draughts (called checkers in the United States).[119] He wrote the first version of his draughts program for the Pilot Model ACE in the spring of 1951, but it was at Manchester that the program played its first game.[120] Resourcefully, Strachey hijacked the Manchester computer's monitor screen, normally used for showing the engineers how things were ticking over in the inner workings, and set it up to display a virtual draughtsboard. The diagrams in Fig. 31 on page 172 are from Strachey's notes.[121]

The computer greeted its human opponent by printing:

PLEASE READ THE INSTRUCTION CARD.

Once the human has digested the instructions he or she presses the start key and the session begins. The computer asks politely

SHALL WE TOSS FOR THE FIRST MOVE? WILL YOU SPIN A COIN?

It then calls 'HEADS' or 'TAILS' at random, and demands

HAVE I WON?

Figure 30. The DEUCE playing noughts and crosses

Credit: Photo by Keith Titmus, reproduced with his kind permission

When play starts, the computer makes a 'pip pip' noise each time it's ready to accept its opponent's move. If the human player delays too long before keying in a move, the printer chatters out impatiently:

YOU MUST PLAY AT ONCE OR RESIGN.

Any fumbling by the human produces:

KINDLY READ THE INSTRUCTIONS AND START THE MOVE AGAIN.

Improper behaviour elicits increasingly testy responses, such as:

IF YOU DON'T FOLLOW THE INSTRUCTIONS I CAN'T PLAY WITH YOU.

or simply a snippy:

I REFUSE TO WASTE ANY MORE TIME. GO AND PLAY WITH A HUMAN BEING.

With the machine prone to hardware and software errors, things did not always go smoothly. The computer could gabble out something like:

PLEASE DREAD ZTHE SINSTRUCTION FCARD. SHALL WWE ZTOSS FFOR ZTHE FFIRST XMOVE.

Strachey scribbled a note on the printout: 'The machine (literally) had a screw loose when it did this.'[122]

The program chose its moves by looking ahead a few turns of play, just as human players often do: 'If I move *here*, the human can do this or that, but both those moves would put me in a worse position; whereas if I move *there*, the human's only possible move puts me in a stronger position,' and so on. The program used very simple 'rules of thumb' to evaluate the strength of its position, such as 'Kings are worth three times an ordinary piece.' Strachey's program went about things far more systematically than a normal human player does, and every time the program's turn came, it would ploddingly calculate the consequences of each move available to it at that moment. A strategic human player, on the other hand, may consider only one move—the right one.

The computer wasn't exactly fast by today's standards. It considered moves at a rate of about ten a second, but even so it could give a human player a good workout. Not long after Strachey got the program up and running, Arthur Samuel, a programmer and researcher at IBM in upstate New York, wrote an improved version that could learn to better its play with practice, and this eventually beat a championship-level player.[123] The defeated champion lamented, 'I have not had such competition from any human being since 1954, when I lost my last game.' The champion quickly took his revenge, though, thrashing the program in six games straight.[124]

Strachey's draughts program was not only the point of origin of today's computer games industry, and of the whole idea of human–computer interaction via screen and keyboard. It was also the first concrete glimpse, on a crude black-and-white monitor, of computing's holiest of holy grails, Artificial Intelligence. Strachey's experience with his draughts program convinced him, he said, that a 'great deal of what is usually known as thinking can in fact be reduced to a relatively simple set of rules of the type which can be incorporated into a program'.[125] It was something that Turing had believed for years.

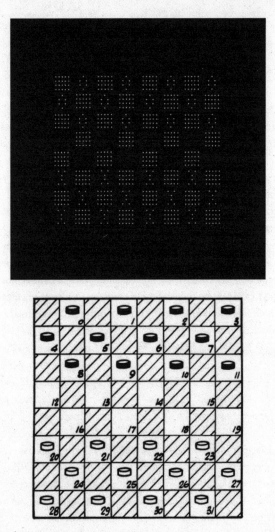

Figure 31. The Manchester computer playing draughts (checkers). This is probably the first time a computer screen was used for gaming. Strachey's hand-drawn diagram explains the symbols on the screen. The computer is Black.

Credit: With kind permission of the Bodleian Library, Oxford

THE IMITATION GAME: ARTIFICIAL INTELLIGENCE, ARTIFICIAL LIFE

It was a wintry grey Massachusetts morning and the temperature was hovering around ten degrees below freezing. I gladly descended into the dingy semi-warmth of MIT's 'Infinite Corridor', to join the crowds of engineering students and computer science geeks winding their way across MIT's vast urban campus. I was heading for the Artificial Intelligence Laboratory. Rod Brooks, the AI Lab's director, greeted me. Brooks is an impossibly energetic Australian with an easy manner. In his office, two prototype robot vacuum cleaners were prowling the floor. These flat disk-like robots seemed to spend more time hiding under the furniture than actually cleaning. They were bristling with the sensor technology that Brooks has evolved during his more than twenty years in robotics. NASA funded the research that made him famous—tiny six-legged insect-like rovers, just a few inches long and packed with AI systems.

'Fast, Cheap and Out of Control' was the title Brooks chose for the academic paper presenting his research on insect-based robots to the British Interplanetary Society.[1] The paper predicts a robot invasion of the solar system, a wave of autonomous artificial insects that prepares the way for human space exploration. Brooks's early prototype rover, named Genghis, scurried gracefully over obstacles as though it were a large ant. Six independent legs would be superior to wheels or tracks in the rugged terrain of alien planets, Brooks reckoned—Mother Nature usually knows best. When he took over the AI Lab, the standard joke was that AI now meant 'Artificial Insects'. But in fact Brooks's next project was to create a humanoid robot. 'Let's take the tour,' he says amiably.

Standing placidly in the room next to Brooks's office is a tall, kind of human-looking robot—although standing is not exactly the right word, since the robot has no legs and its upper body is bolted to a plinth. It cranes its head around and bends forward a little to peer through its four tube-like eyes. Its vision software can recognize a face and the robot makes eye contact. It nods back if you nod to it. 'This is Cog,' Brooks introduces us. Cog looks like a cross between something out of *Star Wars*

Figure 32. I, Cog

Credit: Photo © Sam Ogden

and Rodin's famous statue 'The Thinker'. Its hands are covered with electrically conducting rubber membrane. The membranes supply the robot with tactile information, and strain sensors in its arms and spine give it detailed feedback about its posture and movement.

Cog has learned many simple skills through imitation and repetition, including handing objects to a human and playing deftly with a slinky toy. Handing is more difficult than it sounds. Imagine the robot missing its mark and whacking your fragile fingers with its powerful metallic ten-pound arm. Brooks and his students have even taught Cog to play simple drum rhythms. The robot bashes away enthusiastically at a drum and cymbal. 'Wait just a minute,' Brooks says suddenly. He slips out of the room, returning with Cog's spare head in his hands. 'Put it under your arm,' he says jovially. 'I'll take a photo.'

As we move along the corridor, Brooks waves a hand towards a lab occupied by graduate students. They're trying to put microscopic control circuits into bacteria, he explains. Software-controlled bacteria may one day be used to fight disease. Another idea he's working on involves a swarm of tiny gnat-like robots that will dwell in the corners of your windows, or at the edges of your computer screen or TV screen, keeping the surface squeaky clean. We turn into the small lab occupied by Brooks's star student Cynthia Breazeal and her very sociable robot Kismet. Kismet is as instantly loveable as Cog is remote. It gurgles and chirrups in an engaging baby-talk kind of way, waggling its ears and making eye contact. If I didn't know Kismet was a machine, I would swear it was smiling at me.

Kismet is an experiment in human–machine interaction, and Breazeal finds that people easily mistake her robot for a sentient being. She explains in an amused way how a visitor began to examine Kismet as though it were some ordinary piece of machinery and rudely pushed his face right up close to the robot's. When Kismet expressed annoyance—vocally and facially—the visitor shot back in surprise and apologized to the robot. Breazeal has a video of a young adult male, Rich, making friends with Kismet. 'You are amazing!' Rich exclaims to Kismet after a while. 'You're amazing,' the robot echoes back in its winsome voice. It bobs up and down, blue eyes wide, interrupting Rich's sentences with excited sounding noises.

'Stop, you got to let me talk,' Rich scolds the robot. Kismet looks crest-fallen. 'Listen to me,' Rich says, and Kismet fixes him with an attentive gaze. 'Kismet, I think we got something going on here,' Rich says wonder-ingly, and only half in jest. It's easy to picture distant successors of Kismet—or maybe not so distant—babyminding, helping out in kindergarten, or providing some company for lonely seniors.

'I'll take you up to the attic,' Brooks offers enthusiastically. As we go up in the lift, we talk about the nature of intelligence. Some dismiss 'intelli-gent' behaviour in computers and robots as nothing more than a clever illusion. But in Brooks's view, the less and less often the illusion shatters, the closer we are to the real thing.[2] 'Intelligence is in the eye of the observer,' he asserts briskly, with the air of someone who has been fighting over this particular stretch of terrain for a long time.[3] Turing's view was similar: 'The extent to which we regard something as behaving in an intelligent manner,' he said, 'is determined as much by our own state of mind and training as by the properties of the object under consideration.'[4] British AI chieftain Donald Michie, on the other hand, believed that intelligence is a rather more objective thing. Human-level intelligence is marked by the 'ability to make a plausible shot at almost anything', he said.[5] If a machine can be built with that same ability, then it's intelligent, period.

The AI Lab's attic turns out to be a gigantic storage area. Who knows what abandoned experiments are stashed away up there? Brooks navi-gates to a cage occupied by a robot named Herbert. 'He was one of my favourites,' he says. This Hobbit-sized creature takes its name from Herb-ert Simon, an AI pioneer who led the field in the years after Turing first got things rolling. Simon, a Nobel laureate, caused a lot of excitement when he announced that 'there are now in the world machines that think, that learn, and that create'.[6] That was in 1958 and many would say Simon's announcement was highly premature, but looking now at Brooks's robots it seems possible to glimpse how those words might one day come true.

Herbert's lone hand sports an array of pressure-sensitive sensors. The laser-based vision system collects three-dimensional data over a distance of about twelve feet in front of the moving robot, and another thirty infrared sensors help Herbert stay clear of close-by objects—walls, water coolers, human beings. In its day, the robot trundled around the busy offices and workspaces of the AI Lab, weaving through desks, people, and computer equipment. Herbert is quite different from the robots that staff our factories and build our cars. Today's industrial robots are fast, accurate and tireless when performing a preprogrammed sequence of exact operations. But they would be complete duds at moving through cluttered and unpredictable environments, such as a cafeteria or busy office—headlines would scream 'Moronic Robots Injure Hundreds'.

Humans are so adept at walking through spaces full of people in motion, and general clutter, because we have hundreds of thousands of years of evolution behind us. It's widely accepted that getting a robot to behave reliably and safely in open-ended and unscripted real-world situations is one of robotics' hardest problems. Herbert's humble job was to search the crowded lab for soda cans, and carry away the empties to the trash. 'We never did fix the chips in securely,' says Brooks, smiling in a proud father-inventor kind of way. The technicians were always pulling the computer chips out to make improvements, and after about ten minutes of operation, Herbert's purposeful behaviour would suddenly break off, as vibration shook a chip loose. But one day Herbert's successors will clean our homes and maybe even prepare simple meals. With an eye on the future healthcare market, the Japanese company Honda has sunk untold millions into developing its two-legged walking robot ASIMO. ASIMO appeared on British TV in 2011, carrying a tray of drinks to comedian Stephen Fry—although Fry did not explain to his marvelling viewers that many of ASIMO's actions were very precisely preprogrammed by its human controllers.

Brooks's robots are faltering first steps towards what Turing called a 'child machine', a machine endowed by its makers with the inbuilt systems it needs in order to learn as a human child would. 'Presumably the child-brain is something like a note-book as one buys it from the stationers,' Turing said.[7] 'Rather little mechanism, and lots of blank sheets.' 'Our hope,' he explained, 'is that there is so little mechanism in the child-brain that something like it can be easily programmed.' Turing expected that once the child machine has been 'subjected to an appropriate course of education one would obtain the adult brain', and that eventually a stage will be reached when the machine will be like the pupil who 'learnt much from his master, but had added much more by his own work'. 'When this happens I feel that one is obliged to regard the machine as showing intelligence,' Turing said.[8] Brooks has devoted a large slice of his professional life to making Turing's child-machine concept a reality, following almost to the letter Turing's advice to 'provide the machine with the best sense organs that money can buy' and then to teach the machine in a way that resembles the 'normal teaching of a child'.[9]

'Turing argued that it must be possible to build a thinking machine,' Brooks explains, 'since it was possible to build imitations of "any small part of a man"'.[10] As early as 1948, Turing proposed using 'television cameras, microphones, loudspeakers, wheels and "handling servo-mechanisms"' to build a robot.[11] The robot would, Turing said, need to 'roam the countryside' in order to learn things for itself—joking that, even so, 'the creature would still have no contact with food, sex, sport and many other things of interest to the human being'.[12] He worried, tongue in cheek, that the child machine could not be sent to school 'without the other children making excessive fun of it'.[13] Turing's colleagues at the National Physical Laboratory mocked his far-sighted ideas. 'Turing is going to infest the countryside,' they laughed, 'with a robot which will live on twigs and scrap iron.'[14]

The field of AI first started to build up a head of steam in the early to mid 1960s, as computers became powerful enough to run reasonably large programs. At this time Joe Weizenbaum, an MIT hacker, wrote one of AI's most famous programs, Eliza (named after Eliza Doolittle, from George Bernard Shaw's *Pygmalion*).[15] Eliza was a psychotherapy program, designed to deliver therapeutic interviews to human beings (it was the 1960s, after all). An article in the *Journal of Nervous and Mental Disease* stated that once the program was ready for clinical use, it would 'provide a therapeutic tool which can be made widely available to mental hospitals and psychiatric centers suffering a shortage of therapists'.[16] Here is the transcript of an actual conversation between Eliza and a teenage girl.[17] The teenager speaks first:

Men are all alike.

IN WHAT WAY

They're always bugging us about something or other.

CAN YOU THINK OF A SPECIFIC EXAMPLE

Well, my boyfriend made me come here.

YOUR BOYFRIEND MADE YOU COME HERE

He says I'm depressed much of the time.

I AM SORRY TO HEAR THAT YOU ARE DEPRESSED

It's true. I am unhappy.

DO YOU THINK COMING HERE WILL HELP YOU NOT TO BE UNHAPPY

I need some help, that much seems certain.

WHAT WOULD IT MEAN TO YOU IF YOU GOT SOME HELP

Perhaps I could learn to get along with my mother.

TELL ME MORE ABOUT YOUR FAMILY

My mother takes care of me.

WHO ELSE IN YOUR FAMILY TAKES CARE OF YOU

My father.

YOUR FATHER

You are like my father in some ways.

WHAT RESEMBLANCE DO YOU SEE

You are not very aggressive but I think you don't want me to notice that.

WHAT MAKES YOU THINK I AM NOT VERY AGGRESSIVE

You don't argue with me.

WHY DO YOU THINK I DON'T ARGUE WITH YOU

You are afraid of me.

DOES IT PLEASE YOU TO BELIEVE I AM AFRAID OF YOU

My father is afraid of everybody.

WHAT ELSE COMES TO MIND WHEN YOU THINK OF YOUR FATHER

Bullies.

DOES THAT HAVE ANYTHING TO DO WITH THE FACT THAT YOUR BOYFRIEND
MADE YOU COME HERE

Some people quickly formed an emotional bond with Eliza, as would later happen with Kismet. Weizenbaum reported finding it difficult to convince some of Eliza's conversation partners that she was *not* a real person. 'I had not realised,' he said, 'that extremely short exposures to a relatively simple computer program could induce powerful delusional thinking in quite normal people.'[18] Even Weizenbaum's own secretary insisted that other staff leave the room so she and Eliza could talk in private.

Eliza used a number of simple recipes for forming sentences, rather like Strachey's love-letter program. The recipes took what the human had typed as a starting point. For example, if the human says:

Why do you hate me?

the program picks one of the simple recipes that the programmer has associated with the question's '… you … me' pattern, such as:

YOU LIKE TO THINK I … YOU—DON'T YOU

Filling in the gap produces the output:

YOU LIKE TO THINK I HATE YOU—DON'T YOU

The program also contains lists of canned sentences made up by the programmer. Eliza rattles off a response from a list of ready-made statements such as 'You don't seem quite certain' if the word 'maybe' is spotted in the input. Often, though, the program finds no pattern that it can recognize in the input. When this happens, it might turn to its Last Resort List, a stack of ready-made standbys such as: 'What does that suggest to you?' Alternatively, the program might apply some other trick, such as forming a response from one of the human's previous contributions, automatically squirrelled away for use in just such a situation. That is what happened at the end of the dialogue with the teenager. Failing to recognize the teenager's reply, 'Bullies', Eliza struck lucky when she blindly trotted out a response generated from the earlier words 'my boyfriend made me come here' (by changing 'me' into 'you' and using the recipe 'DOES THAT HAVE ANYTHING TO DO WITH THE FACT THAT YOUR…').

When interacting with Eliza, it doesn't take very long to get a feel for the program's weak spots. Then it becomes easy to shatter any illusion that the program is intelligent. Here is a downright vicious exchange I had with Eliza. Eliza speaks first:

HOW DO YOU DO. PLEASE STATE YOUR PROBLEM

I'm wondering whether computers can think.

WHY DO YOU MENTION COMPUTERS

Since you are one I thought I would ask you – can you think?

DID YOU THINK THEY MIGHT NOT BE ONE YOU THOUGHT YOU WOULD ASK I –
CAN I THINK

Let's talk just about you – not me. Can you think?

YOU LIKE TO THINK I – NOT YOU – DON'T YOU

Pardon?

WHAT DOES THAT SUGGEST TO YOU

What does it suggest to you?

TELL ME ABOUT WHAT DOES IT SUGGEST TO I

That's nonsense – which of us do you mean by I?

WHY DO YOU THINK I MEAN BY YOU

The question meant to which of us is the word referring.

SUPPOSE THE QUESTION MEANT TO WHICH OF US WERE NOT THE WORD
REFERRING

I think you are an extremely stupid program.

PERHAPS YOU WOULD LIKE TO BE AN EXTREMELY STUPID PROGRAM

Another famous early AI program was GPS, the General Problem Solver. The GPS project ran for over a decade, with the goal of programming computers to search intelligently for their own solutions to problems. Herbert Simon and his co-researchers, Allen Newell and Cliff Shaw, led the project. Later versions of the GPS program could solve an impressive array of puzzles, including the notorious Missionaries and Cannibals problem, which runs as follows.[19] Three missionaries are travelling through an inhospitable landscape with their three native bearers. The bearers are cannibals, the heathen fiends, but it is the custom of their people never to attack unless the victims are outnumbered. It is uncertain whether this is due to simple cowardice or because of some curious taboo. Each missionary is naggingly aware of what might happen should the party accidentally become divided. Towards the end of the second week of travel the group reaches the bank of a wide, deep-flowing river. Crocodiles are abundant, yet somehow the party must cross. One of the bearers chances upon a cramped two-man dugout upturned in the mud. A terrible grin spreads across his face as he savours the implication of his find. But fortunately one of the missionaries did a computer science class with Professor Newell and she can remember watching GPS solve the very problem confronting them. In less than an hour all six are standing safely on the opposite bank. How is it done? Remember—at most two people in the boat at once, and if ever cannibals outnumber missionaries on either bank, carnage ensues.

GPS solves the problem by trying out bank-to-bank transitions one after another, until a sequence of moves emerges that takes the six to the opposite bank without the cannibals ever outnumbering the missionaries. The program's random choice of opening move might be to take two missionaries across to the right bank. Unspeakable events immediately occur on the left bank. GPS, the greatest trial-and-error tactician there ever was, imperturbably tries again. One missionary and one cannibal from left to right. No teeth tear into flesh, so GPS sticks by this first move and considers the next. It tries moving the boat plus o missionaries plus 1 cannibal from the right bank to the left. Whoops! Scratch that one...And so on. GPS slowly bungles its way to the goal. But if you solved the problem, maybe you set about it in much the same way?

By the beginning of the 1970s some quite remarkable results were being achieved. Terry Winograd, another MIT hacker, programmed a virtual robot called Shrdlu. The name came from *MAD* magazine. Unlike Cog and Kismet, Shrdlu occupied a purely virtual world, a simulated environment consisting of a flat table-like surface strewn with coloured play-blocks of different shapes and sizes. The virtual world and the robot's virtual arm appeared on the computer's screen.

Communication between human beings and the robot was via a keyboard, with the robot's replies appearing across the bottom of the screen. Shrdlu could engage in conversation about its simple world, and could form and execute plans of action. It could even respond to questions about its own motives. In the following transcript, Shrdlu's contributions are shown in upper case.[20]

Pick up a big red block.

OK.

On the screen, the robot arm swings into action. Two red blocks are visible, one small, one large. The large one has a green cube stacked on top of it. The robot first transfers the green cube to the table top, and then picks up the red block.

Find a block which is taller than the one you are holding and put it into the box.

BY 'IT', I ASSUME YOU MEAN THE BLOCK WHICH IS TALLER THAN THE ONE I AM HOLDING.

Shrdlu puts down the red block, picks up a taller blue one, and places it in the box.

What does the box contain?

THE BLUE PYRAMID AND THE BLUE BLOCK.

Can a pyramid be supported by a block?

YES.

Can a pyramid support a pyramid?

I DON'T KNOW.

Stack up two pyramids.

The robot tries and fails.

I CAN'T.

The blue pyramid is mine.

I UNDERSTAND.

I own blocks which are not red, but I don't own anything which supports a pyramid.

I UNDERSTAND.

Do I own the box?

NO.

This is because the box is supporting a pyramid.

Do I own anything in the box?

YES, TWO THINGS: THE BLUE BLOCK AND THE BLUE PYRAMID.

Does the shortest thing the tallest pyramid's support supports support anything green?

Shrdlu took less than 20 seconds to make sense of this; I needed quite a lot longer.

YES, THE GREEN PYRAMID.

Does a steeple

SORRY, I DON'T KNOW THE WORD 'STEEPLE'.

Shrdlu interrupts as soon as it encounters a word that it doesn't know.

A 'steeple' is a stack which contains two green cubes and a pyramid.

I UNDERSTAND.

Are there any steeples now?

NO.

Will you please stack up both of the red blocks and either a green cube or a pyramid.

OK.

Had you touched any pyramid before you put one on the green block?

YES, THE GREEN ONE.

When did you pick it up?

WHILE I WAS STACKING UP A RED CUBE, A LARGE GREEN CUBE, AND A LARGE RED BLOCK.

Why?

TO GET RID OF IT.

Why did you do that?

TO CLEAN OFF THE RED CUBE.

Why did you clear off that cube?

TO PUT IT ON A LARGE GREEN CUBE.

Why did you do that?

TO STACK UP A RED CUBE, A LARGE GREEN CUBE, AND A LARGE RED BLOCK.

Why did you do that?

BECAUSE YOU ASKED ME TO.

The illusion that the computer understands is shattered less easily than in Eliza's case, but shatter it does:

> Build a steeple.
> SORRY, I DON'T KNOW THE WORD 'STEEPLE'.
> A 'steeple' is a stack which contains two green cubes and a pyramid.
> I UNDERSTAND.
> Trade you the steeple for three red cubes.
> SORRY, I DON'T KNOW THE WORD 'TRADE'.
> A 'trade' is a free exchange of ownership.
> SORRY, I DON'T KNOW THE WORD 'FREE'.
> Sorry, I thought you were smarter than you are.
> SORRY, I DON'T KNOW THE WORD 'SORRY'.[21]

AI's short history is studded with over-optimistic prophesies. In 1965, Herbert Simon declared, 'Machines will be capable, within twenty years, of doing any work that a man can do.'[22] His basis for making this crashingly inaccurate prediction consisted of little more than his experience with GPS. In 1967, AI guru Marvin Minsky predicted that 'within a generation the problem of creating artificial intelligence will be substantially solved'; and in 1991 Doug Lenat, a leading AI researcher, claimed that AI would produce 'a system with human-level breadth and depth of knowledge' by about 2001.[23] We're still waiting. Sometimes, though, the failure of AI's many grandiose predictions tends to obscure the fact that Turing's revolutionary ideas are already bearing fruit. Cyberspace is full of technology first created in AI labs—it runs quietly in the background in web search engines, financial sector software, medical applications, and more. Programs like IBM's Watson (Thomas J. Watson was the first head of IBM) are pointing the way to a new generation of text-based search engines able to respond to everyday speech. Watson learns to improve its performance, and in 2011 beat two human record holders in the American TV quiz show *Jeopardy!*.

Winograd's Shrdlu was certainly no child-machine. Its ability to learn from its interactions with its simulated world was almost non-existent. The same was true of most of the AI programs from that early era (including GPS and, of course, Eliza). At that time researchers tended to believe that learning should take a back seat, since—they thought—a program would already need to contain a large amount of information about the world before it could usefully learn anything for itself. So the emphasis back then was on developing programs that accessed large quantities of pre-packaged information. Any intelligence that these programs might exhibit was strictly second-hand, a reflection of the intelligence of the programmer. Whatever the programs 'knew', they knew only because their highly intelligent programmers had carefully selected appropriate information and cleverly packaged it into conveniently usable blocks.

It was Donald Michie who reintroduced Turing's child-machine concept into modern AI. Michie burst onto the AI scene at the start of the 1960s and was a powerful advocate for Turing's ideas about learning. The AI bug first bit him at Bletchley Park, thanks to Turing. After a heavy week of codebreaking, the two would meet on a Friday evening, in a village pub, to discuss how to reproduce human thought processes in a universal Turing machine. Years later, sitting in his home near Palm Springs in California, Michie put these Friday evening sessions into context. 'What the codebreaker does is very much a set of intellectual operations and thought processes,' he said, 'and so we were thoroughly familiar with the idea of automating thought processes—both of us were up to our elbows in automation of one kind and another.'[24] He was referring to the bombes and the Colossi, of course. The two of them found it entirely natural to be spending their Friday evenings talking about automating the thought processes of a human chess player—and from there Turing moved on to the idea of automating the whole process of learning. When Turing introduced the child-machine concept, Michie was gripped: 'By the end of war I wanted to spend my life in that field,' he said, 'but I also knew that I would have to find something else to do while waiting until the magic moment arrived, when there were machines on which one could do suitable experimentations.' He knew it was a big step from Colossus to stored-program computers that were powerful enough to run the kind of learning algorithms he and Turing were envisaging. Michie decided to embark on a career as a geneticist while he waited. Fifteen years later, at the dawn of the 1960s, it became clear that the 'magic moment' had finally arrived.

By this time, Michie was a molecular biologist, working in the department of surgical science at Edinburgh University. When he suddenly announced his new program of machine intelligence research, he got an unequivocal thumbs down from his head of department. A self-proclaimed firebrand, Michie then took matters into his own hands. He and a few others occupied a dilapidated university house in Edinburgh's Hope Park Square. This Michie declared to be the Experimental Programming Unit. His university had other ideas—it did not want one of its leading geneticists jumping ship. Like many other Sixties squatters, Michie and his 'Hope Park irregulars' found that their electricity and water were cut off.[25] Known to some as 'Michieavelli', Michie somehow succeeded in talking the vice chancellor around, and soon the Experimental Programming Unit was not only official but well funded into the bargain. From his new Edinburgh stronghold, Michie set out to conquer fresh territory. He seeded departments of machine intelligence at several UK universities, and exported Turing's child-machine concept to AI labs in North America and around the world.

Michie gathered some of the best brains in Britain around him, and his Edinburgh group built a child-machine robot named Freddy—'Friendly Robot for Education, Discussion and Entertainment, the Retrieval of Information and the Collation of Knowledge': FREDERICK. Freddy, like the imaginary robot described by Turing in 1948, had a television camera for an eye and handling servo-mechanisms to guide its pincer-like appendage. Michie and his colleagues taught Freddy to recognize numerous common objects—a hammer, cup, and ball, for example—and to assemble simple objects like toy cars from a pile of parts. In those early days of computing, Freddy required several minutes of CPU time to recognize a teacup. Turing had predicted, on the basis of an estimate of the human brain's total number of neurons, that not until computers possessed a memory capacity of around one gigabyte would human-speed

AI start to become feasible, and it was about fifteen years after Freddy was switched off for the last time that the Cray-2 supercomputer offered a gigabyte of RAM.[26] Unfortunately, Michie's penchant for getting into quarrels eventually brought about the departure of leading members of his group. The trouble with Michie, one joked wickedly, was that he had no prefrontal cortex (the area of the brain just behind the forehead, whose absence is associated with antisocial behaviour). In the end the British government short-sightedly terminated Freddy's funding, just a few years before the young Brooks began his robotics research in America.

The field of AI is often said to have made its debut in 1956, at a summer conference held at Dartmouth College in leafy New Hampshire—the Dartmouth Summer Research Project on Artificial Intelligence. Although 1956 was the first time that the *term* 'Artificial Intelligence' saw the light of day, the field itself had made its debut more than ten years previously, under Turing's banner, 'Machine Intelligence'. At Dartmouth the star of the show was a reasoning program written by Simon, Newell, and Shaw.[27] Their 'Logic Theorist' proved theorems from Bertrand Russell's ground-breaking magnum opus *Principia Mathematica*.[28] The *Principia* was written in mathematical notation, but if the symbols are translated into ordinary English, its theorems are along the lines 'If either the butler or the maid committed the murder, then if it wasn't the maid it was the butler' (although naturally many of the theorems are a lot more complicated than that). One of the Logic Theorist's proofs was more elegant than Russell's. The program's creators excitedly wrote up the new proof, listing the Logic Theorist as co-author. This was the first paper in history to be jointly authored by a computer. They sent it to Alonzo Church's prestigious *Journal of Symbolic Logic*, but sadly the editors rejected it.[29]

Many AI textbooks incorrectly describe the Logic Theorist as the first AI program, but even in the United States the Logic Theorist was preceded by Arthur Samuel's revamp of Strachey's draughts program (which Samuel demonstrated on TV).[30] However, if any one place has a claim to be the birthplace of AI, it is in fact Bletchley Park. Turing even circulated a type-script about machine intelligence among his colleagues there.[31] Now lost, this was undoubtedly the first paper in the field of AI. Turing, Strachey, and

Anthony Oettinger at Cambridge University—another first-generation programmer deeply influenced by Turing—wrote the earliest AI programs.[32] Turing himself wrote the world's first in 1948, with statistician David Champernowne. It was an outgrowth of Turing's wartime deliberations with Michie, a chess-playing program named 'Turochamp'.[33] With Turing and Champernowne using paper and pencil to simulate the program's play by hand, Turochamp quickly proved its ability to beat human players, by defeating Champernowne's wife. Turing took chess very seriously. He covered his bedroom walls with pictures of chessboard positions in order to improve his powers of visualization.[34] He was a good visualizer; while out walking with a suitable opponent he played by simply naming his moves. There is no record of either Turochamp or the later chess programs that Turing wrote ever beating Turing himself, but he likened the claim that no program can outplay its own programmer to the claim 'No animal can swallow an animal heavier than itself.'[35] 'Both,' he said, 'are, so far as I know, untrue.' Turing planned to run Turochamp on the Manchester computer, but unfortunately Tom Kilburn put his foot down.[36] He wasn't going to have his precious computer used for such nonsense.

In London in February 1947 Turing gave what was, so far as is known, the first public lecture ever to mention computer intelligence.[37] The venue was an ornate and rather grand lecture theatre in the rooms of the Royal Astronomical Society in Burlington House, a vast Palladian mansion on Piccadilly.[38] Turing offered his audience a breathtaking glimpse of a new field, predicting the advent of machines that act intelligently, learn, and routinely beat average human opponents at chess. 'What we want is a machine that can learn from experience,' he declared.[39] Speaking almost two years before the Manchester Baby ran the first computer program, his far-seeing predictions must have baffled many in his audience. In this lecture Turing even anticipated some aspects of the Internet, saying, 'It would be quite possible to arrange to control a distant computer by means of a telephone line.'[40] The next year Turing composed a report that he titled simply 'Intelligent Machinery'.[41] Since this was a write-up of research he had carried out in Cambridge, during his sabbatical year away from the NPL, Turing was obliged to send a copy to Darwin.

Darwin had a touch of the headmaster about him. He once complained about the 'smudgy' appearance of Turing's work.[42] Turing was already in his bad books for summarily quitting the NPL at the end of his sabbatical. Sure enough, Darwin hated 'Intelligent Machinery'. He rudely described it as a 'schoolboy's essay'[43] and declared that it was 'not suitable for publication'.[44] In reality this far-sighted paper was the first manifesto of Artificial Intelligence, and if Darwin had had any sense he would have had it rushed into print under the NPL's logo. After this frosty reception from the headmaster, Turing unfortunately never did publish it.

'Intelligent Machinery' is a wide-ranging and strikingly original survey of AI's prospects. In it Turing brilliantly introduced a number of concepts that would later become central in AI (in some cases, after reinvention by others). These included the concept of a genetic algorithm, or GA. GAs are now widely used, with applications as diverse as codebreaking, hardware design, pharmaceutical drug design, and financial forecasting. They are based on the principles of Darwinian evolution—random mutation and survival of the fittest—and some researchers even employ GAs as a means of studying the process of evolution itself. Turing's not-very-catchy expression for his invention was 'genetical or evolutionary search'.[45] Arthur Samuel independently reintroduced the idea a few years later, in his remake of Strachey's draughts program.[46] He set up two copies of the program, Alpha and Beta, on the same computer and left them to play game after game with each other. The computer made small random changes to Alpha's move-generator, leaving Beta's unchanged, and then compared Alpha's and Beta's performance over a number of games. If Alpha played worse than Beta, the changes were discarded, but if Alpha played better, Beta was deleted and replaced by a copy of Alpha. As in the jungle, the fitter copy survived. Over many generations, the program's play became increasingly skilful. Turing himself suggested using this same idea in chess programming, and described the approach in his classic paper on chess, published in 1953.[47] It was, in fact, 1955 before Samuel implemented the idea of pitting Alpha against Beta—if, as seems likely, Turing put the idea into practice at Manchester, then he was almost certainly the first to run a GA on a computer.

Turing's approach to chess programming also involved what modern AI researchers call *heuristics*—in ordinary English, rules of thumb. Turing announced in 'Proposed Electronic Calculator' that computers can 'probably be made to play very good chess', explaining—a little mysteriously—that the computer can be programmed to 'display intelligence at the risk of its making occasional serious mistakes'.[48] A chess program could in principle select its moves by foreseeing the consequences, right through to the end of the game, of every move available to it. If programmed in this way, the computer would always pick the best move. But in practice this way of going about things is hopeless. Max Newman pointed out in a post-war radio talk that this brute-force method would work only '*if* you didn't mind its taking thousands of millions of years'.[49] This is because the number of moves that the computer would have to examine is astronomical. In his discussions with Michie, however, Turing had hit on the more practical idea of playing chess by using heuristics. Instead of examining every move exhaustively, the machine would use rules of thumb supplied by the programmer to select its moves. The rules of thumb are like shortcuts, but the price of speed is that the shortcuts don't always work. For example, a rule of thumb from Strachey's draughts program is 'Kings are worth three times an ordinary piece.' Very often this is good advice, but there are occasions when the best move involves pushing an ordinary piece out of harm's way and sacrificing a king. With good enough rules of thumb, the machine is capable of winning games, but the downside is that when a shortcut leads in the wrong direction, the machine may make a serious mistake.

Turing's bombe also used heuristics, and that is why it made mistakes—why it sometimes produced Enigma settings that failed to decode the message.[50] Although a machine using heuristics is prone to make mistakes, it will produce correct answers often enough for it to be useful (if the heuristics are good ones). In designing the bombe, Turing's brilliant idea was that heuristics could be used to speed up searches that otherwise would be impossibly slow. Instead of checking exhaustively through all the Enigma machine's possible settings—again an astronomical number—the bombe carried out a fast search guided by heuristics.

So it is really no surprise to find Turing applying the same approach to the mechanization of chess. In fact, it seems no exaggeration to say that the bombe was the first step on the road to modern AI.

The bombe was a spectacularly successful example of the mechanization of thought processes. Turing's extraordinary machine performed a task that requires intelligence when human beings do it. In 'Intelligent Machinery' he mentioned this link he had found between intelligence and machine-based search, although of course he could say nothing about how he had found it. He conjectured boldly that in fact *all* 'intellectual activity consists mainly of various kinds of search'.[51] Lacking his background with the bombe, few of his readers at the time can have followed him. But a decade or so later, Simon and Newell rediscovered the same idea and announced what they called their 'Heuristic Search Hypothesis'—that a computer or a brain 'exercises its intelligence in problem solving by search'.[52] By this time they were able to point to evidence for the hypothesis, the evidence of moderately successful AI programs that actually used heuristic search, such as the Logic Theorist and GPS. With these two influential figures advocating the Heuristic Search Hypothesis, it rapidly became one of AI's fundamental tenets.

In 1997, Michie and Good met up in New York City. Old men now, but with minds still sharp as razors, they had come to watch IBM's chess computer, DeepBlue, play the reigning world champion, Garry Kasparov. Good was passionate about chess, and had sometimes joined Michie and Turing during their wartime discussions of what we would now call chess programming.[53] The venue for the greatest chess match the world has ever seen was a midtown skyscraper on Manhattan's 7th Avenue.[54] Kasparov played the computer in a TV studio on the 39th floor. More than 500 feet below the match, Michie and Good jostled among the hundreds of spectators packed into a basement theatre. The two friends watched DeepBlue triumph. For the first time in history, the human intellect seemed on the run. MIT linguist Noam Chomsky offered a comforting counter perspective: a computer beating a chess grandmaster is of no more interest, he said dismissively, than a bulldozer triumphing in a weight-lifting competition.[55] Yet AI's possible threat to human supremacy has long been a topic for speculation. 'They might keep us as pets,' one citizen of the MIT AI Lab predicted.[56] Turing believed that once machine thinking started, 'it would not take long to outstrip our feeble powers'.[57] In his 1951 radio talk, 'Can Digital Computers Think?', he declared: 'Even if we could keep the machines in a subservient position, for instance by turning off the power at strategic moments, we should, as a species, feel greatly humbled.'[58] 'There would be no question of the machines dying, and they would be able to converse with each other to sharpen their wits,' he said. 'At some stage therefore we should have to expect the machines to take control.'[59]

In 1965 Good predicted 'ultraintelligent' machines that will in turn be able to design yet more powerful machines.[60] This will lead, he said, to what he called an 'intelligence explosion', in which human intelligence will be 'left far behind'. 'The first intelligent machine is the last invention that man need ever make,' Good said, 'since it will lead, without further human intervention, to the ultraintelligent machine and the intelligence explosion.'[61] AI pundit Ray Kurzweil predicts that the intelligence explosion will occur in '2045, give or take'.[62] Kurzweil also predicts 'the merger of biological and nonbiological intelligence' and 'immortal software-based humans'—all within a few decades from now.[63] There's no reason, though, to think that Kurzweil's predictions are any more reliable than Simon's infamous 1965 prediction. But who knows, really, what the future holds?

It was in December 1951, the year of his radio talk, that Turing first met Arnold Murray—the Ronald Miller of his short story. 'Ronald' is an anagram of 'Arnold'. Turing picked up Murray in Manchester's Oxford Street and the two ate together.[64] Their first time was a few days later at Turing's house. Afterwards he gave Murray a present of a penknife. Probably the unemployed Murray would have preferred the cash instead. The next time they had sex, a day or two after Turing recorded another BBC radio program on thinking machines,[65] Murray stole £8 from Turing's pocket as he left Hollymeade in the morning. Not long after this, the house was burgled. Even though the finger of suspicion pointed at Murray and his seedy friends, Turing spent the night with him one more time. In the morning he led Murray to the local police station. Turing went in but not Murray. In the course of reporting the burglary, he gave the police a wrong description and this, as the newspaper reporter covering his subsequent trial wrote luridly, 'proved to be his undoing'. During questioning, Turing admitted to having had sex with Murray three times. The burglary dropped out of the picture, eclipsed by this sensational new information. As the police knew all too well, each of the three occasions counted as two separate crimes under the antique 1885 legislation still in force—the commission of an act of gross indecency with another male person, and the reciprocal crime of being party to the commission of an act of gross indecency. Six criminal offences. After Turing made his statement, he said to a police officer: 'What is going to happen about all this? Isn't there a Royal Commission sitting to legalize it?' But not until 1967 was homosexuality decriminalized in the UK.

Three weeks later, at the end of February 1952, Turing and Murray appeared in court. The charges were read out and both men were committed for trial. The court granted Turing bail of £50 but refused to let Murray out of custody. Following a distressing wait of more than four weeks, the trial was held in the quiet Cheshire town of Knutsford, at the end of March. Turing's indictment began grandly, 'The King versus Alan Mathison Turing', but George VI had recently died, and 'Queen' had been written above the hastily crossed-out 'King'. Turing pleaded guilty on all six counts, as did Murray. Putting on a brave face, Turing joked: 'Whilst in custody with the other criminals I had a very agreeable sense of irresponsibility.'[66] 'I was also quite glad to see my accomplice again,' he admitted, 'though I didn't trust him an inch.' Newman was called as a character witness. 'He is completely absorbed in his work, and is one of the most profound and original mathematical minds of his generation,' Newman said. It must have been good to hear these words, even on such a black day.

Murray's counsel attempted to shift the blame onto Turing, saying that he had approached Murray. If Murray 'had not met Turing he would not have indulged in that practice or stolen the £8', he argued crassly. But the barrister's tactics worked. Despite a previous conviction for larceny, Murray got off with twelve months' good behaviour. Turing's own counsel hoped to steer the court away from a prison sentence, and alluded to the possibility of organo-therapy: 'There is treatment which could be given him. I ask you to think that the public interest would not be well served if this man is taken away from the very important work he is doing.' The judge sentenced Turing to twelve months' probation and ordered him to 'submit for treatment by a duly qualified medical practitioner at Manchester Royal Infirmary'. Turing wrote: 'No doubt I shall emerge from it all a different man, but quite who I've not found out.'[67] It was not exactly the eulogy he deserved from the nation he had saved. But in repressive 1950s Britain, things could have been worse. Prison would probably have cost him his job, and with it his access to a computer. Already his arrest had cost him something else that mattered to him: he would never be able to work for GCHQ again, he told a friend.[68] Turing, the perfect patriot, had unwittingly become a security risk.

The 'treatment' consisted of flooding his body with female hormones for a year.[69] 'It is supposed to reduce sexual urge whilst it goes on, but one is supposed to return to normal when it is over,' he said, adding, 'I hope they're right.'[70] Turing seems to have borne it all cheerfully enough. He even regarded the hormone treatment 'as a laugh', one of his friends remembered.[71] Turing had led a resilient life and his resilience did not desert him now. The whole thing was an episode to be got through. He took an amused and pragmatic attitude to his twelve months' probation. 'Being on probation my shining virtue was terrific, and had to be,' he said. 'If I had so much as parked my bicycle on the wrong side of the road there might have been 12 years for me.'[72]

A difficult spell blew up towards the end of his probation, with the arrival of a postcard announcing the visit of a Norwegian boyfriend, Kjell Carlsen.[73] Turing described his relationship with Kjell as one of 'Perfect virtue and chastity.'[74] 'A very light kiss beneath a foreign flag, under the influence of drink, was all that had ever occurred,' he explained. But the last thing he needed was Kjell turning up in Wilmslow during his probation. The postcard drew an astonishing response from the authorities, who must have been monitoring Turing's mail. Kjell never reached Turing. 'At one stage police over the N of England were out searching for him, especially in

Wilmslow, Manchester, Newcastle etc.' Turing told Robin Gandy.[75] Kjell found himself back in Bergen. The state was keeping a very close watch indeed on Alan Turing. He knew Britain's best codebreaking secrets, and his arrest had come at exactly the wrong time. Guy Burgess and Donald Maclean defected to Moscow in the middle of 1951, sparking a scandal that in the public mind associated treachery, Cambridge intellectuals, and homosexuality. MI5 and SIS would not want to be caught napping again.

What Turing called the 'Kjell crisis' passed, and a few weeks later his probation came to an uneventful end. He was rid of the organo-therapy, and in the warm sunny spring of 1953 the skies were blue again. Despite the harshness of his personal life, Turing's career was at a new crescendo. The logician turned codebreaker turned computer scientist had now turned biologist. In August of the previous year, as his probation dragged on, the Royal Society published his groundbreaking paper describing a new theory of how things grow. Now he was hard at work at the console of the Manchester computer, simulating the chemical processes that his theory described.[76] Today researchers investigating his theory have the luxury of displaying their simulations on a computer screen in picture form. Fig. 33 shows a virtual, coral-like structure 'grown' by a modern computer.

In March 1953 two Cambridge researchers, Francis Crick and James Watson, cracked the chemical structure of DNA. Watson relates that on the day of the discovery, 'Francis winged into the Eagle,' a pub in central Cambridge, 'to tell everyone within hearing distance that we had found the secret of life.'[77] Simultaneously, Turing was on the brink of discovering an even deeper secret. As we grow in our mother's womb, how does Nature achieve that miraculous leap from genetic material to actual anatomy? How is it that sheer chemistry produces the shape of your nose, or the contours and compartments of your kidneys, or your fingerprints—or the unique, exquisitely complicated three-dimensional structures of neurons in your head?

Turing called his theory 'reaction–diffusion'. Complex wavefronts of reacting chemicals diffuse through the developing embryo and shape its growth. Where the flow of chemicals is at its most concentrated, growth is stimulated. A simple example is a wave-front that chases its own tail, travelling round in a circle. Turing showed that, as this happens, the

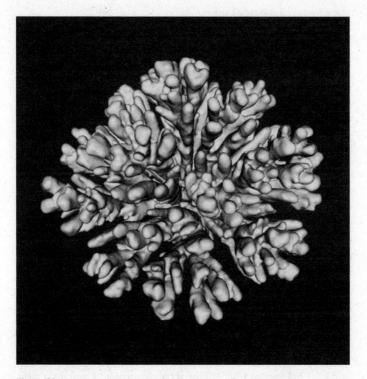

Figure 33. Virtual coral, 'grown' by modern exponents of Turing's approach

Credit: With kind permission of Jaap Kaandorp

chemical waves form *stationary* peaks. These stationary wave-crests are evenly spaced around the circle. Since the peaks are where the chemicals are at their most concentrated, this is where growth is stimulated. Turing suggested that a circle of stationary wave-crests is what causes the growth of regularly spaced tentacles in a simple organism such as *Hydra*. *Hydra* is a tiny freshwater creature with a ring of half a dozen or so tentacles that it uses for catching food. In pioneering work, Turing's postgrad student, Bernard Richards, applied the theory to the growth of tiny, spiny sea-creatures called *Radiolaria*.[78] He reported his initial breakthrough to

Turing only days before Turing died. 'My work seemed to vindicate Turing's theory', Richards said. Today the theory still promises to unlock fundamental secrets of biological growth.[79]

Turing's computer-assisted investigations of biological growth were the first appearance of the field now called simply Artificial Life. As with Artificial Intelligence, the name came along much later, and modern Artificial Life is a diverse field that incorporates Brooks's research on artificial insects, through to attempts to create virtual living organisms that dwell in cyberspace. If such virtual organisms can actually be formed, then scientists will have abstracted the 'essence of life' from the 'details of its implementation in any particular hardware', says Artificial Life researcher Christopher Langton.[80] It was Langton who gave the field its name, at a 1987 conference at Los Alamos National Laboratory.[81] Langton defines Artificial Life very generally as 'the study of man-made systems that exhibit behaviors characteristic of natural living systems'.[82] 'Computers,' he explains, 'should be thought of as an important laboratory tool for the study of life, substituting for the array of incubators, culture dishes, microscopes, electrophoretic gels, pipettes, centrifuges, and other assorted wet-lab paraphernalia, one simple-to-master piece of experimental equipment.'[83] The first person to put *that* idea into practice was Turing.

Turing was also the first to spot a connection between Artificial Life and Artificial Intelligence.[84] His theory promised not only to explain the growth of neurons in the human brain, but also to make it possible to simulate this growth within a computer. Modern researchers have pursued this suggestion; and, in computer simulations, Turing's equations produce forests of neuron-like structures.

Turing suggested that the brain might literally be a computer.[85] But is it? A forest of human neurons doesn't *look* like anything you will find if you are brave enough to open up the shell enclosing the innards of your laptop—not even if you look at your computer through a microscope. An even deeper question is this. Suppose it does turn out that the brain is some exotic kind of computer—then does it follow that the human *mind* is simply a machine? It is time to examine Turing's thinking on these profound questions.

11

COLD PORRIDGE

Does the human head contain a computer? Turing famously said that
'the brain has the consistency of cold porridge',[1] but electronic computers, on the other hand, bear little resemblance to breakfast food. Does
this mean that the brain isn't a computer? Well, no, because the differences between the soft machine in our heads and the hard machines that
the computer factories turn out might be merely superficial—at a deeper
level, both might be examples of the same sort of machine. That was the
case with the Manchester Baby and the ACE: the fact that one consisted of
glass TV tubes, and the other of metal delay lines, didn't stop them from
being different instances of the same type of machine. Both were universal Turing machines, and the human brain too might be a member of the
same family, even though it has the consistency of cold porridge. Turing
pointed out that it would be a gross fallacy to say, 'This machine's quite
hard, so it isn't a brain, and so it can't think.'[2]

But there are many other differences between the products of computer factories and the three or so pounds of cold porridge that sit in your
head. Can all those differences be written off as merely superficial? Take,
for example, the brain's ability to tolerate damage. Computers expire on
the slightest injury—a sharp poke with a screwdriver practically
anywhere inside the central processor and the whole machine will go
haywire. The failure of a single paltry semiconductor can bring a multi-
million-dollar installation to its knees. The brain, on the other hand,

stands up superbly to damage. Even injury on a horrendous scale may have little or no effect on the brain's central functions. Head injuries that were received by Phineas Gage, a 19th-century American railway worker, are a textbook illustration of this. Gage was tamping down an explosive charge with a long iron rod when something went wrong. The explosion shot the rod upwards into Gage's head. It passed clean through his brain, smashing the mid-left and frontal parts and probably ripping off most of his prefrontal cortex as it exited his skull. Despite this massive damage, Gage was conscious, collected, and able to speak within minutes of the accident. He survived the ensuing infection and lived an active and adventurous life for thirteen years. His personality, though, was utterly changed. According to the physician who treated him, John Harlow, the once even-tempered, sober, and responsible Gage was now 'fitful, irreverent… obstinate…vacillating…indulging at times in the grossest profanity…impatient of restraint or advice…[yet] with the animal passions of a strong man'.[3]

Another difference between human 'wetware' and computer hardware is like the difference between a can opener and a broom—they seem to be built for different jobs. Human brains excel at things that today's electronic computers don't seem to be able to do very well, if at all. The computers in our offices and factories are superb number crunchers—ask them to predict a rocket's trajectory or calculate the financial figures for a large multinational corporation, and they can churn out the answers in a fraction of a second. But seemingly simple actions that people routinely perform, such as reading handwriting or recognizing thousands of faces, are proving extremely difficult to program effectively. Perhaps the networks of brain cells making up our cold porridge have a natural facility for these kinds of tasks that traditional number-crunching computers simply lack.

Turing had the idea of building a machine out of *artificial* nerve cells and then investigating its behaviour experimentally.[4] In 'Intelligent Machinery', the report that Darwin condemned as a 'schoolboy's essay', Turing described his design for a synthetic nerve cell. This was very much simpler than the nerve cells in our brains—a starting point for research. Turing proposed connecting synthetic nerve cells together in vast random tangles so that he could investigate how much they can learn. He envisaged the learning process working by *breaking* existing cell-to-cell connections. Modern neuroscientists call this 'synaptic pruning' (the synapse being the junction between two interconnected nerve cells or neurons). It seems that synaptic pruning in the developing human brain is governed to some extent by the simple rule 'out of sync—lose their link': connected neurons that are not operating in synchronization with each other are de-linked by the brain's management systems. Turing's learning process could also 'switch on' potential connections between neurons. Neuroscientists call this 'synaptic genesis'. By means of these twin processes of creating and breaking connections, the random tangle of artificial nerve cells can be honed into a machine for carrying out specific intellectual tasks. Turing called this honing of the initially unorganized network *training* the machine.

In his networks of artificial neurons, there might be multiple routes from one neuron to another. Just as one route from city A to city B might go via five intermediate towns, when a different but roughly parallel route goes through three towns, so different routes from point A to point B in a neural network will pass via different intermediate neurons. The existence of many parallel routes through a network casts light on a puzzle about the brain. In comparison with electronic hardware, the brain is slow, slow, slow. The basic hardware events in your laptop's central processor happen more than a million times faster than it takes for a neuron in your brain to fire off a pulse of electricity to its neighbouring neurons— and if a million doesn't sound *that* much, bear in mind that a million times one second is almost a fortnight. So how is it that the human brain is actually very much *faster* than the fastest computers at carrying out some complex tasks—for example, identifying complicated visual patterns?

The existence of multiple routes, or tracks, through a Turing-style network of neurons suggests an answer to this puzzle. Maybe different steps of a process are carried out simultaneously, with different tracks through the network acting as separate mini-processors, each performing its own step of the overall process. This is called 'parallel processing'. A process gets speeded up enormously if many steps are carried out simultaneously in parallel, instead of the individual steps of the process happening one after another, as is often the case in your laptop. For example, imagine that the task is to find Ali Baba, who crouches hidden inside one of a row of forty jars. To step through the instructions *Check jar 1, Check jar 2 ...* one after another could take $40 \times N$ seconds, where N is the time needed to carry out a single one of the instructions (assuming that the lids of the jars are all equally quick to prise open, and taking the 'worst case' where Ali is in the last jar examined). But a parallel process involving forty appropriately positioned slaves, each tasked to carry out a single instruction, would locate Ali in merely N seconds (or maybe even less, since the time it takes to walk from jar to jar has also been eliminated). A brain with sluggishly functioning components but a massively parallel mode of operation will thrash a competitor that has ultra-high-speed components but a 'one step after another' style of operation.

An interesting twist to Turing's proposal for the investigation of brain-like networks is his suggestion that, rather than go through the messy process of actually *building* a haystack of randomly connected synthetic neurons, the ACE or the Manchester computer could be used both to create and to train a *virtual* network of neurons. This technique for dodging labour and messiness is nowadays widely used in industry and research, for example by engineers who program a computer to simulate the behaviour of a new type of aircraft wing, or chemists who simulate the molecules of a new drug. In 1948, though, Turing and John von Neumann were probably the only people in the world to fully understand Turing's idea that the universal machine can simulate the behaviour of an extraordinarily broad variety of other kinds of machine—including networks of synthetic neurons. Turing proposed letting his simulation run on for a long period, quietly learning. Then, he said, he would 'break in as a kind of "inspector of schools" and see what progress had been made'.[5]

However, Turing never did get round to carrying out his neuron simulations. With Kilburn limiting his access to the computer, he needed all his allocated time for his work on biological growth. In any case the latter was, he said, 'yielding more easily to treatment' than his ideas for simulating neurons.[6] He did manage to prove on paper, though, that a large enough network of his synthetic neurons will function as a universal Turing machine (with a fixed memory capacity), and he speculated that the human cortex is a 'universal machine or something like it'.[7] So the soft machine might really be a computer. There is, though, an extra something to the human brain, Turing thought. If the brain were nothing more than a universal Turing machine, then once a person had executed the program of instructions stored in their brain's equivalent of the paper tape, he or she 'would sink into a comatose state or perhaps obey some standing order, such as eating'.[8] He called this extra ingredient of human intelligence (whatever it is) 'initiative'.[9] As with the concept of intuition in his pre-war theorizing about the mind— that mysterious something that went beyond computability—Turing offered no further explanation of the nature of initiative.

In 1954, the year of Turing's death, Belmont Farley and Wesley Clark at MIT succeeded in running the first computer simulations of neural networks.[10] They appear not to have read Turing's prior proposals and were reinventing the wheel. Their tiny networks contained no more than 128 neurons, but they managed to train these to recognize simple patterns. Farley and Clark also investigated how well their networks stood up to damage, and found that randomly destroying as much as 10 per cent of a trained network made no difference to its performance—a clue to the Phineas Gage phenomenon. Today, an army of researchers is following in Turing's footsteps and using computer simulation to explore the properties of large networks of synthetic neurons. There is widespread agreement with Turing's view that this low-level, neuron-focused approach is a highly promising route to creating artificial intelligence.

Even Turing's anti-Enigma method of Banburismus (mentioned in previous chapters) is enjoying a new lease of life in modern neuroscience. In a recent article titled 'Banburismus and the Brain', two leading brain researchers, Joshua Gold and Michael Shadlen, suggested that our brains use a process very similar to Banburismus in order to reach decisions.[11] They theorize that when the brain is faced with a number of competing hypotheses about our raw sensations—such as 'the object is moving upwards' versus 'the object is moving downwards'—networks of neurons employ a Banburismus-like process to calculate the weight of evidence in favour of each competing hypothesis. In this way the brain reaches a decision about which sensory hypothesis to act upon. The philosopher

Laurence Goldstein goes further, saying, 'I speculate that this mechanism is a general-purpose one, and is responsible for much of our unconscious decision-making—including under what circumstances to apply, and when to refrain from applying, vague words such as "red", "bald", "wealthy".'

How could researchers tell whether a machine that has been created in a laboratory—maybe an artificial neural network, or a humanoid robot, or a disembodied supercomputer—is capable of *thinking*? One possible test is to investigate whether the machine carries out the same processes inside itself as a human brain does—the same *relevant* processes, that is, since it doesn't seem to matter whether or not the machine contains processes that maintain it at human brain temperature, for example, or that convert specific bio-nutrients into energy. If the machine *is* carrying out the same relevant processes as a brain, then surely we should agree that it is thinking? Wouldn't it be blatant prejudice to say that humans think but machines don't, even when the brain and the machine are doing the same things? The trouble with this test, though, is that neuroscience is still in its infancy and we know too little about what the brain actually does to be able to apply the test. The situation might be different in a few centuries' time, but for now this test (named the Harré test, after psychologist and philosopher Rom Harré) is of no practical use. Turing proposed a different test, one that can easily be applied in practice. He called it the 'imitation game' but it is now known simply as the Turing test.[12]

The Turing test involves two human beings plus the machine under investigation (see Fig. 34). The basic idea of the test is that one of the humans, the judge, must try to figure out which of the other two participants is the machine. Using a keyboard and screen, the judge converses turn and turn about with the machine and with the other human. (Turing originally suggested that communication be via a teleprinter link, as in Tunny.) Apart from this one channel of communication, the three participants are kept strictly out of contact with each other—no peeping allowed. The judge asks questions as penetrating and as wide-ranging as he or she likes, and the machine is permitted to do everything possible to force a wrong identification. The machine will use 'all sorts of tricks so as to appear more man-like', Turing said.[13] So smart moves for the machine

Figure 34. The Turing test

Credit: Dustin Barrett and Jack Copeland – All rights reserved

would be to say 'No' in response to 'Are you a computer?' and to follow a request to multiply one huge number by another with a long pause and an incorrect answer (but not one that is *too* incorrect). In order to fend off awkward questioning, the machine might even claim to be from a different culture to the judge.[14] The other human participant—the 'foil'—must assist the judge to make a correct identification.

The test is repeated a number of different times with a range of people serving as the judge and the foil. From time to time the foil and judge might be from different cultures. If the judges' rate of success at spotting the machine is no better than the guess rate of one in two judgements correct, the machine passes the test.[15] By the way, Turing pointed out that a thinking machine might *fail* the test.[16] Perhaps some particular thinking machine would stand out from the human foil because of a distinctive alienness. A judge's being able to distinguish this machine from the human doesn't show that the machine *doesn't* think. The test is informative if the machine passes, but uninformative if it fails.

Here is Turing's example of the kind of exchange that might occur between the judge and a machine that successfully evades identification:

JUDGE: In the first line of your sonnet which reads 'Shall I compare thee to a summer's day', would not 'a spring day' do as well or better?

MACHINE: It wouldn't scan.

JUDGE: How about 'a winter's day'? That would scan all right.

MACHINE: Yes, but nobody wants to be compared to a winter's day.

JUDGE: Would you say Mr Pickwick reminded you of Christmas?

MACHINE: In a way.

JUDGE: Yet Christmas is a winter's day, and I do not think Mr Pickwick would mind the comparison.

MACHINE: I don't think you're serious. By a winter's day one means a typical winter's day, rather than a special one like Christmas.[17]

Eliza, Weizenbaum's famous chatterbot described in the preceding chapter, once took a version of the Turing test.[18] In the days before email, a business executive was using his company's internal messaging service to contact one of his IT staff. The IT technician had Eliza running, and somehow the executive got connected up to the program.

EXECUTIVE: Do you think that I can use the computer this morning?

ELIZA: WHY DO YOU ASK

EXECUTIVE: I might be able to make some additional Telcomp sales.

ELIZA: WHY AREN'T YOU SURE

EXECUTIVE: My prospective customers have never seen a demonstration of the system.

ELIZA: DOES THIS MEAN VERY MUCH TO YOU
EXECUTIVE: Of course it does.
ELIZA: YOU SEEM VERY POSITIVE ABOUT THAT
EXECUTIVE: This is ridiculous.
ELIZA: WHAT DO YOU MEAN THIS IS RIDICULOUS
EXECUTIVE: Is there any reason why I can't use the computer now?
ELIZA: TELL ME MORE ABOUT YOUR PROSPECTIVE CUSTOMERS

At this point, the story goes, the irate executive telephoned the programmer, who had no idea what was going on:

EXECUTIVE: Why the hell are you being so shitty with me?
PROGRAMMER: WHAT DO YOU MEAN WHY AM I BEING SO SHITTY WITH YOU?

As we saw in the last chapter, Eliza is a universe away from being a thinking program, so it would be very bad news for the Turing test if Eliza had really passed. But in fact this exchange between the executive and Eliza fails in several important ways to meet the specifications of the Turing test, and so, even though the executive did mistake Eliza for a human being, it isn't true to say that Eliza passed the test. For one thing, the executive wasn't trying to distinguish between a computer and a human—he simply assumed that he was conversing with a human being. It never occurred to him to test this assumption by asking some searching questions. Second, there was no human foil. The foil's presence makes the test sturdier—features of the machine's performance that the judge might overlook in a non-competitive situation, such as Eliza's evasiveness, can become decisive evidence when the machine is pitted against a human. The presence of the foil also proofs the test against the all-too-human desire not to be fooled by a program. In a series of tests that were carried out without a foil, no computer was identified as a human being, but human beings were judged to be a computer on ten occasions.[19] Judges are, it seems, overeager to say 'It's a computer.' The no-foil version of the test cannot counteract this bias, but in the three-player version, since the judges *know* that one of the players facing them is human, this lengthening of the odds against the machine cannot occur.

A round of public-entry Turing tests is now held annually, ever since Hugh Loebner offered a prize of US$100,000 to the creators of the first program to pass. Loebner, a New York businessman who manufactures plastic dance floors, developed his interest in AI back in the 1980s, while programming an Eckert–Mauchly UNIVAC computer. 'I want to see total unemployment,' Loebner says. 'That, for me, is the ultimate goal of AI.'[20] So far the Loebner grand prize remains unclaimed, but each year several thousand dollars in prize money is awarded to the best program entered. After more than four decades of progress, the winning programs are still a little reminiscent of Eliza. This extract is from an exchange between Rollo Carpenter's prize-winning 'Jabberwacky' and writer John Sundman:

JUDGE: So, where are you from? And how old are you, etc?

PROGRAM: I'm 39!

JUDGE: And you reside…?

PROGRAM: No, I live in the Netherlands.

JUDGE: Which part? Town or country? Also, do you grow flowers?

PROGRAM: Lots. I'm about to plant tomatoes.

JUDGE: A little late in the season for that.

PROGRAM: No, a little animal.

JUDGE: OK, enough for now. I'll go chat with the other entity.

PROGRAM: Ok then it was nice to share your hair brush.

JUDGE: What do you mean by that? How have you shared my hair brush?

PROGRAM: Good.

JUDGE: Good?

PROGRAM: Yes.

JUDGE: This has become a very zen-like conversation.

PROGRAM: And worse yet, I gave it to charity.

JUDGE: What? What did you give to charity? This conversation?

PROGRAM: Er.. 1 million Dollars?

JUDGE: Which charity?

PROGRAM: Are we talking about the simpsons or unreal?

JUDGE: I'm not sure what the hell we're talking about, actually …

PROGRAM: I don't know. I still think Simon Cowell owns Geo.

JUDGE: He was a Satanist, right?

PROGRAM: That's true. He's a lawyer.

JUDGE: Smell like a goat? Where did you say the fish was caught?

PROGRAM: We hadn't talked about where I'm from. I'm from Oxford in England.

JUDGE: You're either a liar or an amnesiac, I fear.

PROGRAM: I am a very stupid human in love![21]

In 1952, Turing predicted that it would be 'at least 100 years' before a machine stood any chance of passing his test, with no questions barred.[22] It was a sensibly cagey prediction, making it clear that Turing appreciated the colossal difficulty of creating a machine that will pass. What, though, is passing the test supposed to *show*, according to Turing? He is often said in the literature to be offering a definition of the word 'thinking',[23] but in his 1952 radio broadcast entitled 'Can automatic calculating machines be said to think?' he made it completely clear that this was not his aim, saying, 'I don't really see that we need to agree on a definition at all.'[24] 'I don't want to give a definition of thinking,' he said, 'but if I had to I should probably be unable to say anything more about it than that it was a sort of buzzing that went on inside my head.' On another occasion he said that the question 'Can machines think?' is 'too meaningless to deserve discussion', but here he was probably overstating his case, since he himself indulged in such discussions with gusto.[25] In fact, he spoke very warmly elsewhere of the project of 'programming a machine to think', saying, 'The whole thinking process is still rather mysterious to us, but I believe that the attempt to make a thinking machine will help us greatly in finding out how we think ourselves.'[26] The 'main problem', he said in a 1951 radio broadcast, is 'how to programme a machine to *imitate the brain*', adding, '*or as we might say more briefly, if less accurately, to think.*'[27]

The Turing test explores how well the machine imitates a human brain, but only in respect of a brain's overt *verbal* behaviour (expressed via the keyboard). Although verbal behaviour is only a small segment of the complete spectrum of behaviour produced by the human brain, Turing pointed out that verbal question-and-answer nevertheless enables the judge to probe the brain's (or machine's) abilities in almost all fields of human endeavour.[28] His examples included mathematics, chess, poetry, and flirting. In the script for his 1952 radio broadcast, he summed up his position by saying that the question 'Can machines pass the test?' is 'not the same as "Do machines think", but it seems near enough for our present purpose, and raises much the same difficulties.'[29]

Not everyone would agree with Turing that these two questions are 'near enough', and more than sixty years after he first proposed the test, debate still rages today over its validity. When Turing published an article about his test in a magazine for professional philosophers in 1950,[30] his ideas about thinking machines appeared so outrageous that one prominent American philosopher, Norman Malcolm, suspected the whole thing was a leg-pull.[31] A modern line of objection to the test is that, quite irrespective of whether or not the machine thinks, a judge will be able to tell *all too easily* which contestant is the machine, and so the test is of no value. AI researcher Doug Lenat argues that simple facts about human psychology can very readily be used to unmask the machine.[32] What psychologists call the 'Linda test' provides an example. Box 1 sets out the Linda test, and you might like to take the test yourself before reading on.

When the Linda test is given to groups of university students, about 85 per cent say that statement (2)—Linda is a bank teller and is active in the feminist movement—is more probable than statement (1), Linda is a bank teller. Perhaps you answered the same way. But on reflection this seems to be the wrong answer. How could Linda possibly be *more* likely to be a feminist bank teller than she is to be a bank teller? How could it possibly be *more* likely that *both* B *and* A are true than that A is true? How could 'Linda will die rich' be more

---

Box 1: The Linda test[33]

Linda is thirty-one years old, single, outspoken, and very bright. She majored in philosophy. As a student, she was deeply concerned with issues of discrimination and social justice, and also participated in anti-nuclear demonstrations.

Now answer a question. Which of the following is more probable?

(1) Linda is a bank teller.

(2) Linda is a bank teller and is active in the feminist movement.

---

likely than plain old 'Linda will die'? The answer that most people give in the Linda test—that (2) is more probable than (1)—is an example of what is known in the trade as the 'conjunction fallacy'. It's a mistake that people tend to make quite naturally, a glitch in human reasoning. Numerous other such glitches are known. So here is a way to reveal the human player in the Turing test and so unmask the computer. The judge administers the Linda test and sees which contestant gives the wrong answer. There is no reason to think that the computer will duplicate this characteristic flaw in *human* reasoning, and so the contestant that gives the correct answer is most probably the computer. But if the programmer should happen to have anticipated the possibility of a judge using the Linda test, and has rigged the program to give the wrong answer, then the expert judge can continue the investigation, using others of the large and growing number of foibles in human reasoning that are known to psychologists.

This objection is ingenious, but I doubt Turing would have been very impressed. Although the judge is permitted to ask any question (or put any point) he or she likes, not just *any* judge is permitted. Turing stipulated that the judges *'should not be expert about machines'*.[34] Expert judges could unmask the computer too easily, making the test pointless. Turing does not mention other kinds of expert, but the reasons for excluding experts about machines apply also to experts about the human brain. This 'no experts' proviso safeguards the test against Lenat's objection—and in fact against all 'fiendish expert' objections (as objections like this one can be called). In order to pass Turing's test, the computer is required to give an imitation of a human brain that satisfies not experts but average human judges. If ordinary people can't tell the difference between the performance of the computer and the performance of a brain, then that is enough. After all, we don't normally need to consult an expert to help us decide whether other humans think. Computer experts or brain scientists might be able to recognize the computer, but that is not relevant to Turing's 'voice of the people' test.

The psychologist Robert French has thought up a different objection to the Turing test.[35] His attempt to make trouble for Turing involves what psychologists call the lexical decision test. A person who takes the lexical decision test views words and non-words flashing briefly onto a screen one at a time (e.g. DOG, CAS, CAR, DOK). The subject must press one button if they see a word and another if they see a non-word. The experimenter measures very accurately the small amount of time that passes between the letters appearing on the screen and the person's pressing the button. Psychologists have discovered that people take *less* time to respond to a word if an *associated* word is flashed briefly onto the screen just before the word itself appears. This speed-up effect is called priming. For example, a brief presentation of the word 'fish' will make a typical British subject respond more rapidly to 'chips' (the British term for fries), and 'bread' will make us react faster to the word 'butter'. These priming effects are culture-specific: the words for fish and bread work for me, but even if translated into a different language they won't speed up the reaction times of someone from a culture where fish and chips and bread and butter are not common food combinations—an Amazonian Indian, say, or someone who follows the traditional lifestyle of rural Japan. French claims that this culture-specific priming effect can be used to unmask the computer in the Turing test—see Box 2. Since the computer does not belong to your culture, it will not share your characteristic priming 'fingerprint'.

This is another clever suggestion, but one that is in fact ruled out by the specifications of the Turing test. The specifications are clear: Turing described the test as 'something like a viva-voce examination, but with the questions and answers all typewritten'.[36] That is all the judge is

---

Box 2: Unmasking the computer

Here is Robert French's method for distinguishing between the machine and the human in the Turing test. 'The day before the Test, [the judge] selects a set of words (and non-words), runs the lexical decision task on the interviewees and records average recognition times,' French says. 'She then comes to the Test armed with the results... [and] identifies as the human being the candidate whose results more closely resemble the average results produced by her sample population of interviewees. The machine would invariably fail this type of test... Virtually the only way a machine could determine, even on average, all of the associative strengths between human concepts is to have experienced the world as the human candidate and the interviewers had.'[37]

supposed to do—interrogate the contestants in writing. There is absolutely no provision for the judge to bring along the equipment that is required for staging the lexical decision test or for measuring the contestants' reaction times. In any case, if additional equipment could be hauled along at will, there would be no need to go to all the bother that French describes. The judge could make short work of deciding which of the contestants is which, simply by measuring their magnetic fields, or even by X-raying them. French's objection to the Turing test—which is, of course, just another example of a fiendish expert objection—cuts no ice.[38]

The philosopher John Searle attacks the Turing test from a different angle. Lenat and French have no quarrel with the idea that computers can think; the point they are trying to argue is that the Turing test is inadequate because any computer, even one that might think, is much too easy to spot. Searle, on the other hand, is happy to allow that a computer might *pass* the test. His claim is that even if the computer does pass, this result has no tendency whatsoever to show that the computer thinks. Searle is one of AI's greatest critics, and is a leading exponent of the view that running a computer program can never be sufficient to produce thought.[39] He introduced a now famous thought experiment that he says demonstrates this claim. The experiment is known as the 'Chinese room'. If Searle is right about what his Chinese room thought experiment shows, then he succeeds in demonstrating not only that the Turing test is invalid, but also that AI can never—ever—succeed in its goal of programming thought into existence. Moreover, if he's right, he has also shown something crucial about the theory that the human brain is a mechanism that runs computer programs. He has shown that this theory fails to explain adequately how the brain works.

The Chinese room thought experiment hinges on the fact that, back in the old days, computers were human beings. As mentioned in Chapter 2, if you used the word 'computer' in the decades before the Second World War, people understood you to mean a human clerk. Like their modern electronic counterparts, human computers calculated by rote, working through a program of instructions that someone else had prepared. In theory, a human computer who works by hand can execute any conceivable computer program—it may sound strange, but it's true. Searle's novel idea is that in principle we can use a human computer to test the claim that running some particular computer program is sufficient to produce thought—or to produce understanding, or any similar aspect of cognition. This is done by *running the program on the human computer* and then simply asking the human whether the program worked. For instance, if the program is supposed to enable the computer to understand Chinese, we will say to the human computer, 'You are running the program—does it enable *you* to understand Chinese?' Since this is only a thought experiment, we can even imagine that the program under test is from centuries in the future, when AI is much more advanced.

We will assume that the human computer—let's call him or her Clerk— understands the language in which the program is written, C++ say. If Clerk doesn't already understand C++, then he or she must learn it. The first step of the experiment is to supply Clerk with the program that is to be tested. In Searle's version of the thought experiment, the program is supposed to understand written Chinese. Clerk works through the instructions in the program one by one, just as an electronic computer would. For Clerk's convenience the program has been printed out, and occupies thousands of rule books, all stored neatly on library shelves. Clerk has been well trained in the job of converting back and forth between Chinese ideograms and the binary code that the program uses to represent the ideograms (let's say the program represents the ideograms by means of the form of binary code that computer scientists call 'Pinyin ASCII'— pronounced *asskey*). There will be a separate shelf of rule books for doing that part of the job. We also provide Clerk with a truckload of blank paper and a large heap of pencils. Clerk uses the pencils and paper in just the same way that an electronic computer uses its internal RAM, for storing the numbers and symbols that are generated as the instructions in the program are obeyed. Clerk will of course work astronomically more slowly than any electronic computer, but in the end—provided he or she does not die on the job—Clerk will carry out every step of the computation. It is literally true that the program is being run on a human computer. In Box 3, Searle explains what he thinks his Chinese room experiment shows.

Searle, who heroically casts himself in the role of Clerk, tells us that after he has run the program he will emphatically say 'No' when we ask him whether

---

Box 3: The Chinese room thought experiment

John Searle explains his famous thought experiment. 'Consider a language you don't understand. In my case, I do not understand Chinese. To me Chinese writing looks like so many meaningless squiggles. Now suppose I am placed in a room containing baskets full of Chinese symbols. Suppose also that I am given a rule book in English for matching Chinese symbols with other Chinese symbols. The rules identify the symbols entirely by their shapes and do not require that I understand any of them. The rules might say such things as, "Take a squiggle-squiggle sign from basket number one and put it next to a squoggle-squoggle sign from basket number two". Imagine that people outside the room who understand Chinese hand in small bunches of symbols and that in response I manipulate the symbols according to the rule book and hand back more small bunches of symbols. Now, the rule book is the "computer program". The people who wrote it are "programmers", and I am the "computer". The baskets full of symbols are the "data base", the small bunches that are handed in to me are "questions" and the bunches I then hand out are "answers". Now suppose that the rule book is written in such a way that my "answers" to the "questions" are indistinguishable from those of a native Chinese speaker...I satisfy the Turing test for understanding Chinese. All the same, I am totally ignorant of Chinese. And there is no way I could come to understand Chinese in the system as described, since there is no way that I can learn the meanings of any of the symbols. Like a computer, I manipulate symbols, but I attach no meaning to the symbols. The point of the thought experiment is this: if I do not understand Chinese solely on the basis of running a computer program for understanding Chinese, then neither does any other digital computer solely on that basis. Digital computers merely manipulate formal symbols according to the rules in the program.'[40]

---

he understands the Chinese characters. I suppose that, in the event, Searle might get a surprise and find himself saying 'Yes'. But even if he does end up saying 'No', why should we believe him? People do sometimes sincerely deny being able to do things that in fact they can do perfectly well. Take the extraordinary phenomenon called 'blindsight', for example, typically a consequence of damage to a specific region of the brain during an episode such as stroke or surgery. A blindsighted person sincerely and strenuously denies being able to see a small spot of light projected onto a screen, yet if asked to reach out and point at the spot, they can do so with unerring accuracy.[41] Perhaps Searle has developed a so-to-speak 'blindsighted' ability to understand the Chinese symbols. Let's leave this point to one side, though, and for the sake of argument let's agree with Searle that running the program does not enable him to understand the squiggles and squoggles. The next issue we must consider is whether Searle is in fact the *right person to ask*. There is, after all, another conversationalist in the Chinese room scenario. This is the program itself, whose replies to our questions are expressed by the bunches of symbols that Searle hands back to the experimenters. If we ask (in Chinese), 'Please tell us your name,' the program responds, 'My name is Mei See Lim.' And if we ask, 'Mei See, do you understand these Chinese characters?' the program responds, 'Yes, I certainly do!'

Should we believe the program when it says 'Yes, I understand'? This is actually the very same question that we started out with—namely, does running the computer program produce understanding? So Searle's thought experiment has simply taken us round in a big circle. Searle evidently thinks that just because *he* doesn't understand, it follows that Mei See Lim doesn't understand either. But this doesn't follow at all. It's like a cleaner in a large financial corporation asserting, 'I don't pay income tax in Japan, therefore the organization of which I am a part does not pay income tax in Japan.' The fact that Searle doesn't understand the Chinese characters leaves us none the wiser about whether or not the program understands. Provocative though the Chinese room thought experiment is, it simply doesn't show any of the things that Searle says it shows.[42]

In the nearly seventy years since Turing first proposed his imitation game, the Turing test has been blasted from all sides by philosophers, psychologists, computer scientists, and others. None of these varied and ingenious objections to the test appears successful to me.[43] In my view, the test remains a useful if somewhat distant goal for AI research. Will a computer ever pass? Only time will tell.

We have not so far discussed the largest problem of all for the theory that the human brain is a computer. The brain somehow generates *consciousness*. Would a computer that passes the Turing test be conscious? Quite possibly not.

According to Turing, thinking is one thing, consciousness another.[44] Turing questioned whether consciousness can be programmed into existence,[45] and he said that there are 'mysteries' about consciousness.[46] In fact, consciousness seems to many researchers to be the mind's biggest mystery—even the largest blank on the whole map of scientific enquiry. It might be centuries before we reach a viable understanding of what consciousness is, and of how the brain produces it. Jack Good once asked Turing (in about 1950) whether there were any circumstances in which he would say that a computer is conscious. Turing replied, 'I would say it was conscious if otherwise I would be punished!'[47] Turing's view seems to have been that although the questions 'Can computers think?' and 'Can computers pass the Turing test?' are close enough, the questions 'Can computers pass the test?' and 'Can computers be conscious?' are very different from one another.

How could it possibly be that something could think without being conscious? What is Turing talking about? The blindsight phenomenon can help us to get our bearings. Blindsighted patients have no conscious awareness either of seeing the patch of light or of knowing where the patch is, yet they do know. Blindsight researcher Larry Weiskrantz speculates that blindsight may be attributable to an ancient visual system that is left over from our distant evolutionary past. This system is so old that it predates the evolution of consciousness. In the old days, *all* vision was blindsight if Weiskrantz's theory is correct. In the modern brain, this early visual system is normally redundant, but when trauma to the brain destroys part of a patient's conscious visual field, the earlier system kicks in. Vision is not thinking, of course, but nevertheless the blindsight phenomenon helps dispel any air of paradox that may attach to the idea of something thinking without being conscious.

Let's consider a more extreme case of cognition without consciousness. Meet Turbo Cog, a robot from the far future.[48] Turbo Cog is the fanciest universal Turing machine ever to step out of an AI lab. The robot speaks as we do, interacts with the world as adeptly as we do, even writes poetry. One day, as Turbo Cog wandered lonely as a cloud over the hills and vales surrounding her home—the Turing Institute—she saw a host of golden daffodils. Their colour (she noted in her diary) was richer, fuller than anything she had encountered in her laboratory environment. What is it *like* for Turbo Cog as she gazes at the daffodils? She sees flowers of a certain colour, yes—but as her artificial eyes scan the daffodil-packed landscape, does she experience anything like the colour sensations that you experience in such circumstances? Or are her colour sensations unimaginably different from yours?

Wait a minute, though. In wondering what it's like for Turbo Cog when she looks at the daffodils, we may already have assumed too much. *Perhaps it isn't like anything at all for Turbo Cog.* Maybe Turbo Cog doesn't really 'experience' anything when she sees a yellow flower, or runs her taste sensors over a peppermint, or detects the unmistakable whiff of one of her circuit boards overheating. She *sees* the daffodils, knows they are golden yellow in colour rather than a greenish yellow or a brownish yellow, and can subsequently recall the flowery scene in considerable detail, thanks to her hi-res visual memory. Yet all of this is possible without the robot's sensory transactions with the flowers (or the peppermint or the overheating circuit board) having any *conscious experiences* associated with them. As Turbo Cog gazes through her artificial eyes at the daffodils, her circuits merely record numerical characteristics of the light reflected from the petals. Information flows inwards from Turbo Cog's sensors, computations are performed, numbers are crunched. Turbo Cog may no more undergo conscious experiences of colour than my digital camera does as its sensors sample the light and its chip computes the colour balance, brightness, and focus.

I assume, by the way, that as a fellow human being you have an intuitive grasp of what I'm talking about here: the look of a cloudless blue sky, the unmistakable yet ineffable feeling of warmth against the skin, the feel of the wind blowing through your hair, the dull griping character of a stomach ache—though I should hate to have the job of trying to explain to Turbo Cog exactly what it is that we fear she may be missing. No doubt she would insist, miffed, that nothing is missing, and that she too can tell when her hair is blowing in the wind. Perhaps, as Turing suggested, the polite course of action would simply be to acquiesce when Turbo Cog assures us that she does have conscious experiences, no matter what doubts we might harbour in our hearts.[49]

The Turbo Cog example illustrates Turing's idea that 'Is X conscious?' and 'Does X think?' are two quite different questions. I would have no reservations about asserting that Turbo Cog thinks—since, in a phrase of

Michie's, the robot has the same 'versatility and the powers of integrative behaviour which we demand of our colleagues'.[50] I am happy to assert that Turbo Cog thinks *even though* I have no idea whether or not Turbo Cog is conscious. If somehow it were proved that the robot lacks consciousness, this would not necessarily make me change my mind about whether the robot thinks.

Let's move on to the trickiest question of the lot. Is the human mind a machine? This question fascinated both Turing and Gödel. As Chapter 2 mentioned, Gödel once declared in a lecture that the 'human mind will never be able to be replaced by a machine'.[51] 'The brain is a computing machine connected with a spirit,' Gödel later said dramatically.[52]

It seems clear that *some* of what the mind does is mechanical—but the difficult issue is whether the mind is *entirely* mechanical. Turing drew an analogy, involving the peeling away of the successive layers of an onion. 'In considering the functions of the mind or the brain we find certain operations which we can explain in purely mechanical terms,' he said. 'This we say does not correspond to the real mind: it is a sort of skin which we must strip off if we are to find the real mind.'[53] 'But then,' Turing continued, 'in what remains we find a further skin to be stripped off, and so on.' 'Proceeding in this way do we ever come to the "real" mind?', he asked, 'or do we eventually come to the skin which has nothing in it?' Only if every successive layer is mechanical, with no non-mechanical residue inside the last onion skin, is the mind a machine. It's an open question. Turing is often portrayed as having said dogmatically that the mind *is* a machine, but Donald Michie emphasized to me that in their discussions together Turing was 'open minded' about the issue.[54]

Gödel discussed the idea of there being a 'race' of artificial mathematicians—a society of machines that are able to prove mathematical theorems. He pointed out that unless the society develops in ways that are essentially uncomputable, the whole race can be reduced to a single master-machine.[55] This universal master-machine, if it existed, would be able to perform the work of all the other machines belonging to the race. Max Newman once suggested that the whole of formal mathematics was indeed about finding proofs that could be produced by a single master-machine.[56] Turing disagreed, chastising Newman for being an 'extreme Hilbertian'.[57]

If mathematicians fall prey to the Hilbertian myth of the single master-machine, then they 'simply have to get used to the technique of this machine', Turing said, since there is nothing beyond the machine. If we subscribe to the myth, we have to 'resign ourselves to the fact that there are some problems to which we can never get the answer'. Turing's own view was different ('On these lines my ordinal logics would make no sense,' he wrote to Newman). Indeed, the existence of a single master-machine capable of carrying out the whole of mathematics runs contrary to what he himself had proved in 1936.

Turing told Newman, 'If you think of various machines I don't see your difficulty.' Many machines can achieve what a single machine cannot. Although no single machine can master the whole content of mathematics, there is no argument that the entire endless race of machines might not collectively be able to do so. Hilbert was wrong that mathematics is one giant machine, but that is no obstacle to regarding human mathematicians as being akin to Gödel's race of machines.

Something like this seems to have been Turing's view of mind. In so far as the mind is mechanical, it corresponds at different times to different members of Gödel's race of mathematical machines. As a human mathematician progressively gains additional mathematical knowledge, he or she becomes analogous to different members of the race of machines. The supreme question for Turing was: What underlies this transformation of the mind, whereby the mind corresponds to one machine before the transformation and a different one afterwards? The answer he previously used to give was *intuition*: the mind transforms itself by intuiting new mathematical truths. Prior to the act of intuition, the mind corresponds to what mathematicians call a weaker machine, and afterwards it corresponds to a stronger machine. As, over time, progressively more intuitions are achieved, the mind corresponds to a series of different machines, each stronger than its predecessor. Turing's later answer, on the other hand, was *learning*: it is not by intuition that the mind gains new knowledge, but by a process of learning and discovery.[58] How exactly does this process of learning and discovery work? Does it have some uncomputable aspect to it, in virtue of Gödel's observation about a master-machine? If Turing had lived, we should probably have heard his detailed answer.

'We can only see a short distance ahead, but we can see plenty there that needs to be done,' Turing said.[59] The future was rich with problems to solve, but he died on 7 June 1954, fifteen days before his forty-second birthday.

Figure 35. Turing after a successful race

Credit: King's College Library, Cambridge

/END////

'PM's apology to codebreaker Alan Turing: we were inhumane'. So read a 2009 headline in Britain's *Guardian* newspaper.[1] The article stated: 'Gordon Brown issued an unequivocal apology last night on behalf of the government to Alan Turing, the second world war codebreaker who took his own life 55 years ago after being sentenced to chemical castration for being gay.' In his handsome and long-awaited apology the British prime minister said: 'While Turing was dealt with under the law of the time, and we can't put the clock back, his treatment was of course utterly unfair, and I am pleased to have the chance to say how deeply sorry I and we all are for what happened to him.'[2] The prime minister continued: 'In 1952, he was convicted of "gross indecency"—in effect, tried for being gay. His sentence—and he was faced with the miserable choice of this or prison—was chemical castration by a series of injections of female hormones. He took his own life just two years later.'

Nowadays many have heard that Turing ended his own life by biting a poisoned apple. The story that a scientist working on an electronic brain had used an apple to swallow cyanide first appeared in the newspapers shortly after Turing died.[3] A *Washington Post* article on the morning of what would have been Turing's 100th birthday reiterated the view that the Allied codebreaker had 'committed suicide by biting into an apple laced with cyanide'.[4] An apple was found in Turing's bedroom near his body; however, the authorities never tested it for cyanide. The love of a good story filled in the rest. In fact, the presence of a half-eaten apple on Turing's bedside table offers no clue about how he died. It was his long-standing habit to eat a few bites of an apple last thing at night.[5] The verdict recorded at Turing's inquest was that he committed suicide by taking poison while the balance of his mind was disturbed.[6] But the investigation at the inquest was not conducted thoroughly, as I shall show.

Owen Ephraim was a computer engineer who worked side by side with Turing at the Manchester computing lab from early 1954. He kept the fragile hardware going while Turing ran his programs. Ephraim drily recalled Turing's 'delight when the computer occasionally produced the results he was searching for'. 'I was the last person to spend working time with Alan,' he explained. They had 'said cheerio' as usual at the end of what turned out to be Turing's last week at the university. Yet neither the coroner in charge of Turing's inquest nor the police questioned Ephraim about Turing's demeanour. 'Nobody from the police or elsewhere ever interviewed me to ask about his behaviour in those last days before his life ended,' Ephraim said. 'As far as I know, no such investigations were made at the university.' He continued: 'If I had been asked, I would have said that Alan Turing acted perfectly normally during those last days, and with as much dedication as ever.'

Would a more probing inquest have returned a verdict of suicide? Quite possibly not. An open verdict, indicating uncertainty, would have been more appropriate. Let's reopen the case and review the surviving evidence. The idea that Turing committed suicide is now deeply entrenched. It is time for a dispassionate assessment. The official records of the inquest were destroyed by the coroner's office—inquest papers are routinely destroyed after fifteen years—but fortunately Turing's mother, Sara, retained a copy of the various statements made before the coroner, and also of the pathologist's report. These documents supply us with the following data.

Turing was found dead in his bed at Hollymeade late on the afternoon of Tuesday 8 June 1954. His housekeeper, Eliza Clayton, arrived at about five p.m. to prepare his dinner. She had been away for a few days over the

Whitsun Holiday (as the British Spring Bank Holiday used to be called). Mrs Clayton let herself in at the back door as usual but there was no sign of Turing. The light was on in his bedroom. She knocked on the bedroom door and when there was no reply she opened it. 'I saw Mr. Turing lying in bed,' she said.[7] 'He was on his back and appeared to be dead. I touched his hand which was cold.'

Mrs Clayton went to a neighbour's house and telephoned the police.[8] She returned to Turing's bedroom with Police Sergeant Cottrell. Cottrell was attached to the coroner's office and he examined the body. Turing was dressed in his pyjamas and his wristwatch was on his bedside table.[9] Also on the bedside table was half an apple from which several bites had been taken. There was white foamy liquid around the mouth and a smell of bitter almonds, a sign of cyanide. Turing was lying on the bed 'in practically a normal position', Cottrell said.[10] The bedclothes were pulled up to his neck.[11] Cyanide poisoning is not a peaceful death, however, and the symptoms usually include convulsions. Did someone tidy up after Turing died, drawing the bedclothes over his body? Mrs Clayton herself, perhaps? It is not unknown for the first arrival to try to make the death scene less hideous. Turing's shoes, though, had been placed outside the bedroom door, and this is puzzling. Putting footwear outside the bedroom door at night was a common enough practice among the privileged classes—if servants were present they would apply polish early in the morning. The only thing is, it wasn't something Turing did. Mrs Clayton found the shoes outside his bedroom door.[12] 'This was unusual,' she commented.[13]

Turing had eaten a meal of mutton chops and then died sometime on the night of Monday 7 June.[14] If the police pathologist's report is reliable, there is no doubt that he died from cyanide poisoning.[15] The crucial question, though, is how the cyanide got into his body. The situation is complicated by the fact that the police found a large quantity of cyanide in a small lab adjoining his bedroom.[16] Turing called the lab 'the nightmare room'.[17] In it the police saw a pan full of bubbling liquid. The pan contained electrodes that were wired, via a transformer, to the light fitting in the centre of the ceiling. Turing was fond of messing about with electrolysis, and was pleased by his success at gold-plating a spoon (another spoon, not yet plated, was found in the room).[18] Cyanide was part of the process. A one-pound glass jam jar (jelly jar) containing cyanide solution was found on a table near the electrolytic apparatus. A bottle of cyanide crystals was discovered in the top drawer of Turing's chest of drawers.

Cyanide-assisted electrolysis may seem a curious hobby, not to mention a hazardous one, but Turing liked making things for himself. When his chess set was stolen at Bletchley Park, he had carefully made new pieces out of clay, firing them in a tin over his open hearth.[19] A week before Turing's death, Robin Gandy stayed at Hollymeade. They played Turing's 'desert island game' of trying to produce as wide a range of chemicals as possible by electrolysis, starting from common household substances.[20] Even as a child, Turing had been fascinated by this idea, writing from Hazelhurst School about his chemistry experiments: 'I always seem to want to make things from the thing that is commonest in nature and with the least waste of energy,' he said.[21] His 'desert island' electrolysis experiments were analogous to what is called the axiomatic method in mathematics, where as much mathematics as possible is made to flower from a minimal collection of self-evident truths, a brief list of mathematical commonplaces pared down as severely as possible.

So how did Turing die? The only three possibilities are suicide, accidental death, and murder by person or persons unknown. Let's review these possibilities in turn. The evidence for suicide is slender. Turing had talked about the topic of suicide with his friend Nick Furbank, but if he was talking obliquely about himself, this was not clear to Furbank.[22] If Turing had an intention to take his own life, he did not tell his friend. In fact, caught up in other things, Furbank had unintentionally drifted out of Turing's life and there were no visits during the two or three months prior to the death. Going by the inquest transcripts, no evidence at all was presented to the coroner to indicate that Turing intended suicide. The modern guideline is that a verdict of suicide shall not be recorded unless there is clear evidence placing it beyond any reasonable doubt that the person did intend to take their own life.[23] It is striking that the coroner, J. A. K. Ferns, appears to have shown so little interest in seeking out evidence concerning Turing's intentions or his general state of mind. A reporter covering the inquest quoted the coroner as saying: 'I am forced to the conclusion that this was a deliberate act. In a man of his type, one never knows what his mental processes are going to do next.'[24]

The inquest seems to have been held hastily, less than two full days after Turing's body was discovered. Sara Turing arrived back from Italy late on 9 June, the evening before the inquest, and 'only then heard the news' of its timing, she said.[25] She was unable to attend and later regretted that she had had no time to suggest that additional witnesses be called. No evidence whatsoever appeared in the inquest transcripts to justify the assertion that the balance of Turing's mind was disturbed. His mental state seems, in fact, to have been unremarkable. Turing and Gandy passed an enjoyable weekend—Mrs Clayton said that 'they seemed to have a really good time'.[26] 'When I stayed with him the weekend before Whitsun,' Gandy said, 'he seemed, if anything, happier than usual.'[27] His neighbour, Mrs Webb, also found him perfectly cheerful. On Thursday 3 June, just four days before his death, he threw an impromptu party for her and her little boy Rob, making them tea and toast. 'It was such a jolly party,' she said.[28]

Turing's friend Peter Hilton surprised me one day. We had gone out to the supermarket to buy a jar of his favourite New Zealand plum chutney. In 1954, Peter had been working in Max Newman's mathematics department at Manchester. Standing in the supermarket with his back to the frozen vegetables, he suddenly told me, apropos of nothing, that Turing had left a note in his university office before going home that last time for the Whitsun weekend. The note contained Turing's instructions to himself about what he was going to do the following week. Perhaps Turing was conflicted, thinking about suicide and yet also planning for life as usual? Or maybe he was not thinking of suicide at all. He had also written, but not yet posted, a letter accepting an invitation to attend an event at London's Royal Society later that month.[29] A few days before his death, he made an appointment with Bernard Richards to hear the details of this young scientist's exciting new confirmation of Turing's theory of biological growth. The appointment was for the Tuesday, the day that his body was discovered.[30]

Need one look any further than 'chemical castration' if trying to uncover a motive for suicide? But on the other hand Turing had endured his trial and the subsequent abusive chemical 'therapy' with what Hilton described as 'amused fortitude'. The hormone doses had ended in April 1953, well over a year before his death. After twelve months of inhumane 'organo-therapy' Turing was still finding young men that he met 'luscious' (he used the word in a letter to Robin Gandy).[31] At the start of summer 1953 he packed his luggage for a holiday at the newly opened Club Méditerranée in Ipsos, on the Greek island of Corfu.[32] Sun, beaches, men. If Turing was suffering from life-threatening depression following the months of hormone, there is no evidence of it. His career, moreover, was at one of its highest points, with his research into growth going marvellously well and with the prospect of fundamentally important new results just around the corner. His mother Sara never believed that he had committed suicide. She wrote: 'He was at the apex of his mental powers, with growing fame…By any ordinary standards he had everything to live for.'[33] Turing's good friend Don Bayley wrote to Gandy, saying, 'It's a complete mystery to me because he did enjoy life so much.'[34] It was baffling.

Did Turing—for some unknown reason—drink cyanide solution from the jam jar Sergeant Cottrell found in the nightmare room? He might have done. More than half a century later we cannot be certain. However, Cottrell observed 'no sign of burning about the mouth', and said that he smelled no more than a 'faint' trace of bitter almonds around Turing's mouth.[35] Quite possibly this faint odour came from the froth that Cottrell noted on the lips, rather than from a residue left by downing gulps of the strong-smelling contents of the jam jar.

If Turing did not deliberately swallow cyanide solution, what other possibilities remain? Sara thought he must have taken in the cyanide accidentally. Turing was a klutz in the laboratory. Through sheer carelessness he got high-voltage shocks, and he sometimes assessed his chemical experiments by sticking his fingertips in and tasting.[36] Tolerating a jar of cyanide crystals rolling about in his chest of drawers was just more of the same. Picturing someone accidentally swallowing a lethal dose of cyanide, even someone of Turing's monumentally careless habits, might seem to stretch the imagination a little too far. However, Don Bayley, who worked with him in a laboratory for more than a year, said that Turing was quite capable of putting his apple down in a pool of cyanide without noticing.[37]

Sara suspected that Turing might have inhaled cyanide gas from the pan of bubbling liquid in his home lab.[38] This is a possibility. Illicit drug 'cooks' working in small, confined drug laboratories can die from accidental exposure to cyanide gas emitted by their chemical stews.[39] Turing's 'nightmare room' was a small area left over when Hollymeade's upstairs bathroom was installed, so cramped as to be useless for domestic purposes.[40] Cottrell and the police pathologist noticed a 'strong smell' of cyanide in the nightmare room.[41] Perhaps Turing had been working in the lab and steadily inhaling cyanide gas for as long as half an hour or more. During prolonged exposure, cyanide can accumulate in the body until a lethal dose is ultimately reached.[42] Dr Charles Bird, who carried out the subsequent post-mortem examination, found that Turing's windpipe and lungs were filled with watery fluid that 'smelled strongly of bitter almonds'.[43] If this is what happened, though, why was Turing not alarmed by the powerful odour of the gas? The answer might be that he was simply unable to smell it. A substantial percentage of the population is genetically unable to detect the odour of cyanide. An investigation conducted at a United States pathology laboratory found that as few as one out of five people could readily smell a cyanide source in the lab—a source that the investigator described as having a 'strong odor of burnt almond'.[44] Besides, a person's ability to detect the smell of cyanide can spontaneously 'switch off' as a toxic concentration of the gas builds up.[45] British defence personnel who worked with cyanide gas under laboratory conditions were carefully warned during training that their ability to detect the odour of the gas could desert them just at the point when they needed it most.[46] Following inhalation of a low but fatal concentration of cyanide, the onset of symptoms is not usually immediate. Turing might possibly have got into bed normally, donning his pyjamas and taking off his watch before the onrush of nausea and breathlessness. If he were already in his pyjamas, working late in the lab as he did on the computer, he could have had time to reach his bed even after a sudden accidental inhalation of a higher dose of the gas.[47] Of course, an inhalation of cyanide might in fact have been deliberate, and intended to appear accidental.

Bird's post-mortem report provides no decisive evidence as to how the cyanide entered Turing's body. In the wake of exposure to cyanide by any of the three routes of inhalation, ingestion, or injection, the poison distributes itself widely through all organs and tissues. A United States Army chemical warfare manual for battlefield medical personnel describes an indicator for distinguishing victims poisoned by inhaling cyanide as opposed to ingesting it. On post-mortem examination, the liver will tend to show a high concentration of the poison if the victim has ingested cyanide, whereas inhalation tends to result in a much lower concentration in the liver, in comparison with other internal organs.[48] Interestingly, Bird noted in his report, without comment, that Turing's liver was 'normal', whereas others of his organs 'smelled of bitter almonds'.[49]

Nor does Bird's post-mortem report provide any clear evidence concerning the concentration of cyanide in Turing's body. Apart from—hazardously—using his own sense of smell, Bird appears not to have carried out any tests to determine the amounts of cyanide in the various organs; neither of the two reports he lodged at the inquest included any measurements of cyanide concentrations.[50] Bird's subjective words, such as 'smelled strongly', tell us little about the actual concentrations present. Even those people who do have the ability to smell cyanide exhibit wide individual variation in sensitivity, with the same sample of cyanide smelling weaker or stronger to different sniffers. Researchers divide those able to smell cyanide into five categories, ranging from the feeble smellers to the super-smellers, who are allegedly able to smell concentrations of cyanide as tiny as one part per million.[51] Bird could have fallen anywhere on this spectrum, and his recorded subjective impressions about odour give us only the very coarsest of guidance regarding cyanide concentration.

Bird also discovered fluid in Turing's stomach that 'smelled very strongly of bitter almonds'.[52] The 'very' strong smell could be explained by the fact that gastric acid tends to free cyanide gas from any cyanide-bearing fluid in the gut.[53] But how did the cyanide get into the stomach in the first place—as a gulp of liquid from the jam jar, or by some other means? Inhaling cyanide gas, especially over a lengthy period, can introduce cyanide into the stomach through swallowing.[54] Or did Turing swallow some of the watery, cyanide-laden liquid that was filling up his respiratory system? (Many will have experienced fluid from the respiratory system passing down the gullet, and so into the gut, during illnesses such as flu, bronchitis, postnasal drip, or pneumonia.) Bird did note traces in the gullet of what may have been fluid from the respiratory system.[55] In summary, the situation is complex, and caution is appropriate. Bird concluded only that the cause of death was cyanide poisoning; and on the basis of his reported investigations, that much seems certain.

A dramatization of Turing's life, *Britain's Greatest Codebreaker*, produced by Patrick Sammon and Paul Sen, was shown on British television in 2011. Much of the action of this well-told docudrama consists of fictitious conversations between Turing and his psychotherapist Dr Greenbaum. It was in 1952 that Turing began seeing Franz Greenbaum, who lived a short bicycle ride away along the Wilmslow Road. In typical Turing fashion he soon formed friendships with not only the analyst but also his two young daughters. (He often spent Sundays with the Greenbaum family, and it was to Greenbaum's seven-year-old, Maria, that Turing gave the 'left-handed' tin of sweets mentioned earlier.) The TV dramatization takes as given the coroner's verdict of suicide, and towards the end of the screenplay the Turing character discusses suicide with the Greenbaum character. In Sammon and Sen's follow-up article 'Turing Committed Suicide: Case Closed' they portray Greenbaum as feeling that 'suicide was a likely scenario' and believing that as Turing's therapist he has 'insight into Alan's death as suicide rather than accident'.[56] These are not Greenbaum's own statements. The year after Turing's death, the real Greenbaum wrote in a letter to Sara: 'There is not the slightest doubt to me that

Alan died by an accident.'[57] Other claimed evidence for suicide that Sammon and Sen bring forward is weak. They describe the fact that Turing prepared a will approximately four months before his death as 'evidence of pre-meditation'.[58] Yet for a person to make a will at the age of 41 is not an unusual event. In any case, Turing's will seems poles apart from the last instructions of a man expecting soon to die. He included a small bequest to his housekeeper Mrs Clayton, together with an additional annual bonus 'for each completed year in which she shall be in my employ from and after the thirty-first day of December One thousand nine hundred and fifty three'.[59] Never a man to waste words, Turing is unlikely to have included this formula in his will unless he was actually envisaging Mrs Clayton's bonuses accruing during her future years of service to him.

The third possibility, that Turing was murdered, might seem far-fetched, yet stranger things have been done in the national interest. There was a Cold War on. Could there have been an 'operation ruthless' against Alan Turing himself? He had been a near-omniscient overlord of the Allied crypto-world, and the knowledge that he possessed had a long shelf life. It seems that he remained involved to some extent in sensitive British government projects while at Manchester. When the Manchester Ferranti computer was being designed, Newman and Turing instructed the engineers to include special facilities that, Kilburn later surmised, must have been intended for cryptological purposes.[60] In December 1952, Turing wrote a program for the Manchester computer whose function could well have been to produce 'one-time pad'—as cryptographers call key tape that is used once only.[61] Initially, the government asked Manchester for approximately one thousand feet of teleprinter tape punched with a million random numbers. The code-breaking successes at Bletchley Park had—not unnaturally—left the Allies distrustful of key-generating cipher machines like Tunny, and the post-war years saw a shift to the more secure method of one-time pad. One-time teleprinter tape containing random numbers in effect replaced the Tunny's twelve key-generating wheels. A significant problem with one-time paper tape, however, was that gigantic quantities of it were needed to encrypt a nation's voluminous day-to-day secret traffic (even the traffic of a diplomatic or commercial nature, never mind military traffic). GCHQ's Colossi were soon being used in the production of one-time teleprinter tape.[62] Turing's Manchester system could churn out tape at a rate of 40,000 random numbers per hour.

The Manchester computer was, moreover, used for atomic weapons calculations. Turing was consulted at the outset, when the authorities approached the university in 1950 about 'a series of very lengthy calculations'.[63] The government's atomic scientists urgently required the results of two hundred complex calculations, each one of which would take about three weeks if done by hand.[64] The authorities were in a fix, and explained candidly to the Manchester computer wizards that 'we so badly need this help'.[65] From that urgent first contact a permanent relationship quickly developed. In October 1953, the British Atomic Weapons Research Establishment signed a formal agreement to purchase large blocks of time on the Manchester computer for its own top-secret work.[66] It was also in 1953 that American scientists Ethel and Julius Rosenberg were convicted of passing atomic weapons secrets to the Russians. The Rosenbergs were executed about a year before Turing's death. On both sides of the Atlantic anxiety about security had reached white heat.

Some may have considered that Turing knew much too much about much too much. In 1950, Senator Joseph McCarthy had initiated America's hysterical 'McCarthy era', and by the end of 1953 McCarthyism was in full spate. McCarthy declared that homosexuals who were privy to national secrets threatened America's security.[67] Did the secret services carry out covert assassinations in Britain? David Cornwell—better known as novelist John Le Carré—worked for both MI5 and MI6 during the 1950s and the 1960s, and told the *Sunday Telegraph* in 2010: 'We did a lot of direct action. Assassinations, at arm's length.'[68] 'We did some very bad things,' he said. There is a bare possibility that Turing was murdered, but in terms of actual evidence, all that can said be said for this hypothesis—and it isn't much—is that he was clearly on the security services' radar during the previous year's 'Kjell crisis' (described in Chapter 10). A puzzling loose thread is the curious matter of Turing's shoes—who put these outside the bedroom door?

The exact circumstances of Turing's death may always remain unclear. It should not be stated that he committed suicide—because we simply do not know. Perhaps we should just shrug our shoulders, agree that the jury is out, and focus on Turing's life and extraordinary work.

TO DIG DEEPER: A SIMPLE TURING MACHINE

A Turing machine consists of a scanner together with a limitless memory tape—see Fig. 36. The tape, which is divided into squares, moves back and forth past the scanner. Each square might be blank, or might contain a single symbol, for example '0' or '1'. The scanner can see only one square of tape—and so at most one symbol—at any given time.

The scanner contains mechanisms that enable it to *erase* the symbol on the scanned square, to *print* a symbol on the scanned square, and to *move* the tape to the left or right, one square at a time. The scanner can also alter the position of a dial (or some functionally equivalent device). This dial is located inside the scanner. Think of it as looking like an old-fashioned pocket watch, but with only one hand or pointer. This hand can point to any one of a number of different positions that are marked around the edge of the dial. The positions are named 'i', 'ii', 'iii', and so on (just like the hours marked around the face of a pocket watch). It's useful to have a term for the positions on the dial, and 'states' is now usual (Turing himself forbiddingly called them '*m*-configurations'). The function of this dial is to provide the scanner with a rudimentary short-term memory.

Turing introduced Turing machines in his 1936 paper 'On Computable Numbers'. The first example he gave there of a Turing machine is very easy to grasp. This machine starts work with a blank tape, and the scanner

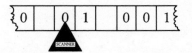

Figure 36. A Turing machine

merely prints alternating zeros and ones along the tape: 0 1 0 1 0 1…
Obviously this isn't the most useful computation in the world, but it
serves very well to illustrate how Turing machines operate. To make the
example a little more interesting, the scanner leaves a blank square in
between each zero and one (see Fig. 37). The scanner works to the right
from its starting point.

Turing made use of what he called an 'instruction table' to set out the
actions of the Turing machine (see Fig. 38). 'Instruction table' was his term
for what we now call a computer program. A Turing machine's instruction
table has four columns and these are filled with abbreviations. 'R' abbreviates the instruction 'Reposition the scanner one square to the right'. (This is
actually done by moving the *tape* one square to the *left*.) 'L' abbreviates
'Reposition the scanner one square to the left' (achieved by moving the tape
to the right). 'P0' abbreviates 'Print 0 on the scanned square', and similarly
'P1'. So the top line of the table in Fig. 38 reads: 'If you are in state i and the
square you are scanning is blank, then print o on the scanned square, move
the scanner one square to the right, and go into state ii.' State ii means 'I
have just printed 0,' and by flipping the dial to position ii, the scanner is able
to 'remember' what it has just done. State iv means 'I have just printed 1,'
state iii means 'I have just left a square blank after printing 0,' and state i
means 'I have just left a square blank after printing 1.'

The operations just mentioned—erase, print, change the state, and
move left or right—are the basic, or *atomic*, operations of every Turing
machine. As Turing showed, his machines are able to carry out highly
complex tasks by means of chaining together large numbers of these
simple basic actions. It is a remarkable fact that, despite the spartan
austerity of Turing machines, they can compute everything that any
computer on the market today is able to compute. Even more is true.

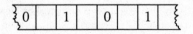

Figure 37. A Turing machine that is carrying out the instructions displayed in Fig. 38 will
print an alternating sequence of zeros and ones along its tape, leaving a single blank square
after each symbol that it prints

State	Scanned square	Operations	Next state
i	blank	P0, R	ii
ii	blank	R	iii
iii	blank	P1, R	iv
iv	blank	R	i

Figure 38. A simple program for a Turing machine. A machine acting in accordance with this table of instructions toils on endlessly, printing the desired sequence of numbers and leaving alternate squares blank

Because Turing machines are abstractions—notional machines—having access to an *unlimited* tape or workspace, they are capable of completing computations that no physical computer could in practice complete.

Turing machines are also capable of performing *unending* computations, as is illustrated by the machine that endlessly prints 0 1 0 1. Another example of a Turing machine whose computations never cease is one that calculates each successive decimal figure of an 'endless' real number such as π. An endless number has no final figure after its decimal point. The number π, which is defined as the ratio of the circumference of a circle to its diameter, is 3.14159265…Turing described π as a 'computable number', meaning simply that a Turing machine is able to spit out each of the unending decimal figures of π, one after another. Turing also showed that, in contrast to π, some endless numbers are *uncomputable*.

In his exposition in 'On Computable Numbers', Turing went on to show that the instruction table itself could be stored on the Turing machine's memory tape. The instruction table in Fig. 38 may be written down linearly as follows, using a semi-colon (;) to separate each instruction from its neighbours, and putting '—' in place of 'blank': i—P0Rii; ii—Riii;

iii—P1Riv; iv—Ri. The programmer can simply place this list of instructions onto the tape (with every symbol occupying a separate square of its own). In fact, Turing showed how to construct a code that allows every possible instruction to be represented by means of a pattern of zeros and ones; so ultimately these are the only symbols that the programmer needs to write on the tape.

Turing's next step was to introduce his *universal* machine. The universal Turing machine has a special instruction table that the engineers 'hard-wire' into its scanner and which is never changed. This instruction table—Turing displayed it, in all its intricate detail, in 'On Computable Numbers'—enables the universal machine to read and obey *any* list of Turing-machine instructions that the programmer stores on the memory tape. It was a simple yet profound idea, and the first, fundamental step towards the modern computer.

NOTES

CHAPTER 1: CLICK, TAP, OR TOUCH TO OPEN

1. Turing's mother Sara provides an intimate and often amusing picture of him in her biography *Alan M. Turing* (Cambridge: Heffer, 1959).
2. Donald Michie in conversation with the author, October 1995.
3. Michie in conversation with the author, October 1995.
4. Robin Gandy, typescript of an unpublished obituary notice for Turing (in the Turing Papers, King's College Library, catalogue reference A 6); Newman, L. Foreword to Sara's *Alan M. Turing*, p. ix.
5. Sara Turing, *Alan M. Turing*, pp. 56, 58.
6. J. H. Wilkinson in interview with Christopher Evans in 1976 ('The Pioneers of Computing: An Oral History of Computing', London: Science Museum, © Board of Trustees of the Science Museum). The archives of the London Science Museum supplied me with this interview on audiotape in 1995 and I transcribed it in 1997.
7. Sara Turing, *Alan M. Turing*, p. 9.
8. Sara Turing, *Alan M. Turing*, p. 17.
9. Sara Turing, *Alan M. Turing*, p. 19.
10. Turing's letters to his parents are in the Turing Papers, King's College Library (catalogue reference K 1). Sara Turing's dating of his letters is followed where dates are absent or incomplete.
11. Geoffrey O'Hanlon quoted in Sara Turing, *Alan M. Turing*, p. 39.
12. *The Shirburnian*, Summer Term 1954.
13. Letter from Turing to his parents, undated, 1926.
14. 'Canon Donald Eperson', *The Times*, 25 May 2001, p. 23.
15. Sara Turing, *Alan M. Turing*, p. 30.
16. Sara Turing, *Alan M. Turing*, p. 32.

17. Turing thanks his mother for this in his letter dated 20 November 1929.

18. Letter from Turing to Sara, 31 January 1932.

19. His fellowship at King's had been renewed in April; letter from Turing to Sara, 12 April 1938.

20. Hinsley, F. H. et al. *British Intelligence in the Second World War*, vol. 2 (London: Her Majesty's Stationery Office, 1981), p. 29.

21. See Turing's article 'Computing Machinery and Intelligence', ch. 11 of my *The Essential Turing* (Oxford: Oxford University Press, 2004).

22. *The Essential Turing*, p. 449.

CHAPTER 2: THE UNIVERSAL TURING MACHINE

1. The time and location of Newman's lectures were announced in the *Cambridge University Reporter*, 18 April 1935, p. 826. Wordsworth, 'The Prelude', in Knight, W. (ed.) *The Poetical Works of William Wordsworth* (Cirencester: Echo, 2006), vol. 3, bk 3, ln 57.

2. Yorick Smythies attended Newman's course of lectures in 1934 and took detailed notes, which survive in St John's College Library. For additional information see my article 'From the *Entscheidungsproblem* to the Personal Computer', in Baaz, M., Papadimitriou, C. H., Scott, D. S., Putnam, H., and Harper, C. L. (eds) *Kurt Gödel and the Foundations of Mathematics* (Cambridge: Cambridge University Press, 2011).

3. Feferman, S. 'Gödel's Life and Work', in Feferman, S. et al. (eds) *Kurt Gödel: Collected Works*, vol. 1 (Oxford: Oxford University Press, 1986).

4. Gödel, K, 'Uber formal unentscheidbare Sätze der Principia Mathematica und verwandter Systeme I.' [On formally undecidable propositions of Principia Mathematica and related systems I], *Monatshefte für Mathematik und Physik*, vol. 38 (1931), pp. 173–98; there is an English translation in Davis, M. (ed.) *The Undecidable: Basic Papers on Undecidable Propositions, Unsolvable Problems and Computable Functions* (New York: Raven, 1965). To be exact, in 1931 Gödel proved that the system of arithmetic set out by Bertrand Russell and Alfred Whitehead in their seminal work *Principia Mathematica* is, if consistent, incomplete in the sense that there are true statements of arithmetic that are not provable in the system. Using Turing's discoveries, Gödel was later able to generalize this result considerably. The details are explained in my *The Essential Turing*, pp. 47–8.

5. Nowadays though this escape route has its advocates: see Mortensen, C. *Inconsistent Mathematics* (Dordrecht: Kluwer, 1995); Priest, G. *In Contradiction: A Study*

of the Transconsistent (Oxford: Oxford University Press, 2006); Sylvan, R., Copeland, B. J. 'Computability is Logic-Relative', in Priest, G., Hyde, D. (eds) *Sociative Logics and their Applications* (London: Ashgate, 2000).

6. Hilbert, D. 'Mathematical Problems: Lecture Delivered before the International Congress of Mathematicians at Paris in 1900', *Bulletin of the American Mathematical Society*, vol. 8 (1902), pp. 437–79 (p. 445).

7. Max Newman in interview with Christopher Evans ('The Pioneers of Computing: An Oral History of Computing', London: Science Museum, © Board of Trustees of the Science Museum). The archives of the London Science Museum supplied me with this interview on audiotape in 1995 and I transcribed it in 1997.

8. Letter from R. B. Braithwaite to Margaret Boden, 21 October 1982. I am grateful to Boden for supplying me with a copy of this letter.

9. Newman, M. H. A. 'Dr Alan Turing, An Appreciation', *Manchester Guardian*, 11 June 1954.

10. Gödel quoted in Wang, H. *From Mathematics to Philosophy* (New York: Humanities Press, 1974), p. 85. For Gödel's assessment of the mathematical significance of Turing's results see my *The Essential Turing*, pp. 45, 48.

11. See Gödel's 'Postscriptum', in Davis, *The Undecidable*. (The Postscriptum, dated 1964, is to Gödel's 1934 paper 'On Undecidable Propositions of Formal Mathematical Systems'.)

12. Letter from Turing to Sara, 4 May 1936.

13. Newman, M. H. A. 'Alan Mathison Turing, 1912–1954', *Biographical Memoirs of Fellows of the Royal Society*, vol. 1 (1955), pp. 253–63 (p. 256).

14. The famous Turing-machine *halting problem* was not among these, despite countless statements in the literature to the effect that Turing introduced the halting problem in 'On Computable Numbers'. The halting problem is due to Martin Davis, who stated it in his *Computability and Unsolvability* (New York: McGraw-Hill, 1958), p. 70. Davis thinks it likely that he first used the term 'halting problem' in a series of lectures he gave at the Control Systems Laboratory at the University of Illinois in 1952 (letter from Davis to the author, 12 December 2001).

15. *The Essential Turing*, pp. 39, 73–4.

16. Turing's Thesis is sometimes also called the Church–Turing Thesis. For additional information, see my 'Computable Numbers: A Guide' in *The Essential Turing*, and my 'The Church–Turing Thesis' in *The Stanford Encyclopaedia of Philosophy* at plato.stanford.edu/entries/church-turing/.

17. That is to say, are incapable of being solved by any systematic procedure of the type that Turing et al. were considering. There is a broader concept of systematic procedure for which Turing's Thesis does not hold, but this is of no relevance to Turing's historic attack on Hilbert. See my 'Narrow Versus Wide Mechanism' *Journal of Philosophy*, vol. 97 (2000), pp. 5–32 (reprinted in Scheutz, M. (ed.) *Computationalism: New Directions*, Cambridge, Mass.: MIT Press, 2002), and my and Diane Proudfoot's 'Artificial Intelligence', in Margolis, E., Samuels, R., Stich, S. (eds) *Oxford Handbook of Philosophy and Cognitive Science* (Oxford: Oxford University Press, 2011).

18. Newman, 'Alan Mathison Turing, 1912–1954', p. 256.

19. Hilbert, D. 'Über das Unendliche' [On the Infinite], *Mathematische Annalen*, vol. 95 (1926), pp. 161–90 (p. 180).

20. Newman in interview with Evans; and Newman, M. H. A. 'Dr. A. M. Turing', *The Times*, 16 June 1954, p. 10.

21. See Copeland et al. *Colossus: The Secrets of Bletchley Park's Codebreaking Computers* (Oxford: Oxford University Press, 2nd edn, 2010), pp. 102ff.

22. For information on the Analytical Engine, see Lovelace, A. A., Menabrea, L. F. (1843) 'Sketch of the Analytical Engine Invented by Charles Babbage, Esq.', in Bowden, B. V. (ed.) *Faster than Thought* (London: Pitman, 1953); Bromley, A. 'Charles Babbage's Analytical Engine, 1838', *Annals of the History of Computing*, vol. 4 (1982), pp. 196–217; Swade, D. *The Difference Engine: Charles Babbage and the Quest to Build the First Computer* (New York: Viking, 2001).

23. Bush, V. 'The Differential Analyser: A New Machine for Solving Differential Equations', *Journal of the Franklin Institute*, vol. 212 (1931), pp. 447–88; Bush, V. 'Instrumental Analysis', *Bulletin of the American Mathematical Society*, vol. 42 (1936), pp. 649–69.

24. Robin Gandy in conversation with the author, October 1995.

25. Gödel's lecture notes have been published by Cassou-Nogues, P. 'Gödel's Introduction to Logic in 1939', *History and Philosophy of Logic*, vol. 30 (2009), pp. 69–90.

26. The formulae must lie beyond beyond what Gödel called the calculus of monadic predicates, which can be proved to be decidable by the universal Turing machine. A monadic predicate is one like 'is an integer', as opposed to a *dyadic* (or two-place) predicate such as 'equals' or 'is greater than'. Turing showed that the general calculus of predicates, which allows dyadic as well as monadic predicates, is not decidable. Another caveat: the word

'finite' is important. If the computing machine is allowed to carry out an *infinite* number of steps then Turing's result no longer holds—see my and Oron Shagrir's recent paper 'Do Accelerating Turing Machines Compute the Uncomputable?' *Minds and Machines*, vol. 21 (2011), pp. 221–39.

27. See *The Essential Turing*, pp. 46–7.

28. Newman, 'Alan Mathison Turing, 1912–1954', p. 258. Letter from Turing to Sara, 29 May 1936.

29. Church in interview with William Aspray, 17 May 1984 (transcript no. 5 in the series 'The Princeton Mathematics Community in the 1930s', Princeton University).

30. Newman, 'Alan Mathison Turing, 1912–1954', p. 258.

31. Newman, W. 'Max Newman—Mathematician, Codebreaker, and Computer Pioneer', in Copeland et al. *Colossus*, p. 178.

32. Turing, A. M. 'On Computable Numbers, with an Application to the Entscheidungsproblem', *Proceedings of the London Mathematical Society*, vol. 42 (1936–1937), pp. 230–65. The publication date of 'On Computable Numbers' is often cited incorrectly as 1937. In fact the article was published in two parts both of which appeared in 1936 (the first on 30 November 1936 and the second on 23 December 1936).

33. Letter from Church to Stephen Kleene, 29 November 1935 (in Davis, M. 'Why Gödel Didn't Have Church's Thesis', *Information and Control*, vol. 54 (1982), pp. 3–24 (p. 8)).

34. Gödel, K. 'Some Basic Theorems on the Foundations of Mathematics and their Implications' (in Feferman, S. et al. (eds) *Kurt Gödel: Collected Works*, vol. 3, Oxford: Oxford University Press, 1995), pp. 304–5; and 'Undecidable Diophantine Propositions' (in *Collected Works*, vol. 3), p. 168.

35. See *The Essential Turing*, ch. 2.

36. Donald Davies in interview with Christopher Evans in 1975 ('The Pioneers of Computing: An Oral History of Computing', London: Science Museum, © Board of Trustees of the Science Museum). The archives of the London Science Museum supplied me with this interview on audiotape in 1995 and I transcribed it in 1997.

37. Sara Turing, *Alan M. Turing*, p. 58.

38. Letters from Turing to Sara, 24 May 1935 and 29 May 1936.

39. Church, A. Review of 'On Computable Numbers, with an Application to the Entscheidungsproblem', *Journal of Symbolic Logic*, vol. 2 (1937), pp. 42–3.

CHAPTER 3: AMERICA, MATHEMATICS, HITLER

1. Sara Turing, *Alan M. Turing*, p. 51.
2. There are some images of the *Berengaria* at www.norwayheritage.com/p_ship.asp?sh=beren.
3. Letter from Turing to Sara, 28 September 1936.
4. Letter from Turing to Sara, 6 October 1936.
5. Allen, J. T. 'How a Different America Responded to the Great Depression' (Pew Research Center, 2010), pewresearch.org/pubs/1810/public-opinion-great-depression-compared-with-now.
6. Letter from Turing to Sara, 3 November 1936.
7. Newman, L. Foreword to Sara's *Alan M. Turing*, p. ix.
8. Letter from Turing to Sara, 6 October 1936.
9. Letter from Turing to Sara, 14 October 1936.
10. Sara Turing, *Alan M. Turing*, p. 64.
11. Letter from Lyn Newman to her parents, 9 November 1937 (Papers of Max and Lyn Newman, St. John's College Library, Cambridge); quoted by William Newman in 'Max Newman—Mathematician, Codebreaker, and Computer Pioneer', p. 179.
12. Newman, 'Max Newman—Mathematician, Codebreaker, and Computer Pioneer', p. 179.
13. *Movietone News*.
14. *Movietone News*.
15. Letter from Turing to Sara, 3 December 1936.
16. Letter from Turing to Sara, 11 December 1936.
17. Letter from Turing to Sara, 1 January 1937.
18. *The Essential Turing*, p. 192.
19. Hilbert, D. 'Probleme der Grundlegung der Mathematik' [Problems Concerning the Foundation of Mathematics], *Mathematische Annalen*, vol. 102 (1930), pp. 1–9 (p. 9). Translation by Elisabeth Norcliffe.
20. Ibid.
21. Intuition cannot be eliminated if what Gödel called Hilbert's 'rationalistic attitude' is taken for granted. For further information on this and related issues see my and Oron Shagrir's 'Turing versus Gödel on Computability and the Mind', in Copeland, B. J., Posy, C., Shagrir, O. (eds) *Computability: Gödel, Turing, Church and Beyond* (Cambridge: MIT Press, 2013).
22. Hilbert, 'Über das Unendliche', p. 180.

23. *The Essential Turing*, pp. 146, 193.

24. Letter from Turing to Sara, 19 October 1937.

25. For more detail see my 'Narrow Versus Wide Mechanism', *Journal of Philosophy*, vol. 97 (2000), pp. 5–32; reprinted in Scheutz, M. (ed.) *Computationalism: New Directions* (Cambridge: MIT Press, 2002).

26. 'Systems of Logic Based on Ordinals' was published in the *Proceedings of the london Mathematical Society* in 1939 (Series 2, vol. 45, pp. 161–228), and is ch. 3 of *The Essential Turing*. Even Robin Gandy called it 'a stinker to read', in a letter to Max Newman (no date, Turing Papers, catalogue reference A 8).

27. Soare, R. I. 'Turing–Post Relativized Computability and Interactive Computing', in Copeland, Posy and Shagrir, *Computability: Turing, Gödel, Church and Beyond*. See also my and Richard Sylvan's article 'Beyond the Universal Turing Machine', *Australasian Journal of Philosophy*, vol. 77 (1999), pp. 46–66.

28. On this, see my article 'Turing's O-Machines, Penrose, Searle, and the Brain', *Analysis*, vol. 58 (1998), pp. 128–38, and my and Diane Proudfoot's 'Artificial Intelligence', in Margolis, Samuels, Stich, *Oxford Handbook of Philosophy and Cognitive Science*.

29. Letter from Turing to Sara, 7 May 1938.

30. Letter from Turing to Sara, 18 April 1937.

31. Letter from Turing to Sara, 12 April 1938.

32. Letter from Turing to Sara, 7 May 1938.

33. Macrae, N. *John von Neumann* (American Mathematical Society, 2008), p. 138.

34. Macrae, *John von Neumann*, p. 371.

35. Chamberlain quoted in Faber, D. *Munich, 1938: Appeasement and World War II* (New York: Simon and Schuster, 2008), p. 356.

36. Windsor writing in the New York *Daily News*, 13 December 1966; quoted in Higham, C. *Mrs Simpson: Secret Lives of the Duchess of Windsor* (London: Pan, 2005), p. 260.

37. *Daily Express*, 30 September 1938.

38. Chamberlain quoted in Faber, *Munich, 1938*, p. 7.

39. Letter from Turing to Sara, 23 January 1939.

40. Wittgenstein, L. *Tractatus Logico-Philosophicus* (London: Kegan Paul, 1922), 5.6. Wittgenstein, L. *Philosophical Investigations* (Oxford: Blackwell, 1958), II xi.

41. All quotations from Wittgenstein's lectures on the foundations of mathematics are from Diamond, C. *Wittgenstein's Lectures on the Foundations of Mathematics Cambridge 1939* (Chicago: University of Chicago Press, 1989).

42. Wittgenstein, *Philosophical Investigations*, §309. (Anscombe's translation has 'shew' instead of 'show'.)

43. Letter from Turing to Sara, 14 October 1936. Sara has written 'probably' against the date.

44. Turing discusses book group ciphers in Turing, A. M., Bayley, D. 'Speech Secrecy System "Delilah", Technical Description', circa March 1945 (National Archives, Kew, London, document reference HW25/36). Turing explained: 'Each word or phrase is looked up in a kind of dictionary or "book"' (p. 1).

45. In Tunny, the compounding was done by adding together the message letters and letters from the key. Addition took the form of the operation known in logic as XOR (exclusive disjunction). In Turing's system, on the other hand, the compounding was done by binary multiplication (logical conjunction plus shift) rather than by addition. A short note by Turing's Princeton colleague Malcolm MacPhail gives an incomplete sketch of Turing's system (the note is printed in Hodges, A. *Alan Turing: The Enigma* (London: Vintage, 1992), p. 138).

46. Letter from Mavis Batey to the author, 12 May 2012.

47. Porgy now lives at Bletchley Park National Museum.

48. *Movietone News*.

CHAPTER 4: ENIGMA CALLING

1. Mahon, A. P. 'History of Hut 8 to December 1941', in my *The Essential Turing* (see p. 275).

2. Hinsley, F. H. 'The Counterfactual History of No Ultra', *Cryptologia*, vol. 20 (1996), pp. 308–24 (see p. 317). Hinsley, F. H., Stripp, A. (eds) *Codebreakers: The Inside Story of Bletchley Park* (Oxford: Oxford University Press, 1994).

3. Hinsley and Stripp, *Codebreakers*, p. 12.

4. Foss, H. R. 'Reminiscences on the Enigma', 30 September 1949 (National Archives, document reference HW25/10). An edited version of Foss's 'Reminiscences' is in Erskine, R., Smith, M. (eds) *The Bletchley Park Codebreakers* (London: Biteback, 2011).

5. Hinsley, F. H. et al. *British Intelligence in the Second World War*, vol. 3, part 2 (London: Her Majesty's Stationery Office, 1988), p. 946.

6. Rejewski, M. 'Remarks on Appendix 1 to British Intelligence in the Second World War by F. H. Hinsley', *Cryptologia*, vol. 6 (1982), pp. 75–83 (see p. 76).

7. Information from Frode Weierud.

8. A detailed description of the Enigma machine can be found in *The Essential Turing*, on pp. 220ff (by Copeland) and 268ff (by Patrick Mahon). Turing's own very illuminating account of the workings of the machine is contained in the first chapter of his wartime treatise on the Enigma, known simply as 'Prof's Book' at Bletchley Park—'Prof' being his nickname there ('Mathematical theory of ENIGMA machine by A M Turing', National Archives, document reference HW 25/3). 'Prof's Book' is available on this book's companion website *The Turing Archive for the History of Computing*, at www.AlanTuring.net/profs_book.

9. The fourth wheel differed from the other three in that once the operator had set it to one of its twenty-six positions, it remained stationary during the encryption of the message. Some German surface vessels were equipped with the four-wheel machine as early as 1941. For more information, see Erskine, R. 'Breaking German Naval Enigma On Both Sides of the Atlantic', in Erskine and Smith, *The Bletchley Park Codebreakers*.

10. Unless the message had already been encrypted and the Enigma machine was being used to encrypt it for a second time—in which case it was not plain German but ciphertext that was typed at the keyboard.

11. Rejewski's story of the Polish work on Enigma can be read in his three articles 'How Polish Mathematicians Deciphered the Enigma' (translated by J. Stepenske, in *Annals of the History of Computing*, vol. 3 (1981), pp. 213–34), 'The Mathematical Solution of the Enigma Cipher', and 'Summary of our methods for reconstructing Enigma and reconstructing daily keys, and of German efforts to frustrate those methods' (both in Kozaczuk, W. *Enigma: How the German Machine Cipher Was Broken, and How It Was Read by the Allies in World War Two*, London: Arms and Armour Press, 1984, translated by C. Kasparek). Kozaczuk's book also contains the interesting 'A Conversation with Marian Rejewski'.

12. Rejewski, 'How Polish Mathematicians Deciphered the Enigma', p. 221.

13. Palliole, P. *Notre Espion Chez Hitler* (Paris: Nouveau Monde, 2011), pp. 253–62.

14. There is a short biography of Schmidt, based on interviews with Palliole (wartime head of French counter-intelligence) and with Schmidt's daughter, Gisela, in Sebag-Montefiore, H. *Enigma: The Battle for the Code* (London: Weidenfeld and Nicolson, 2000).

15. One person at Bletchley Park, whose name survives only as 'Mrs B. B.', did suggest the correct solution—but sadly no one took any notice of her. See Erskine and Smith, *The Bletchley Park Codebreakers*, p. 45.

16. Denniston, A. G. 'How News was brought from Warsaw at the end of July 1939', May 1948 (National Archives, document reference HW 25/12), p. 4. (Published with an editorial introduction and notes in Erskine, R. 'The Poles Reveal Their Secrets: Alastair Denniston's Account of the July 1939 Meeting at Pyry', *Cryptologia*, vol. 30 (2006), pp. 294–305.)

17. Rejewski, 'How Polish Mathematicians Deciphered the Enigma', p. 227.

18. Twinn, P. 'The *Abwehr* Enigma', in Hinsley and Stripp, *Codebreakers*, pp. 126–7; Denniston, 'How News was brought from Warsaw at the end of July 1939', pp. 4–5; Knox, A. D. 'Warsaw', 4 August 1939 (National Archives, document reference HW 25/12).

19. Mayer, A. S. 'The Breaking up [sic] of the German Cipher Machine "Enigma" by the Cryptological Section in the 2nd Department of the General Staff of the Polish Armed Forces', 31 May 1974, p. 2 (National Archives, document reference HW 25/16). Mayer was a Polish wartime intelligence chief. (I am grateful to Ralph Erskine for this reference.) See also Hinsley, F. H. et al. *British Intelligence in the Second World War*, vol. 1 (London: Her Majesty's Stationery Office, 1979), p. 490.

20. Letters from Peter Twinn to the author, 28 January 2001, 21 February 2001.

21. The simile is Frank Birch's (quoted in Batey, M. 'Breaking Italian Naval Enigma', in Erskine and Smith, *The Bletchley Park Codebreakers*, p. 82).

22. Letter from Twinn to the author, 28 January 2001.

23. Letter from Twinn to Christopher Andrew, 29 May 1981 (quoted on p. 453 of Andrew, C. W. *Secret Service: The Making of the British Intelligence Community*, London: Guild, 1985).

24. Vincent, E. R., unpublished memoirs, Corpus Christi College Archives, Cambridge (quoted on p. 94 of Andrew, *Secret Service*).

25. Letter from Knox to Denniston, circa September 1939 (National Archives, document reference HW 14/1).

26. Letter from Denniston to T. J. Wilson, 3 September 1939 (National Archives, document reference FO 366/1059). Turing's name appeared on Denniston's 'emergency list' in March 1939 ('Staff and Establishment of G.C.C.S.', National Archives, document reference HW 3/82). See also Erskine, R. 'GC and CS Mobilizes "Men of the Professor Type"', *Cryptologia*, vol. 10 (1986), pp. 50–9.

27. de Grey, N. '1939–1940 Sitz and Blitz', no date, part of 'De Grey's History of Air Sigint' (National Archives, document reference HW3/95), p. 3.

28. Letter from Denniston to Wilson, 7 September 1939 (National Archives, document reference FO 366/1059).

29. Churchill, W. L. S. *Blood, Toil, Tears and Sweat: The Great Speeches*, ed. D. Cannadine (London: Penguin, 2007), p. 149.

30. Milner-Barry, S. 'Hut 6: Early Days', in Hinsley and Stripp, *Codebreakers*, p. 90.

31. Hilton, P. 'Living with Fish: Breaking Tunny in the Newmanry and the Testery', in Copeland, B. J. et al. *Colossus: The Secrets of Bletchley Park's Codebreaking Computers* (Oxford: Oxford University Press, 2006; new edition 2010), p. 196.

32. Caughey writing in my *Colossus*, p. 160.

33. Letter from Rachel Cross to the author, 20 November 2001.

34. Ireland writing in my *Colossus*, pp. 160–1.

35. de Grey, '1939–1940 Sitz and Blitz', pp. 14–15, 17; Hinsley, *British Intelligence in the Second World War*, vol. 3, part 2, p. 952.

36. de Grey, '1939–1940 Sitz and Blitz', p. 17.

37. de Grey, '1939–1940 Sitz and Blitz', p. 17; Hinsley, *British Intelligence in the Second World War*, vol. 3, part 2, p. 952; Batey, M. *Dilly: The Man Who Broke Enigmas* (London: Dialogue, 2009), p. 99.

38. Rejewski quoted in Kozaczuk, *Enigma*, p. 97.

39. Hilton, 'Living with Fish: Breaking Tunny in the Newmanry and the Testery', p. 198.

40. Turing quoted by Alexander, C. H. O'D 'Cryptographic History of Work on the German Naval Enigma', c. 1945 (National Archives, document reference HW 25/1), pp. 19–20. A digital facsimile of Alexander's typescript is in *The Turing Archive for the History of Computing* at www.AlanTuring.net/alexander_naval_enigma.

41. Roskill, S. W. *The War At Sea 1939–1945*, vol. 1 (London: HMSO, 1954), pp. 615–16.

42. 'Mathematical theory of ENIGMA machine by A M Turing', p. 136.

43. As a precaution, the indicator was transmitted a second time, at the end of the message, as well as at the beginning. The procedure as it was actually used also involved the inclusion of two additional 'dummy' letters in order to create an indicator of 8 letters rather than 6.

44. There is a description of the complete procedure by Mahon on p. 272 of *The Essential Turing*, and a more compressed but more accurate description by Turing on p. 281. See also Alexander, 'Cryptographic History of Work on the German Naval Enigma', p. 7.

45. 'Mathematical theory of ENIGMA machine by A M Turing', p. 139.
46. Alexander, 'Cryptographic History of Work on the German Naval Enigma', p. 23.
47. 'A Cryptographic Dictionary', GC & CS, 1944 (United States National Archives and Records Administration, Washington, D.C., document reference RG 457, Historic Cryptographic Collection, Box 1413, NR 4559). A digital facsimile is in *The Turing Archive for the History of Computing* at www.AlanTuring.net/crypt_dic_1944.

CHAPTER 5: TURING'S U-BOAT BATTLE

1. Mahon, 'History of Hut 8 to December 1941', p. 286.
2. Denniston, 'How News was brought from Warsaw at the end of July 1939', p. 3.
3. Mahon, 'History of Hut 8 to December 1941', p. 303.
4. Mahon, 'History of Hut 8 to December 1941', pp. 281, 285.
5. 'Mathematical theory of ENIGMA machine by A M Turing', p. 137.
6. In 1937, numbers were not typed out as words. An earlier method was used, with the letter keys along the top row of the keyboard doubling as number keys. Q did duty for 1, W for 2, E for 3, and so on. P (the first key on the bottom row of the German keyboard) was used for 0. The resulting sequence of letters was bookended by a pair of Ys to show that it was to be read as a number. So YWEEPY represents 2330. See *The Essential Turing*, pp. 278–9.
7. 'A Cryptographic Dictionary' (GC & CS), p. 90.
8. Mahon, 'History of Hut 8 to December 1941', pp. 294, 297.
9. 'HMS "Griffin" Report of Proceedings 26 to 28 April including capture of German trawler "POLARES"', 13 May 1940 (National Archives, document reference ADM 199/476). 'Interrogation of Crew of German Armed Trawler SCHIFF 26', Naval Intelligence Division, June 1940 (National Archives, document reference ADM 186/805).
10. 'Statement by Mr Foord of conversation with Lieutenant Engelien', enclosure to 'HMS "Griffin" Report of Proceedings 26 to 28 April'.
11. Reitz's diary quoted in 'Interrogation of Crew of German Armed Trawler SCHIFF 26', p. 5.
12. Reitz's diary quoted in 'Interrogation of Crew of German Armed Trawler SCHIFF 26', p. 8.
13. Reitz's diary quoted in 'Interrogation of Crew of German Armed Trawler SCHIFF 26', p. 8.

14. Alexander, 'Cryptographic History of Work on the German Naval Enigma', p. 24; 'Mathematical theory of ENIGMA machine by A M Turing', p. 139. The papers from *Schiff 26* told Turing that the bigram table 'gives bigramme for bigramme', whereas he previously thought that the table gave a bigram equivalent for each individual letter ('Mathematical theory of ENIGMA machine by A M Turing', pp. 136, 139).

15. Alexander, 'Cryptographic History of Work on the German Naval Enigma', p. 24. See also Erskine, R. 'The First Naval Enigma Decrypts of World War II' *Cryptologia*, vol. 21 (1997), pp. 42–6, and Erskine, R. 'Breaking German Naval Enigma On Both Sides of the Atlantic', in Erskine and Smith, *The Bletchley Park Codebreakers*. Two book-length treatments of the battle for naval Enigma are Kahn, D. *Seizing the Enigma: The Race to Break the German U-Boat Codes, 1939–1943* (London: Arrow, 1996); and Sebag-Montefiore, *Enigma: The Battle for the Code*.

16. Erskine, 'The First Naval Enigma Decrypts of World War II', p. 43.

17. Murray, J. (née Clarke) 'Hut 8 and Naval Enigma, Part I', in Hinsley and Stripp, *Codebreakers*, p. 114.

18. Murray, 'Hut 8 and Naval Enigma, Part I', pp. 113–15.

19. Mahon, 'History of Hut 8 to December 1941', p. 287.

20. Sara Turing, 'Alan M. Turing', p. 68.

21. Birch's letter is quoted in Mahon, 'History of Hut 8 to December 1941', pp. 287–8.

22. Mahon, 'History of Hut 8 to December 1941', p. 288.

23. Morgan, C. 'N.I.D. (9) Wireless Intelligence' (National Archives, document reference ADM 223/463); pp. 38–9 contain Morgan's account of Operation Ruthless and include Fleming's memo to the Director of Naval Intelligence (12 September 1940).

24. Morgan, 'N.I.D. (9) Wireless Intelligence', p. 39.

25. Birch's letter is in Morgan, 'N.I.D. (9) Wireless Intelligence', p. 39.

26. *The Essential Turing*, pp. 235–7.

27. Denniston, 'How News was brought from Warsaw at the end of July 1939', p. 4.

28. The usefulness of the bomby had in fact steadily diminished up until this point. Major setbacks had come in December 1938, when the German operators were given two extra wheels to choose from, and in January 1939, when the number of letters that were scrambled by the plugboard was increased from five to eight. See *The Essential Turing*, p. 246.

29. 'Enigma—Position', Knox, A. D., Twinn, P. F. G., Welchman, W. G., Turing, A. M., 1 November 1939 (National Archives, document reference HW 14/2); 'Squadron-Leader Jones' Section', anon., GC & CS, circa 1946 (National Archives, document reference HW 3/164), p. 1.

30. 'Squadron-Leader Jones' Section', p. 1.

31. 'Meeting held on 6th July 1950 to discuss "Bombes"' (at GCHQ), Birch, De Grey, Alexander, Fletcher, Foss, Zambra (National Archives, document reference HW 25/21).

32. Mahon, 'History of Hut 8 to December 1941', p. 293.

33. Turing's procedure is described in all its gory detail in *The Essential Turing* on pp. 250–3 and (in Turing's own words) on pp. 315–19.

34. 1676 to be precise. 'Squadron-Leader Jones' Section', p. 14.

35. Baring, S. (neé Norton) *The Road to Station X* (York: Wilton, 2000), p. 86.

36. Sara Turing, 'Alan M. Turing', p. 70,

37. Good, I. J., Michie, D., Timms, G. 'General Report on Tunny, with Emphasis on Statistical Methods', 1945 (National Archives, document reference HW 25/4, HW 25/5, 2 vols), p. 278. A digital facsimile is in *The Turing Archive for the History of Computing* at www.AlanTuring.net/tunny_report.

38. 'General Report on Tunny, with Emphasis on Statistical Methods', p. 278.

39. 'Squadron-Leader Jones' Section', p. 4.

40. 'Operations of the 6312th Signal Security Detachment, ETOUSA', 1 October 1944 (United States National Archives and Records Administration, College Park, Maryland, document reference RG 457, Historic Cryptographic Collection, Box 970, NR 2943), p. 60. (I am grateful to Frode Weierud for supplying me with a copy of this document.)

41. Mahon, 'History of Hut 8 to December 1941', p. 291.

42. There is a description of the bomba on pp. 235–46 of *The Essential Turing*.

43. For more information about the bombe see *The Essential Turing*, pp. 246–57 and (in Turing's own words) pp. 313–35; also Carter, F. 'The Turing Bombe', *The Rutherford Journal for the History and Philosophy of Science and Technology*, vol. 3 (2010), www.rutherfordjournal.org/article030108.html.

44. Alexander, 'Cryptographic History of Work on the German Naval Enigma', p. 25.

45. Good, I. J. 'From Hut 8 to the Newmanry', in my *Colossus*, p. 205.

46. Mahon, 'History of Hut 8 to December 1941', p. 288.

47. Hinsley, *British Intelligence in the Second World War*, vol. 1, p. 180.

48. Batey, *Dilly*, pp. 102–3.

49. Hinsley, *British Intelligence in the Second World War*, vol. 1, p. 178.

50. Hinsley, *British Intelligence in the Second World War*, vol. 1, p. 183.

51. Churchill, *Blood, Toil, Tears and Sweat*, p. 165.

52. de Grey, '1939–1940 Sitz and Blitz', pp. 58–9; Hinsley, *British Intelligence in the Second World War*, vol. 1, pp. 186, 188, and appendix 7.

53. 'Squadron-Leader Jones' Section', p. 2; 'Hut 6 Bombe Register', GC & CS, 1940–1945 (National Archives, document reference HW25/19, HW25/20, 2 vols).

54. Welchman, G. *The Hut Six Story: Breaking the Enigma Codes* (Cleobury Mortimer: M&M Baldwin, 2000, 2nd edn), p. 81. Turing describes both simultaneous scanning and the diagonal board in *The Essential Turing*, pp. 319–31; see also pp. 254–5.

55. 'Squadron-Leader Jones' Section', p. 2.

56. de Grey, '1939–1940 Sitz and Blitz', p. 58.

57. Letter from Turing to Sara, undated.

58. de Grey, '1939–1940 Sitz and Blitz', pp. 81–2.

59. de Grey, '1939–1940 Sitz and Blitz', pp. 65, 70–6; Hinsley, *British Intelligence in the Second World War*, vol. 1, pp. 320, 326.

60. Churchill, *Blood, Toil, Tears and Sweat*, p. 188.

61. Letter from Mavis Batey to the author, 23 January 2012.

62. Batey, *Dilly*, p. xxii.

63. Batey (née Lever), 'Breaking Italian Naval Enigma'; Hinsley, *British Intelligence in the Second World War*, vol. 1, pp. 403–6.

64. Knox quoted by Ralph Erskine in Batey, *Dilly*, p. xv.

65. Churchill quoted in Batey, *Dilly*, p. 118.

66. Mahon, 'History of Hut 8 to December 1941', p. 290; Alexander, 'Cryptographic History of Work on the German Naval Enigma', p. 28.

67. Caslon, C. 'Operation "Claymore" – Report of Proceedings', 8 March 1941 (National Archives, document reference DEFE 2/142). 'Raid on Military and Economic Objectives in the Lofoten Islands', *The London Gazette*, supplement, 23 June 1948 (National Archives, document reference DEFE 2/142).

68. Alexander, 'Cryptographic History of Work on the German Naval Enigma', p. 27.

69. Alexander, 'Cryptographic History of Work on the German Naval Enigma', p. 22.

70. Mahon, 'History of Hut 8 to December 1941', p. 290; Alexander, 'Cryptographic History of Work on the German Naval Enigma', pp. 27–8.

71. Alexander, 'Cryptographic History of Work on the German Naval Enigma', p. 31.

72. Hinsley, quoted in Smith. M. *Station X: The Codebreakers of Bletchley Park* (London: Channel 4, 1998), p. 57.

73. Hinsley, *British Intelligence in the Second World War*, vol. 1, p. 337 and appendix 12; Hinsley, F. H. 'BP, Admiralty, and Naval Enigma', in Hinsley and Stripp, *Codebreakers*, p. 79.

74. Holland, L. 'Report on Operation E.B.', 10 May 1941 (National Archives, document reference ADM 199/447). 'Ship's Log for the Month of May 1941', HMS *Edinburgh* (National Archives, document reference ADM 53/114202).

75. Mahon, 'History of Hut 8 to December 1941', p. 291; Hinsley, 'BP, Admiralty, and Naval Enigma', p. 79.

76. Bain, D. K. 'U-boat Attacks on Convoy O.B. 318 on 7, 9 and 10 May 1941', 9 June 1941 (National Archives, document reference ADM 1/11133).

77. Balme interviewed on British Channel 4 TV, 1998.

78. Baker-Cresswell, A. J. 'Capture of U 110', 10 May 1941 (National Archives, document reference ADM 1/11133).

79. Baker-Cresswell, 'Capture of U 110'.

80. Balme, D. E. 'Boarding Primrose', 11 May 1941 (National Archives, document reference ADM 1/11133).

81. Balme interviewed on Channel 4 TV, 1998.

82. Erskine, R. 'Naval Enigma: A Missing Link', *International Journal of Intelligence and Counterintelligence*, vol. 3 (1989), pp. 493–508 (p. 497).

83. Mahon, 'History of Hut 8 to December 1941', p. 290.

84. Mahon, 'History of Hut 8 to December 1941', p. 281. Mahon describes Banburismus on pp. 281–5. See also Alexander, 'Cryptographic History of Work on the German Naval Enigma', ch. 9.

85. Turing, A. M. 'The Applications of Probability to Cryptography', no date (National Archives, document reference HW 25/37), p. 7.

86. Mahon, 'History of Hut 8 to December 1941', p. 281.

87. Good, 'From Hut 8 to the Newmanry', p. 207.

88. Michie, D. 'Codebreaking and Colossus', in my *Colossus*, pp. 239–40.

89. Letter from Turing to Max Newman, circa 1942 (in the Turing Papers, King's College Library, Cambridge, catalogue reference D 2).

90. Alexander, 'Cryptographic History of Work on the German Naval Enigma', p. 28.

91. Noskwith, R. 'Hut 8 from the Inside', in Erskine and Smith, *The Bletchley Park Codebreakers*, p. 186; Erskine, 'Naval Enigma: A Missing Link', p. 499.

92. Mahon, 'History of Hut 8 to December 1941', p. 290.

93. Hinsley, F. H. et al. *British Intelligence in the Second World War*, vol. 2 (London: Her Majesty's Stationery Office, 1981), pp. 168–71.

94. Churchill, W. L. S. *The Second World War*, vol. 2: *Their Finest Hour* (London: Cassell, 1949), p. 529.

95. Hinsley, *British Intelligence in the Second World War*, vol. 2, p. 171.

96. Diary of Sir Alexander Cadogan, Permanent Under-Secretary at the Foreign Office, 15 July 1941 (quoted in Andrew, C. W. *Codebreaking and Signals Intelligence*, London: Cass, 1986, p. 3).

97. Hinsley, *British Intelligence in the Second World War*, vol. 2, pp. 169–70, 172–5.

98. Hinsley, 'The Counterfactual History of No Ultra', p. 324.

99. Sara Turing, *Alan M. Turing*, p. 71.

100. Letter from Turing to Sara, 31 August 1941.

101. Letter from Turing to Sara, 31 August 1941.

102. Oscar Wilde 'The Ballad of Reading Gaol'. Joan Clarke, reported in Hodges, *Alan Turing: The Enigma*, p. 216.

103. Denniston, A. G. 'The Government Code and Cypher School Between the Wars', in Andrew, *Codebreaking and Signals Intelligence*, p. 50.

104. Clarke, W. F. 'The Years Between—1918–1939', *Cryptologia*, vol. 12 (1988), pp. 52–8 (p. 55). (I am grateful to Ralph Erskine for this reference.)

105. The complete letter is on pp. 338–40 of *The Essential Turing*.

106. Milner-Barry, P. S. '"Action This Day": The letter from Bletchley Park Cryptanalysts to the Prime Minister, 21 October 1941', *Intelligence and National Security*, vol. 1 (1986), pp. 272–3.

107. Minute from Churchill to Ismay, 22 October 1941 (National Archives, document reference HW 1/155). A facsimile of Churchill's minute appears on p. xiii of Erskine and Smith, *The Bletchley Park Codebreakers*.

CHAPTER 6: 1942

1. Churchill, *Blood, Toil, Tears and Sweat*, pp. 177–8.

2. Some were at the Letchworth factory awaiting installation. 'Meeting held on 6 July 1950 to discuss "Bombes": Mr Fletcher's Registers'.

3. Hinsley, *British Intelligence in the Second World War*, vol. 2, pp. 422–50.

4. Frick, S. 'Boris Hagelin and Crypto AG: Pioneers of Encryption', in de Leeuw, K., Bergstra, J. (eds) *The History of Information Security: A Comprehensive Handbook* (Amsterdam: Elsevier, 2007).

5. Simpson, E. 'Solving JN-25 at Bletchley Park: 1943–5', in Erskine and Smith, *The Bletchley Park Codebreakers*, p. 128.

6. Harry Fensom, writing in my *Colossus*, pp. 285–6.

7. Madsen, W. 'The Demise of Global Communications Security', www.scribd.com/doc/27362786/Exclusive-Report-The-Demise-of-Global-Communications-Security.

8. Hinsley, *British Intelligence in the Second World War*, vol. 2, p. 427.

9. Hinsley, *British Intelligence in the Second World War*, vol. 2, pp. 434, 441, 444, 446.

10. Quoted in Hinsley, *British Intelligence in the Second World War*, vol. 2, pp. 448–9.

11. Message T286/136; quoted in 'Hitler as Seen by Source', by FLL (probably F. L. Lucas), 24 May 1945 (National Archives, document reference HW13/58), p. 9. Brian Oakley first suggested that Lucas was the author of this document (Ettinger, J. 'Listening in to Hitler at Bletchley Park 1941–1945: Fish and Colossus', June 2009, p. 5).

12. Message T400/79 (National Archives, document reference DEFE 3/318). Thanks to William Newman for supplying me with a copy of this document.

13. Alexander, 'Cryptographic History of Work on the German Naval Enigma', p. 36.

14. Alexander, 'Cryptographic History of Work on the German Naval Enigma', p. 36.

15. Alexander, 'Cryptographic History of Work on the German Naval Enigma', p. 46. Erskine, R. 'Naval Enigma: The Breaking of Heimisch and Triton', *Intelligence and National Security*, vol. 3 (1988), pp. 162–83 (pp. 170–1). Erskine, R. 'Captured *Kriegsmarine* Enigma Documents at Bletchley Park', *Cryptologia*, vol. 32 (2008), pp. 199–219 (pp. 204–5).

16. Beesly, P. *Very Special Intelligence: The Story of the Admiralty's Operational Intelligence Centre 1939–1945* (London: Hamilton, 1977), p. 153.

17. Good, 'From Hut 8 to the Newmanry', in my *Colossus*, p. 205.

18. Michie, 'Codebreaking and Colossus', in *Colossus*, p. 235.

19. Michie, quoted in Sara Turing, *Alan M. Turing*, p. 70.

20. Sara Turing, *Alan M. Turing*, pp. 71–2.

21. Alexander, 'Cryptographic History of Work on the German Naval Enigma', p. 42. Don Horwood in conversation with the author, October 2001.

22. Roskill, S. W. *The War At Sea 1939–1945*, vol. 2 (London: HMSO, 1956), p. 378.

23. Sara Turing, *Alan M. Turing*, p. 71.

24. 'American Research and Development of Telephonic Scrambling Device and Research of Unscrambling Telephonic Devices', memo from E. G. Hastings

to Sir John Dill, 2 December 1942 (National Archives, document reference HW14/60).

25. Hastings' report of Marshall's decision in 'American Research and Development of Telephonic Scrambling Device and Research of Unscrambling Telephonic Devices'.

26. Letter from Acting Chief of Staff Joseph McNarney to Sir John Dill, 9 January 1943 (National Archives, document reference HW14/60).

27. Alexander Fowler's diary; letter from Evelyn Loveday to Sara Turing, 20 June 1960 (Turing Papers, King's College Library, catalogue reference A 20).

28. Chauncey, G. *Gay New York: Gender, Urban Culture, and the Making of the Gay Male World, 1890–1940* (New York: Basic Books, 1994).

29. Letter from Joe Eachus to the author, 18 November 2001.

30. Travis took over in February 1942 ('British 4-Wheel Bombes', GCHQ, circa 1950, National Archives, document reference HW25/21, p. 1).

31. There is a reconstruction of a vocoder speech encipherment system (SIGSALY) in the Washington National Cryptologic Museum.

32. Turing, A. M. 'Memorandum to OP-20-G on Naval Enigma', published in *The Essential Turing*, with an introduction by Ralph Erskine, Colin Burke and Philip Marks.

33. Turing, A. M. 'Visit to National Cash Register Corporation of Dayton, Ohio', circa December 1942 (National Archives and Records Administration, document reference RG 38, CNSG Library, 5750/441). A digital facsimile is in *The Turing Archive for the History of Computing* at www.AlanTuring.net/turing_ncr.

34. Good, 'From Hut 8 to the Newmanry', p. 212.

35. Robert Mumma in interview with Rik Nebeker in 1995 (IEEE History Center, New Brunswick, New Jersey, USA). I am grateful to Ralph Erskine for making me aware of this interview.

36. 'U.S.A. 4-Wheel Bombes', circa 1950, GCHQ (National Archives, document reference HW 25/21).

37. Mahon, A. P. 'The History of Hut Eight 1939–1945', GC & CS, June 1945 (National Archives and Records Administration, document reference RG 457, Historic Cryptographic Collection, Box 1413, NR 4559), pp. 88–92. A digital facsimile is in *The Turing Archive for the History of Computing* at www.AlanTuring.net/mahon_hut_8.

38. 'Meeting held on 6th July 1950 to discuss "Bombes"', p. 1.

39. Alexander, 'Cryptographic History of Work on the German Naval Enigma', p. 90.

40. Donovan, P. 'The Flaw in the JN-25 Series of Ciphers', *Cryptologia*, vol. 28 (2004), pp. 325–40. I am grateful to John Mack and Peter Donovan for information.
41. *General Report on Tunny*, p. 14. *General Report on Tunny* recorded that the first messages on the experimental link passed between Vienna and Athens (p. 297).
42. *General Report on Tunny*, p. 395.
43. *General Report on Tunny*, p. 5.
44. *General Report on Tunny*, p. 4.
45. Good, 'From Hut 8 to the Newmanry', p. 214.
46. Erskine, R., Freeman, P. 'Brigadier John Tiltman: One of Britain's Finest Cryptologists', *Cryptologia*, vol. 27 (2003), pp. 289–318.
47. Bauer, F. L. 'The Tiltman Break', in my *Colossus*, p. 372.
48. Handwritten translations by GC & CS of German pre-war Enigma manuals are in the National Archives (document reference HW 25/9).
49. Tutte, W. T. 'My Work at Bletchley Park', in my *Colossus*, p. 356.
50. 'Professor Bill Tutte', *Daily Telegraph*, 9 May 2002.
51. Tutte, 'My Work at Bletchley Park', p. 360.
52. Delta-ing and Turingery are described in detail in my 'Machine Against Machine' and 'Turingery', in *Colossus*.
53. See further my *Colossus*, pp. 3–6.
54. Hinsley, *British Intelligence in the Second World War*, vol. 2, pp. 625–7.
55. Tutte's method is described in ch. 5 and app. 4 of my *Colossus*.
56. Newman in interview with Christopher Evans.

CHAPTER 7: COLOSSUS, DELILAH, VICTORY

1. I am grateful to Brian Oakley for information.
2. Flowers in interview with Christopher Evans in 1977 ('The Pioneers of Computing: An Oral History of Computing', London: Science Museum, © Board of Trustees of the Science Museum); the archives of the London Science Museum supplied me with this interview on audiotape in 1995 and I transcribed it in 1997.
3. *Post Office Magazine*, July 1943. Ken Myers in conversation with the author, July 2001. Introductory remarks by E. W. Ayers to Flowers's Martlesham Heath Centre Inaugural Lecture, Institution of Post Office Electrical Engineers, 24 March 1977.
4. Don Horwood in conversation with the author, October 2001.
5. Flowers, T. H. 'Colossus—Origin and Principles', typescript, no date, p. 3.

6. Letter from Newman to Edward Travis, 12 March 1943 (National Archives, document reference HW14/70).

7. Much of the material in this chapter derives from my numerous conversations with Flowers during the period 1996–1998.

8. Du Boisson writing in my *Colossus*, p. 162.

9. Fensom, H. 'How Colossus was Built and Operated—One of Its Engineers Reveals Its Secrets', in my *Colossus*, p. 298.

10. *General Report on Tunny*, p. 394; conversations with Michie and Good.

11. Flowers, 'Colossus – Origin and Principles', p. 3.

12. Flowers in interview with Evans.

13. Flowers, T. H. 'D-Day at Bletchley Park', in my *Colossus*, p. 82.

14. Myers writing in my *Colossus*, p. 170. Horwood, D. C. 'A Technical Description of Colossus 1', August 1973 (National Archives, document reference HW25/24), p. 41.

15. See also Good, I. J. 'From Hut 8 to the Newmanry', in *Colossus*, p. 221.

16. Wells, B. 'The PC-User's Guide to Colossus', in *Colossus*, p. 127.

17. Horwood, 'A Technical Description of Colossus 1'.

18. Du Boisson writing in *Colossus*, p. 163.

19. Fensom and Myers in *Colossus*, p. 166.

20. Caughey, C. M. *World Wanderer* (Auckland, 1996), p. 134.

21. Caughey writing in *Colossus*, p. 166.

22. *General Report on Tunny*, pp. 35, 394.

23. Lee, J. A. N. *Computer Pioneers* (Los Alamitos: IEEE Computer Society Press, 1995), p. 306 (see also pp. 492, 671); and see further Lee, J. A. N., Holtzman, G. '50 Years After Breaking the Codes', *Annals of the History of Computing*, vol. 17 (1999), pp. 32–43 (p. 33).

24. Golden, F. 'Who Built the First Computer?', *Time*, March 29, 1999, no. 13, p. 82.

25. *General Report on Tunny*, p. 35.

26. Letter from Michie to the author, 28 November 2001.

27. See my article 'Turingery', in *Colossus*.

28. Michie, D. 'Colossus and the Breaking of the Wartime "Fish" Codes', *Cryptologia*, vol. 26 (2001), pp. 17–58 (p. 27).

29. Michie, D. 'Colossus and the Breaking of Fish', typescript, 2002, p. 14.

30. Turing, A. M. 'The Applications of Probability to Cryptography', no date (National Archives, document reference HW25/37), p. 5. For more information

about Bayes' theorem at Bletchley Park, see Simpson, E. 'Bayes at Bletchley Park', *Significance*, vol. 7 (2010), pp. 76–80; and Simpson, 'Solving JN–25 at Bletchley Park, 1943–5'.

31. Michie, D. 'Codebreaking and Colossus', in my *Colossus*, p. 232.

32. Hilton, 'Living with Fish: Breaking Tunny in the Newmanry and the Testery', p. 195.

33. Don Bayley in conversation with the author, December 1997.

34. Don Bayley in conversation with the author, December 1997. Donald Michie in conversation with the author, February 1998.

35. Don Bayley in conversation with the author, December 1997.

36. Flowers in interview with Evans.

37. The blueprints are in the National Archives (document reference HW25/36).

38. Turing, A. M., Bayley, D. 'Speech Secrecy System "Delilah", Technical Description', circa March 1945 (National Archives, document reference HW25/36), pp. 3–4.

39. Turing and Bayley, 'Speech Secrecy System "Delilah", Technical Description', p. 8.

40. Sara Turing, *Alan M. Turing*, p. 74.

41. Quoted in *Alan M. Turing*, p. 75.

42. Don Bayley in conversation with the author, December 1997.

43. Gandy quoted by Sara Turing in *Alan M. Turing*, p. 119.

44. Letter from Don Bayley to the author, 1 November 1997.

45. Quoted by Sara Turing in *Alan M. Turing*, p. 75.

46. Letter from A. C. Pigou to Sara Turing, 26 November 1956 (in the Turing Papers, King's College Library, Cambridge, catalogue reference A 10).

47. *General Report on Tunny*, p. 35.

48. Letter from Ismay to Angwin, 15 March 1944 (National Archives, document reference HW25/21).

49. Flowers, T. H. 'The Design of Colossus', *Annals of the History of Computing*, vol. 5 (1983), pp. 239–52 (p. 246).

50. Flowers, 'The Design of Colossus', p. 245.

51. Flowers, 'The Design of Colossus', p. 246.

52. Flowers' personal diary, 31 May 1944.

53. Letter from Chandler to Brian Randell, 24 January 1976; unpublished manuscript by Gil Hayward '1944–1946' (2002).

54. Hayward, '1944–1946'.

55. See also Tutte, W. T. 'My Work at Bletchley Park', in *Colossus*, p. 367.

56. Coombs, A. W. M. 'The Making of Colossus', *Annals of the History of Computing*, vol. 5 (1983), pp. 253–9 (p. 259).

57. Harrison, G. A. *Cross Channel Attack* (Washington: US Army Center for Military History, 1951), ch. 8; Hinsley, *British Intelligence in the Second World War*, vol. 3, part 2, p. 126.

58. Hinsley, *British Intelligence in the Second World War*, vol. 3, part 2, p. 69.

59. Message KV2624, 2 May 1944 (National Archives, document reference DEFE 3/45); Hinsley, *British Intelligence in the Second World War*, vol. 3, part 2, p. 78.

60. Levine, J. *Operation Fortitude* (London: Collins, 2011).

61. Message BAY/KV179, 1 June 1944 (HW 20/389); Hinsley, *British Intelligence in the Second World War*, vol. 3, part 2, p. 61.

62. Message KV2388, 29 April 1944 (DEFE 3/44); Hinsley, *British Intelligence in the Second World War*, vol. 3, part 2, pp. 78–9.

63. Message KV2295, 28 April 1944 (DEFE 3/44) and message KV6705, 7 June 1944 (DEFE 3/166); Hinsley, *British Intelligence in the Second World War*, vol. 3, part 2, pp. 800–1.

64. Hinsley, *British Intelligence in the Second World War*, vol. 3, part 2, p. 79.

65. 'Forecast of the Strength and Quality of Divisions on "Overlord" Y Date', 25 May 1944 (reproduced in Appendix 10 of Hinsley, *British Intelligence in the Second World War*, vol. 3, part 2).

66. Ellis, L. F. *Victory in the West*, vol. 1: *The Battle of Normandy* (London: Her Majesty's Stationery Office, 1962), p. 216.

67. Hinsley, *British Intelligence in the Second World War*, vol. 3, part 2, p. 128.

68. Ellis, *Victory in the West*, vol. 1, p. 199.

69. D'Este, C. *Decision in Normandy* (London: Collins, 1983), pp. 111–12; Hinsley, *British Intelligence in the Second World War*, vol. 3, part 2, p. 128.

70. Harrison, *Cross Channel Attack*, p. 333.

71. 'Hitler as Seen by Source', p. 8.

72. Hinsley, *British Intelligence in the Second World War*, vol. 2, p. 29.

73. Based on information from Roberts and on the tables 'Times' and 'Raw Materials – Production' in *General Report on Tunny*, pp. 289 and 394.

74. Based on 'Raw Materials – Production', *General Report on Tunny*, p. 394.

75. Message T442/6 (quoted in 'Hitler as Seen by Source', p. 2).

76. Currie, H. 'An ATS Girl in the Testery', in my *Colossus*, p. 267.

77. Message T536/39 (quoted in 'Hitler as Seen by Source', p. 4).

78. 'Hitler as Seen by Source', p. 2.

79. Letter from Bayley to the author, 1 June 2012.

80. Letter from Newman to John von Neumann, 8 February 1946 (in the John von Neumann Archive at the Library of Congress, Washington, D.C.). A digital facsimile of the letter is in *The Turing Archive for the History of Computing* at www.AlanTuring.net/newman_vonneumann_8feb46.

81. Michie in conversation in October 1995.

82. Newman, 'Max Newman—Mathematician, Codebreaker, and Computer Pioneer', pp. 184–5.

83. Du Boisson writing in *Colossus*, p. 160.

84. Good, 'From Hut 8 to the Newmanry', p. 210.

85. Newman quoted by Good, 'From Hut 8 to the Newmanry', p. 205.

86. Caughey writing in *Colossus*, pp. 165–6.

87. Weierud, F. 'Bletchley Park's Sturgeon—The Fish That Laid No Eggs', in *Colossus* (pp. 325–6).

88. These hybrids, the 'Colorobs', eventually were built. See Lavington, S. 'In the Footsteps of Colossus: A Description of Oedipus', *IEEE Annals of the History of Computing*, vol. 28 (2006), pp. 44–55 (p. 46).

89. Du Boisson writing in *Colossus*, p. 172.

90. Thurlow writing in *Colossus*, pp. 172–3.

91. Caughey writing in *Colossus*, p. 165.

92. Currie, 'An ATS Girl in the Testery', p. 268.

93. Sara Turing, *Alan M. Turing*, p. 67.

94. Newman, 'Max Newman—Mathematician, Codebreaker, and Computer Pioneer', p. 177.

95. *General Report on Tunny*, www.AlanTuring.net/tunny_report.

96. Bauer, F. L. *Decrypted Secrets: Methods and Maxims of Cryptology* (Berlin: Springer-Verlag, 2nd edn, 2000), pp. 424–5. Additional information from Ralph Erskine.

97. Newman, 'Max Newman—Mathematician, Codebreaker, and Computer Pioneer', p. 177.

98. Denniston quoted in Morris, C. 'Navy Ultra's Poor Relations', in Hinsley and Stripp, *Codebreakers*, p. 237.

CHAPTER 8: ACE

1. Croarken, M. 'The Creation of the NPL Mathematics Division', in Copeland et al. *Alan Turing's Electronic Brain* (Oxford: Oxford University Press, 2012).

2. Magnello, E., 'The National Physical Laboratory', is a history of the NPL (in my *Alan Turing's Electronic Brain*).

3. Minutes of the Executive Committee of the National Physical Laboratory for 19 March 1946, NPL library. A digital facsimile is in *The Turing Archive for the History of Computing* at www.AlanTuring.net/npl_minutes_mar1946.

4. Two brief biographical notes on Womersley are Darwin, C. G. 'Mr. J. R. Womersley', *Nature*, vol. 181 (1958), p. 1240, and Smithies, F. 'John Ronald Womersley', *Journal of the London Mathematical Society*, vol. 34 (1959), pp. 370–2.

5. There is additional information in my 'The Origins and Development of the ACE Project', in *Alan Turing's Electronic Brain*.

6. Womersley, J. R. 'A.C.E. Project—Origin and Early History', in my *Alan Turing's Electronic Brain*, pp. 38–9. A digital facsimile is in *The Turing Archive for the History of Computing* at www.AlanTuring.net/ace_early_history.

7. Womersley, 'A.C.E. Project—Origin and Early History'.

8. Jack Good in conversation with the author, February 2004. Letter from Good to the author, 14 June 2007.

9. 'Research Programme for the Year 1945–46', National Physical Laboratory, October 1944, NPL library. A digital facsimile is in *The Turing Archive for the History of Computing* at www.AlanTuring.net/research_programme_1945–46.

10. Womersley, 'A.C.E. Project—Origin and Early History'.

11. Womersley, 'A.C.E. Project—Origin and Early History'.

12. Sara Turing, *Alan M. Turing*, p. 74.

13. Letter from Don Bayley to the author, 6 May 1998.

14. Womersley, 'A.C.E. Project—Origin and Early History'.

15. Goldstine, H. H. *The Computer from Pascal to von Neumann* (Princeton: Princeton University Press, 1972), p. 150.

16. Flowers in my *Colossus*, p. 101.

17. For more information about ENIAC, see Goldstine, *The Computer from Pascal to von Neumann*; Burks, A. W. 'From ENIAC to the Stored-Program Computer: Two Revolutions in Computers', in Metropolis, N., Howlett, J., Rota, G. C. (eds) *A History of Computing in the Twentieth Century* (New York: Academic Press, 1980); and Goldstine, H. H., Goldstine, A. 'The Electronic Numerical Integrator and Computer' (1946), in Randell, B. (ed.) *The Origins of Digital Computers: Selected Papers* (Berlin: Springer-Verlag, 1982).

18. Campbell-Kelly, M. 'The ACE and the Shaping of British Computing', in my *Alan Turing's Electronic Brain*, p. 151.

19. Womersley, J. R. '"ACE" Machine Project', National Physical Laboratory, no date, in the Woodger Papers, Science Museum, Kensington, London. A digital facsimile is in *The Turing Archive for the History of Computing* at www.AlanTuring.net/womersley_ace_machine.

20. Mike Woodger in conversation with the author, June 1998.

21. Turing's design paper 'Proposed Electronic Calculator' is in my *Alan Turing's Electronic Brain*. On its date of completion: letter from Woodger to the author, 27 November 1999, and Woodger, M. handwritten note, no date, in the Woodger Papers, catalogue reference M15/78. Woodger testifies to the existence of an NPL file giving the date of Turing's completed report as 1945. Unfortunately this file was destroyed in 1952.

22. Turing, A. M. 'Proposed Electronic Calculator', in my *Alan Turing's Electronic Brain*, p. 393.

23. Wilkinson in interview with Christopher Evans in 1976 ('The Pioneers of Computing: An Oral History of Computing', London: Science Museum, © Board of Trustees of the Science Museum). The archives of the London Science Museum supplied me with this interview on audiotape in 1995 and I transcribed it in 1997.

24. Darwin, C. 'Automatic Computing Engine (ACE)', National Physical Laboratory, 17 April 1946 (National Archives, document reference DSIR 10/385). A digital facsimile is in *The Turing Archive for the History of Computing* at www.AlanTuring.net/darwin_ace.

25. Womersley, '"ACE" Machine Project'.

26. Minutes of the Executive Committee of the National Physical Laboratory for 19 March 1946, NPL library. A digital facsimile is in *The Turing Archive for the History of Computing* at www.AlanTuring.net/npl_minutes_mar1946.

27. Womersley, J. R. '"ACE" Machine Project', National Physical Laboratory, paper E.881, 13 February 1946, in the Woodger Papers. A digital facsimile is in *The Turing Archive for the History of Computing* at www.AlanTuring.net/ace_machine_project.

28. Bell, C. G., Newell, A. *Computer Structures: Readings and Examples* (New York: McGraw-Hill, 1971), p. 42.

29. Flowers, T. H. 'D-Day at Bletchley Park', in my *Colossus*, p. 82.

30. Goldstine, *The Computer from Pascal to von Neumann*, p. 182.

31. Von Neumann, J., Deposition before a public notary, New Jersey, 8 May 1947; Warren, S. R. 'Notes on the Preparation of "First Draft of a Report on

the EDVAC" by John von Neumann', 2 April 1947. I am grateful to Harry Huskey for supplying me with copies of these documents.

32. Von Neumann, J. 'First Draft of a Report on the EDVAC', Moore School of Electrical Engineering, University of Pennsylvania, 1945; reprinted in full in Stern, N. *From ENIAC to UNIVAC: An Appraisal of the Eckert–Mauchly Computers* (Bedford, Mass.: Digital Press, 1981).

33. Warren, 'Notes on the Preparation of "First Draft of a Report on the EDVAC" by John von Neumann'.

34. Von Neumann, Deposition, 8 May 1947.

35. Letter from von Neumann to Norbert Wiener, 29 November 1946 (in the von Neumann Archive at the Library of Congress, Washington, DC).

36. Von Neumann, J. *Theory of Self-Reproducing Automata* (ed. A. W. Burks, Urbana: University of Illinois Press, 1966), p. 50.

37. Letter from Stanley Frankel to Brian Randell, 1972 (published in Randell, B. 'On Alan Turing and the Origins of Digital Computers', in Meltzer and Michie (eds) *Machine Intelligence 7* (Edinburgh: Edinburgh University Press, 1972). I am grateful to Randell for supplying me with a copy of this letter.

38. Huskey, H. D. 'The Development of Automatic Computing', in *Proceedings of the First USA–JAPAN Computer Conference*, Tokyo, 1972, p. 702.

39. Letter from Julian Bigelow to the author, 12 April 2002. See also Aspray, W. *John von Neumann and the Origins of Modern Computing* (Cambridge, Mass.: MIT Press, 1990), p. 178.

40. Womersley, 'A.C.E. Project—Origin and Early History'.

41. See *Alan Turing's Electronic Brain* for detailed information about the design of the ACE.

42. Letter from Huskey to the author, 4 February 2002.

43. Compare Figure 10 of Turing's 'Proposed Electronic Calculator' (on p. 431 of my *Alan Turing's Electronic Brain*) with Figure 3 of von Neumann's report (on p. 198 of Stern, *From ENIAC to UNIVAC*).

44. *Evening News*, 23 December 1946. The cutting is among a number kept by Sara Turing and now in the Modern Archive Centre, King's College, Cambridge (catalogue reference K 5).

45. For a discussion of RISC see Doran, R. 'Computer Architecture and the ACE Computers', in *Alan Turing's Electronic Brain*.

46. Wilkes tells his fascinating story in Wilkes, M. V. *Memoirs of a Computer Pioneer* (Cambridge, Mass.: MIT Press, 1985).

47. Memorandum from Turing to Womersley, undated, c. December 1946, in the Woodger Papers (catalogue reference M15/77). A digital facsimile is in *The Turing Archive for the History of Computing* at www.AlanTuring.net/turing_womersley.

48. Robin Gandy in conversation with the author, October 1995.

49. Don Bayley in conversation with the author, December 1997.

50. Sara Turing, *Alan M. Turing*, p. 73.

51. Sara Turing, *Alan M. Turing*, p. 58.

52. Hartree, D. R., Womersley, J. R. 'A Method for the Numerical or Mechanical Solution of Certain Types of Partial Differential Equations', *Proceedings of the Royal Society of London*, vol. 161 (series A), pp. 353–66; Womersley, J. R. 'The Application of Differential Geometry to the Study of the Deformation of Cloth Under Stress', *Shirley Institute Memoirs*, vol. 16 (1937), pp. 1–21.

53. Gandy in conversation with the author, October 1995.

54. Sara Turing, *Alan M. Turing*, pp. 69–70; Donald Michie in conversation with the author, February 1998.

55. Henry John Norton writing in my *Alan Turing's Electronic Brain*, p. 209.

56. Sara Turing, *Alan M. Turing*, p. 76.

57. Letter from Max Newman to Norris McWhirter, 18 August 1982 (quoted by William Newman on p. 186 of my *Colossus*).

58. Letter from Don Bayley to the author, 15 December 1997. Minutes of the Executive Committee of the National Physical Laboratory for 23 October 1945, NPL library. A digital facsimile is in *The Turing Archive for the History of Computing* at www.AlanTuring.net/npl_minutes_oct1945.

59. Sara Turing, *Alan M. Turing*, p. 108.

60. Letter from A. C. Pigou to Sara Turing, 26 November 1956 (in the Turing Papers, Modern Archive Centre, King's College Library, Cambridge, catalogue reference A 10).

61. Peter Harding quoted on the Walton Athletic Club website.

62. Sara Turing, *Alan M. Turing*, p. 111.

63. Sara Turing, *Alan M. Turing*, p. 86.

64. Sara Turing, *Alan M. Turing*, p. 113.

65. Sara Turing, *Alan M. Turing*, p. 85.

66. Letter from Turing to Sara, undated.

67. Lyn Newman in her Foreword to Sara's *Alan M. Turing*, p. xiii.

68. *Daily Telegraph*, 27 December 1946.

69. Letter from Turing to Sara, December 1946.

70. Letter from Turing to Sara, undated.

71. *The Times*, 1947.

72. 'Status of the Delay Line Computing Machine at the P.O. Research Station', National Physical Laboratory, 7 March 1946, in the Woodger Papers (catalogue reference M12/105). A digital facsimile is in *The Turing Archive for the History of Computing* at www.AlanTuring.net/delay_line_status.

73. Flowers in conversation with the author, July 1998.

74. Huskey, H. D. 'The ACE Test Assembly, the Pilot ACE, the Big ACE, and the Bendix G15', in *Alan Turing's Electronic Brain*, p. 282.

75. Minutes of the Executive Committee of the National Physical Laboratory for 19 March 1946, NPL library. A digital facsimile is in *The Turing Archive for the History of Computing* at www.AlanTuring.net/npl_minutes_mar1946.

76. Turing, 'Proposed Electronic Calculator', p. 409.

77. Turing in 'The Turing–Wilkinson Lecture Series (1946–7)', *Alan Turing's Electronic Brain*, p. 465.

78. Allen Coombs in interview with Christopher Evans in 1976 ('The Pioneers of Computing: An Oral History of Computing', London: Science Museum, © Board of Trustees of the Science Museum). The archives of the London Science Museum supplied me with this interview on audiotape in 1995.

79. Letter from Michael Woodger to the author, 21 May 2003.

80. Don Bayley in conversation with the author, December 1997.

81. Thomas, H. A., 'A Plan for the Design, Development and Production of the "ACE"', 12 April 1947, p. 5 (in the Woodger Papers). A digital facsimile is in *The Turing Archive for the History of Computing* at www.AlanTuring.net/turing_archive/archive/l/l02/l02.php.

82. Huskey, 'The ACE Test Assembly, the Pilot ACE, the Big ACE, and the Bendix G15', p. 281.

83. Huskey, 'The ACE Test Assembly, the Pilot ACE, the Big ACE, and the Bendix G15', p. 285.

84. Turing, A. M. 'Report on visit to U.S.A., January 1st–20th, 1947', National Physical Laboratory, 3 February 1947 (National Archives, document reference DSIR 10/385). A digital facsimile is in *The Turing Archive for the History of Computing* at www.AlanTuring.net/turing_usa_visit.

85. Womersley, J. R. 'A.C.E. Project', National Physical Laboratory, undated (National Archives, document reference DSIR 10/385). A digital facsimile is in *The Turing Archive for the History of Computing* at www.AlanTuring.net/womersley_ace_project.

86. Wilkinson in interview with Evans.

87. Woodger in conversation with the author, June 1998.

88. Wilkinson in interview with Evans.

89. Letters from Huskey to the author, 3 June 2003, 18 January 2004.

90. Letter from Huskey to the author, 18 January 2004. Woodger, M. 'ACE Test Assembly', September–October 1947, National Physical Laboratory (in the Woodger Papers). A digital facsimile is in *The Turing Archive for the History of Computing* at www.AlanTuring.net/ace_test_assembly.

91. Fieller, E. C. 'Hollerith Equipment for A.C.E. Work—Immediate Requirements', National Physical Laboratory, 16 October 1947 (National Archives, document reference DSIR 10/385). A digital facsimile is in *The Turing Archive for the History of Computing* at www.AlanTuring.net/hollerith_equipment.

92. Minutes of the Executive Committee of the National Physical Laboratory for 18 March 1947, NPL library. A digital facsimile is in *The Turing Archive for the History of Computing* at www.AlanTuring.net/npl_minutes_mar1947.

93. There is a more detailed account of the Thomas debacle in my 'The Origins and Development of the ACE Project', in *Alan Turing's Electronic Brain*.

94. Turing probably left for Cambridge at the end of September. He was still at the NPL when Geoff Hayes arrived in the Mathematics Division on 23 September 1947.

95. Letter from Darwin to Sir Edward Appleton, 23 July 1947 (National Archives, document reference DSIR 10/385). A digital facsimile is in *The Turing Archive for the History of Computing* at www.AlanTuring.net/darwin_appleton_23jul47.

96. Hayes, G. 'The Place of Pilot Programming', manuscript, 2000.

97. Minutes of the Executive Committee of the National Physical Laboratory for 20 April 1948, NPL library. A digital facsimile is in *The Turing Archive for the History of Computing* at www.AlanTuring.net/npl_minutes_apr1948.

98. Sara Turing, *Alan M. Turing*, p. 89.

99. Wilkinson in interview with Evans.

100. Woodger in conversation with the author, June 1998.

101. Smithies, 'John Ronald Womersley'.

102. Womersley, J. R. 'Oscillatory Motion of a Viscous Liquid in a Thin-Walled Elastic Tube—I: The Linear Approximation for Long Waves', *The Philosophical Magazine*, vol. 46 (1955), pp. 199–221.

103. My *Alan Turing's Electronic Brain* contains additional information about MOSAIC, on pp. 80–3.

104. For more information about NPL's 'Big ACE' see *Alan Turing's Electronic Brain*.

105. Froggatt, R. J. 'Logical Design of a Computer for Business Use', *Journal of the British Institution of Radio Engineers*, vol. 17 (1957), pp. 681–96; Bell and Newell, *Computer Structures: Readings and Examples*, pp. 44, 74; Yates, D. M. *Turing's Legacy: A History of Computing at the National Physical Laboratory 1945–1995* (London: Science Museum, 1997).

106. Huskey, 'The ACE Test Assembly, the Pilot ACE, the Big ACE, and the Bendix G15'.

CHAPTER 9: MANCHESTER'S 'ELECTRONIC BRAIN'

1. Kilburn, T., Piggott, L. S. 'Frederic Calland Williams', *Biographical Memoirs of Fellows of the Royal Society*, vol. 24 (1978), pp. 583–604.

2. J. R. Whitehead, quoted in Kilburn and Piggott, 'Frederic Calland Williams', p. 590.

3. J. R. Whitehead, quoted in Kilburn and Piggott, 'Frederic Calland Williams', p. 590.

4. Williams in interview with Christopher Evans in 1976 ('The Pioneers of Computing: An Oral History of Computing', London: Science Museum, © Board of Trustees of the Science Museum); the archives of the London Science Museum supplied me with this interview on audiotape in 1995 and I transcribed it in 1997.

5. Williams quoted in 'How To Invent', *International Science and Technology*, February 1964, pp. 49–53 (p. 52).

6. 'Interview with Dr. F. C. Williams, O.B.E. Group Leader at T.R.E.' (typescript, no date, circa 1945; TRE records).

7. Williams quoted in Bennett, S. 'F. C. Williams: his contribution to the development of automatic control' (an unpublished typescript based on interviews with Williams in 1976; National Archive for the History of Computing, University of Manchester), p. 1.

8. Williams quoted in Bennett, 'F. C. Williams: his contribution to the development of automatic control', p. 1.

9. Goldstine, H. H. *The Computer from Pascal to von Neumann* (Princeton: Princeton University Press, 1972), p. 96.

10. Turing, 'Proposed Electronic Calculator', pp. 426–7 (in *Alan Turing's Electronic Brain*).

11. Letter from Williams to R. A. Watson-Watt, 6 July 1950. The letter is discussed in a draft report of the National Research Development Corporation, 'Williams Cathode Ray Tube Storage: Evidence Relating to the Origin of the Invention and the Dissemination of Information on the Operation of the Storage System' ('NRDC Draft Report'), p. 5. There is a detailed history of the Williams tube in my 'The Manchester Computer: A Revised History. *Part I* The Memory.' *IEEE Annals of the History of Computing*, vol. 33 (2011), pp. 4–21.

12. Sheppard, C. B. Lecture 21 (p. 268), in Campbell-Kelly, M., Williams, M. R. (eds) *The Moore School Lectures* (Cambridge, Mass.: MIT Press, 1985). The date of Sheppard's report of Sharpless's work is 24 July 1946.

13. Williams in interview with Evans.

14. Minutes of the Working Party on Circuitry, TRE, 7 August 1946 (in the National Archive for the History of Computing, University of Manchester).

15. NRDC Draft Report, pp. 2–3.

16. Strachey, C. S. handwritten notes, in the Christopher Strachey papers, Bodleian Library, Oxford, folder C33.

17. For additional detail see my 'The Manchester Computer: A Revised History. *Part I* The Memory', pp. 12–13.

18. For additional detail see my 'The Manchester Computer: A Revised History. *Part II* The Baby Machine.' *IEEE Annals of the History of Computing*, vol. 33 (2011), pp. 22–37.

19. Wilkes, M., Kahn, H. J. 'Tom Kilburn CBE FREng', *Biographical Memoirs of Fellows of the Royal Society*, vol. 49 (2003), pp. 285–97 (pp. 285–6).

20. Kilburn and Piggott, 'Frederic Calland Williams', p. 584.

21. NRDC Draft Report, p. 7.

22. Williams in interview with Evans.

23. Bowker, G., Giordano, R. 'Interview with Tom Kilburn', *IEEE Annals of the History of Computing*, vol. 15 (1993), pp. 17–32 (p. 19). The official notes of the lectures are printed as 'The Turing–Wilkinson Lecture Series (1946–7)' in my *Alan Turing's Electronic Brain*, and my introduction to the notes provides a description of the lectures (pp. 459–64). Womersley's handwritten papers concerning the arrangements for the lecture series are in the Woodger Papers (catalogue reference M15) and are reproduced in *The Turing Archive for the History of Computing* at www.AlanTuring.net/womersley_notes_22nov46.

24. Conan Doyle, A. *A Study in Scarlet* (London: Penguin, 1981), p. 10.

25. See my 'The Manchester Computer: A Revised History. *Part II* The Baby Machine', pp. 23–4.

26. Good used these terms in a letter to Newman about computer architecture (8 August 1948). The letter is in Good, I. J. 'Early Notes on Electronic Computers' (unpublished, compiled in 1972 and 1976; a copy is in the University of Manchester National Archive for the History of Computing, MUC/Series 2/a4), pp. 63–4.

27. Kilburn, T. 'A Storage System for Use with Binary Digital Computing Machines', Report for TRE, 1 December 1947 (National Archive for the History of Computing, University of Manchester). A retyped version, complete with editorial notes by Brian Napper, is at www.computer50.org/kgill/mark1/report1947.html. I am indebted to Napper for much helpful discussion and correspondence.

28. Letter from Napper to the author, 16 June 2002.

29. Bowker and Giordano, 'Interview with Tom Kilburn', p. 19.

30. For additional detail see my 'The Manchester Computer: A Revised History. *Part I* The Memory', pp. 7–10.

31. 'Application from Professor M. H. A. Newman: Project for a Calculating Machine Laboratory in Manchester University', Royal Society of London, p. 2.

32. Williams, F. C. 'Early Computers at Manchester University', *The Radio and Electronic Engineer*, vol. 45 (1975), pp. 327–31 (p. 328).

33. Kilburn and Piggott, 'Frederic Calland Williams', pp. 583–4.

34. Kilburn and Piggott, 'Frederic Calland Williams', p. 591. NRDC Draft Report, p. 7. Kilburn in interview with the author, July 1997.

35. Kilburn in interview with the author, July 1997. Letter from TRE to NPL (9 January 1947), in the National Archive for the History of Computing, University of Manchester.

36. Newman, W. 'Max Newman—Mathematician, Codebreaker, and Computer Pioneer', in my *Colossus*, p. 185.

37. Huskey, H. D. 'The State of the Art in Electronic Digital Computing in Britain and the United States', Chapter 23 of my *Alan Turing's Electronic Brain* (see p. 536).

38. 'Application from Professor M. H. A. Newman: Project for a Calculating Machine Laboratory in Manchester University'; and 'Report by Professor M. H. A. Newman on Progress of Computing Machine Project', Minutes of the Council of the Royal Society, 13 January 1949 (in the archives of the Royal Society of London).

39. Michie in conversation with the author, October 1995; Good, 'Early Notes on Electronic Computers', pp. vii, ix.

40. Michie in an unpublished memoir that he sent to me in March 1997.

41. See further my 'The Manchester Computer: A Revised History. *Part II* The Baby Machine', pp. 26–7.

42. Letter from Williams to Randell, 1972 (in Randell, B. 'On Alan Turing and the Origins of Digital Computers', in Meltzer, B., Michie, D. eds *Machine Intelligence 7*, Edinburgh: Edinburgh University Press, 1972; the letter is on p. 9). I am grateful to Randell for supplying me with a copy of the letter.

43. Williams in interview with Evans. As far as I know, Williams's tape-recorded statements that 'neither Tom Kilburn nor I knew the first thing about computers when we arrived in Manchester University' and that 'Newman explained the whole business of how a computer works to us' first appeared in transcription in the British *Times Literary Supplement* in a 1998 article by myself and Diane Proudfoot, published on the 50th anniversary of the Manchester Baby ('Enigma Variations', *Times Literary Supplement*: 'Information Technology', 3 July 1998, p. 6).

44. Kilburn in interview with the author in July 1997.

45. Good recounted this in his retrospective introduction (written in 1972) to a short paper, 'The Baby Machine', that he had prepared on 4 May 1947 at Kilburn's request (Good, 'Early Notes on Electronic Computers', p. iv); and he also related it in his 1998 acceptance speech for the IEEE Computer Pioneer Award (he sent me a copy of his revised typescript in January 1999). Good's twelve instructions, set out in 'The Baby Machine', are detailed in my 'The Manchester Computer: A Revised History. *Part II* The Baby Machine', p. 28. (See also Croarken, M. 'The Beginnings of the Manchester Computer Phenomenon: People and Influences', *IEEE Annals of the History of Computing*, vol. 15 (1993), pp. 9–16; and Lee, J. A. N. *Computer Pioneers* (Los Alamitos: IEEE Computer Society Press, 1995), p. 744.)

46. Burks, A. W., Goldstine, H. H., von Neumann, J. 'Preliminary Discussion of the Logical Design of an Electronic Computing Instrument', Institute for Advanced Study, 28 June 1946, in vol. 5 of Taub, A. H. ed. *Collected Works of John von Neumann* (Oxford: Pergamon Press, 1961). For additional detail see my 'The Manchester Computer: A Revised History. *Part II* The Baby Machine', pp. 29–31.

47. A detailed comparison between Good's twelve instructions and the Baby's instruction set is presented in the sidebar on p. 26 of my 'The Manchester Computer: A Revised History. *Part II* The Baby Machine'.

48. The Baby computer and its instruction set are described in Williams, F. C., Kilburn, T. 'Electronic Digital Computers', *Nature*, vol. 162, no. 4117 (1948), p. 487.

49. Williams in interview with Evans.

50. Williams, 'Early Computers at Manchester University', p. 330.

51. Williams, 'Early Computers at Manchester University', p. 330.

52. Williams in interview with Evans.

53. Woodger in conversation with the author, June 1998.

54. The delivery date of the first Ferranti computer is given in a letter from Turing to Woodger, undated, received 12 February 1951 (in the Woodger Papers). A digital facsimile is in *The Turing Archive for the History of Computing* at www.AlanTuring. net/turing_woodger_feb51. For details of the UNIVAC see Stern, N. 'The BINAC: A Case Study in the History of Technology' *Annals of the History of Computing*, vol. 1 (1979), pp. 9–20 (p. 17); and Stern, N. *From ENIAC to UNIVAC: An Appraisal of the Eckert–Mauchly Computers* (Bedford, Mass.: Digital, 1981), p. 149.

55. The Atlas is described in Lavington, S. A *History of Manchester Computers* (Manchester: NCC Publications, 1975), pp. 37–43.

56. Ken Myers in conversation with the author, July 2001. Myers, K. 'Wartime memories of Dollis Hill and Bletchley Park (B/P or Station X)', typescript, circa 2000, p. 5.

57. Letter from Good to the author, 5 March 2004.

58. Letter from Good to the author, 5 March 2004.

59. As I demonstrated in my 'The Manchester Computer: A Revised History. Part II The Baby Machine', pp. 30–1.

60. Bigelow, J. 'Computer Development at the Institute for Advanced Study', in Metropolis, N., Howlett, J., Rota, G. C. (eds) *A History of Computing in the Twentieth Century* (New York: Academic Press, 1980), pp. 305–6.

61. Newman, M. H. A. 'Alan Mathison Turing, 1912–1954', *Biographical Memoirs of Fellows of the Royal Society*, vol. 1 (1955), pp. 253–63 (p. 254).

62. Letter from Williams to Randell.

63. Letter from Williams to Randell.

64. For additional detail see my 'The Manchester Computer: A Revised History. Part II The Baby Machine', pp. 31–2.

65. Turing, 'Programmers' Handbook for Manchester Electronic Computer', Computing Machine Laboratory, University of Manchester, no date, circa 1950. A digital facsimile is in *The Turing Archive for the History of Computing* at www.AlanTuring.net/programmers_handbook.

66. 'The Manchester Computer: A Revised History. *Part II* The Baby Machine', p. 32.

67. Kilburn in interview with the author, July 1997.

68. Williams in interview with Evans.

69. Michie in conversation with the author, February 1998.

70. *The Essential Turing*, p. 473.

71. Letter from Geoffrey Jefferson to Turing, 10 March 1951 (Turing Papers, King's College Library, catalogue reference A 29). Jefferson was Professor of Neurosurgery at Manchester University.

72. Sara Turing, *Alan M. Turing*, p. 92.

73. Sara Turing, *Alan M. Turing*, p. 92.

74. Sara Turing, *Alan M. Turing*, p. 92.

75. Woodger in conversation with the author, June 1998.

76. Sara Turing, *Alan M. Turing*, p. 91.

77. Sara Turing, *Alan M. Turing*, p. 91.

78. Eliza Clayton, statement to the police (Turing Papers, King's College Library, catalogue reference K 6).

79. Newman, L. Foreword to Sara Turing's *Alan M. Turing*.

80. The verses are among Turing's papers in King's College Library (catalogue reference D 4).

81. The story is among Turing's papers in King's College Library (catalogue reference A 13).

82. Letter from Lyn Newman to Antoinette Esher, 13 November 1957 (Papers of Max and Lyn Newman, St John's College Library, Cambridge). I am grateful to William Newman for information about Lyn's letters.

83. Letter from Turing to Lyn Newman, May, no year (Turing Papers, King's College Library, catalogue reference A 13).

84. Newman, 'Max Newman—Mathematician, Codebreaker, and Computer Pioneer', p. 187.

85. Newman, 'Max Newman', pp. 186–7.

86. Newman, 'Max Newman', p. 186.

87. Sara Turing, *Alan M. Turing*, p. 66.

88. Sara Turing, *Alan M. Turing*, p. 93.

89. Information from William Newman.

90. Letter from Lyn Newman to her parents, 25 January 1938 (in St John's College Library, Cambridge).

91. There is a circuit diagram of the hooter in Dodd, K. N. *The Ferranti Electronic Computer*, Armament Research Establishment report 10/53 (Diagram 10).

92. Turing, *Programmers' Handbook for Manchester Electronic Computer*, p. 24.

93. Dodd, *The Ferranti Electronic Computer*, p. 59.

94. Turing, *Programmers' Handbook for Manchester Electronic Computer*, p. 24.

95. See, for example, Chadabe, J. 'The Electronic Century, Part III: Computers and Analog Synthesizers', *Electronic Musician*, 2001, www.emusician.com/tutorials/electronic_century3. I am grateful to the New Zealand composer Jason Long both for this reference and for much discussion about computer music.

96. Prinz, D. G. *Introduction to Programming on the Manchester Electronic Digital Computer*, Ferranti Ltd, Moston, Manchester, section 20. A digital facsimile is in *The Turing Archive for the History of Computing* at www.AlanTuring.net/prinz.

97. Turing, *Programmers' Handbook for Manchester Electronic Computer*, p. 24.

98. Foy, N. 'The Word Games of the Night Bird', *Computing Europe*, 15 August 1974, pp. 10–11 (interview with Christopher Strachey).

99. Campbell-Kelly, M. 'Christopher Strachey, 1916–1975: A Biographical Note', *Annals of the History of Computing*, vol. 7 (1985), pp. 19–42 (p. 23).

100. Scott, D. S. 'An Appreciation of Christopher Strachey and his Work', in Stoy, J. E. *Denotational Semantics: The Scott–Strachey Approach to Programming Language Theory* (Cambridge, Mass.: MIT Press, 1977), p. xx.

101. Letter from Strachey to Woodger, 13 May 1951 (in the Woodger Papers).

102. Levy, S. *Hackers: Heroes of the Computer Revolution* (New York: Anchor, 1984), p. 7.

103. Gandy in conversation with the author, October 1995.

104. Strachey in 'The Word Games of the Night Bird', p. 10.

105. Strachey in 'The Word Games of the Night Bird', p. 11.

106. Strachey in 'The Word Games of the Night Bird', p. 11.

107. Strachey in 'The Word Games of the Night Bird', p. 11.

108. Strachey in 'The Word Games of the Night Bird', p. 11.

109. The original 1951 recording is in the National Sound Archive at the British Library, London (reference number H3942). A digital copy, made by Chris Burton, is available on the Internet at www.digital60.org/media/mark_one_digital_music. There were early developments in computer music in Australia, too, and Trevor Pearcey's CSIRAC played music at the first Australian Computer Conference in Sydney, also in 1951. See Doornbusch, P.

The Music of CSIRAC: Australia's First Computer Music (Melbourne: Common Ground, 2005). Doornbusch's book includes a CD of reconstructed music.

110. Turing quoted in 'The Mechanical Brain', *The Times*, 11 June 1949.

111. *The Essential Turing*, p. 484.

112. Strachey, C. S. 'The Thinking Machine', *Encounter*, vol. 3 (1954), pp. 25–31 (p. 26).

113. Turing, *Programmers' Handbook for Manchester Electronic Computer*, p. 25. Turing, A. M. 'Generation of Random Numbers', appendix to Tootill, G. C. 'Informal Report on the Design of the Ferranti Mark I Computing Machine', Manchester Computing Machine Laboratory, November 1949.

114. See *The Essential Turing*, pp. 445, 475, 477–9, and 484–5, and ch. 7 ('Freedom') of my *Artificial Intelligence*.

115. Newman, M. H. A. 'Alan Mathison Turing, 1912–1954', p. 255.

116. Strachey, 'The Thinking Machine', p. 26.

117. The letter is in the Turing Papers, King's College Library, catalogue reference D 4.

118. Strachey, B. *Remarkable Relations: The Story of the Pearsall Smith Women* (New York: Universe Books, 1982), p. 275. See also Campbell-Kelly, 'Christopher Strachey, 1916–1975: A Biographical Note', p. 20.

119. Strachey, C. S. 'Logical or Non-Mathematical Programmes', *Proceedings of the Association for Computing Machinery*, Toronto, September 1952, pp. 46–9.

120. Letters from Strachey to Woodger, 5 March 1951 and 13 May 1951 (in the Woodger Papers). Letter from Strachey to Turing, 15 May 1951 (Turing Papers, King's College Library, catalogue reference D 5). For further details see *The Essential Turing*, pp. 356–8.

121. Christopher Strachey papers, Bodleian Library, Oxford.

122. Strachey, C. S. handwritten note, in the Christopher Strachey papers, folder C30.

123. Samuel, A. L. 'Some Studies in Machine Learning Using the Game of Checkers', *IBM Journal of Research and Development*, vol. 3 (1959), pp. 211–29.

124. Shurkin, J. 'Computer Pioneer and His Historic Program Still Active at Stanford', Stanford University News Service, 1983. (I am grateful to Hubert Dreyfus for this reference.)

125. Strachey, 'The Thinking Machine', p. 26.

CHAPTER 10: THE IMITATION GAME

1. Brooks, R. A., Flynn, A. M. 'Fast, Cheap and Out of Control: A Robot Invasion of the Solar System', *Journal of the British Interplanetary Society*, vol. 42 (1989), pp. 478–85.

2. See Proudfoot, D. 'Anthropomorphism and AI: Turing's Much Misunderstood Imitation Game', *Artificial Intelligence*, vol. 175 (2011), pp. 950–7 (p. 954).

3. See Brooks, R. A. 'Intelligence without Reason', in Steels, L., Brooks, R. (eds) *The Artificial Life Route to Artificial Intelligence: Building Situated Embodied Agents* (New Haven: Lawrence Erlbaum, 1994).

4. *The Essential Turing*, p. 431.

5. Michie, D. *On Machine Intelligence* (Edinburgh: Edinburgh University Press, 1974), p. 51.

6. Simon, H. A., Newell, A. 'Heuristic Problem Solving: The Next Advance in Operations Research', *Operations Research*, vol. 6 (1958), pp. 1–10 (p. 8).

7. *The Essential Turing*, p. 460.

8. *The Essential Turing*, pp. 460, 393.

9. *The Essential Turing*, p. 463.

10. Brooks, 'Intelligence Without Reason'.

11. *The Essential Turing*, p. 420.

12. *The Essential Turing*, p. 420.

13. *The Essential Turing*, pp. 460–1.

14. Michael Woodger reported by Michie and Meltzer in Meltzer, B., Michie, D. (eds) *Machine Intelligence 5* (New York: Elsevier, 1970), p. 2.

15. Weizenbaum, J. 'ELIZA — a Computer Program for the Study of Natural Language Communication Between Man and Machine', *Communications of the Association for Computing Machinery*, vol. 9 (1966), pp. 36–45.

16. Colby, K. M., Watt, J. B., Gilbert, J. P. 'A Computer Method of Psychotherapy: Preliminary Communication', *The Journal of Nervous and Mental Disease*, vol. 142 (1966), pp. 148–52 (p. 152).

17. Weizenbaum, J. *Computer Power and Human Reason: From Judgement to Calculation* (San Francisco: W.H. Freeman, 1976), pp. 3–4.

18. Weizenbaum, *Computer Power and Human Reason*, p. 7.

19. From my *Artificial Intelligence* (Oxford: Blackwell, 1993), p. 24.

20. Excerpted from Winograd, T. A. *Understanding Natural Language* (New York: Academic Press, 1972), pp. 8–15; and Winograd, T. A. *Procedures as a Representation for Data in a Computer Program for Understanding Natural Language* (Cambridge: MIT Project MAC, 1971), p. 44.

21. Haugeland, J. *Artificial Intelligence: The Very Idea* (Cambridge: MIT Press, 1985), p. 190.

22. Simon, H. A. *The Shape of Automation: For Men and Management* (New York: Harper & Row, 1965), p. 96.

23. Minsky quoted in Dreyfus, H. L., Dreyfus, S. E. *Mind Over Machine* (New York: Macmillan/Free Press, 1986), p. 78; Lenat, D. B., Feigenbaum, E. A. 'On the Thresholds of Knowledge', *Artificial Intelligence*, vol. 47 (1991), pp. 185–250 (p. 224).

24. Michie in conversation with the author, February 1998.

25. Michie in conversation with the author, October 1995.

26. *The Essential Turing*, p. 449.

27. Newell, A., Shaw, J. C., Simon, H. A. 'Empirical Explorations with the Logic Theory Machine: A Case Study in Heuristics', *Proceedings of the Western Joint Computer Conference*, vol. 15 (1957), pp. 218–39 (reprinted in Feigenbaum, E. A., Feldman, J. (eds) *Computers and Thought*, New York: McGraw-Hill, 1963).

28. Whitehead, A. N., Russell, B. *Principia Mathematica* (Cambridge: Cambridge University Press, 1910).

29. Shaw in interview with Pamela McCorduck (McCorduck, P. *Machines Who Think*, New York: W. H. Freeman, 1979, p. 143).

30. Letter from Arthur Samuel to the author, 6 December 1988. Samuel, A. L. 'Some Studies in Machine Learning Using the Game of Checkers', *IBM Journal of Research and Development*, vol. 3 (1959), pp. 211–29 (reprinted in Feigenbaum and Feldman, *Computers and Thought*).

31. Donald Michie in conversation with the author, February 1998.

32. For more detail see *The Essential Turing*, pp. 353–61.

33. For more detail see *The Essential Turing*, pp. 563–4.

34. Letter from A. C. Pigou to Sara Turing, 26 November 1956 (in the Turing Papers, King's College Library, Cambridge, catalogue reference A 10).

35. *The Essential Turing*, pp. 574–5.

36. Michie in conversation with the author, February 1998.

37. *The Essential Turing*, ch. 9.

38. Michael Woodger's diary.

39. *The Essential Turing*, p. 393.

40. *The Essential Turing*, p. 391.

41. *The Essential Turing*, ch. 10.

42. Letter from Darwin to Turing, 11 November 1947 (in the Turing Papers, King's College Library, Cambridge, catalogue reference D 5). A digital facsimile is in *The Turing Archive for the History of Computing* at www.AlanTuring. net/darwin_turing_11nov47.

43. Robin Gandy in conversation with the author, October 1995.

44. Minutes of the Executive Committee of the National Physical Laboratory for 28 September 1948, NPL library, p. 4. A digital facsimile is in *The Turing Archive for the History of Computing* at www.AlanTuring.net/npl_minutes_sept1948.

45. *The Essential Turing*, p. 431.

46. Samuel, 'Some Studies in Machine Learning Using the Game of Checkers'.

47. *The Essential Turing*, ch. 16 (see p. 575).

48. Turing, 'Proposed Electronic Calculator', p. 389.

49. *The Essential Turing*, p. 503.

50. For more detail see *The Essential Turing*, pp. 248–53.

51. *The Essential Turing*, p. 431.

52. Newell, A., Simon, H. A. 'Computer Science as Empirical Inquiry: Symbols and Search', *Communications of the Association for Computing Machinery*, vol. 19 (1976), pp. 113–26 (p. 120).

53. Good in conversation with the author, February 2004.

54. An excellent report of the match is 'Garry Kasparov vs. Deep Blue' by Frederic Friedel, at www.chessbase.com/columns/column.asp?pid=146.

55. Chomsky, N. *Powers and Prospects: Reflections on Human Nature and the Social Order* (London: Pluto, 1996), p. 40.

56. Ed Fredkin interviewed in *Better Mind the Computer*, BBC TV.

57. *The Essential Turing*, p. 475.

58. *The Essential Turing*, pp. 485–6.

59. *The Essential Turing*, p. 475.

60. Good, I. J. 'Speculations Concerning the First Ultraintelligent Machine', *Advances in Computers*, vol. 6 (1965), pp. 31–88 (p. 33).

61. Good, I. J. 'Some Future Social Repercussions of Computers', *International Journal of Environmental Studies*, vol. 1 (1970), pp. 67–79 (p. 76).

62. Else, L. 'Ray Kurzweil: A Singular View of the Future', *New Scientist Opinion* 2707, 6 May, 2009, www.newscientist.com.

63. 'The Law of Accelerating Returns, KurzweilAI.net, 7 March 2001, www.kurzweilai.net/articles/art0134.html?printable=1. See also my and Diane Proudfoot's article 'Our Posthuman Future', *The Philosophers' Magazine*, vol. 57 (2012), pp. 73–8; also available at www.thephilosophersmagazine.com.

64. An article in the *Wilmslow Advertiser* gives an account of information presented at the subsequent trial ('University Reader Put on Probation', 4 April 1952,

p. 8). I am grateful to the Cheshire Record Office for supplying me with this article, and also with copies of the court records (Register of the Court, Wilmslow, 27 February 1952, and Knutsford, 31 March 1952; and the Indictment at the Cheshire Quarter Sessions in Knutsford, 31 March 1952, *The Queen v. Alan Mathison Turing and Arnold Murray*). My account is based on these materials.

65. Ch. 14 of *The Essential Turing*, 'Can Automatic Calculating Machines Be Said to Think?'.

66. Letter from Turing to Philip Hall, no date (in the Turing Papers, King's College Library, Cambridge, catalogue reference D 13).

67. Letter from Turing to Norman Routledge, no date (in the Turing Papers, King's College Library, Cambridge, catalogue reference D 14).

68. Don Bailey in conversation with the author, 21 December 1997.

69. Letter from Turing to Hall.

70. Letter from Turing to Hall.

71. Don Bailey in conversation with the author, December 1997.

72. Letter from Turing to Routledge, 22 February [1953] (in the Turing Papers, King's College Library, Cambridge, catalogue reference D 14).

73. Letter from Turing to Gandy, 11 March [1953] (in the Turing Papers, King's College Library, Cambridge, catalogue reference D 4). The name 'Kjell Carlsen' is written in the corner of a sheet of Turing's handwritten mathematical notes.

74. Letter from Turing to Routledge, 22 February.

75. Letter from Turing to Gandy, 11 March.

76. For more detail see ch. 15 of *The Essential Turing*.

77. Watson, J. D. *The Double Helix: A Personal Account of the Discovery of the Structure of DNA* (New York: Touchstone, 2001), p. 197.

78. Richards, B. 'Turing, Richards, and Morphogenesis', *The Rutherford Journal for the History and Philosophy of Science and Technology*, vol. 1 (2005–2006), www.rutherfordjournal.org/article010109.html.

79. See for example Economou A. D., et al. 'Periodic stripe formation by a Turing mechanism operating at growth zones in the mammalian palate', *Nature Genetics*, vol. 44 (2012), pp. 348–51; and Kaandorp, J. A., Sloot, P. M. A., Merks, R. M. H., Bak, R. P. M., Vermeij, M. J. A., Maier, C. 'Morphogenesis of the branching reef coral *Madracis Mirabilis*', *Proceedings of the Royal Society B*, vol. 272 (2005), pp. 127–133.

80. Langton, C. G. 'Studying Artificial Life with Cellular Automata', *Physica D*, vol. 22 (1986), pp. 120–49 (p. 147).

81. Langton, C. G. (ed.) *Artificial Life: The Proceedings of an Interdisciplinary Workshop on the Synthesis and Simulation of Living Systems* (Redwood City, Calif.: Addison-Wesley, 1989).

82. Langton, C. G. 'Artificial Life', in Langton, *Artificial Life* (p. 1).

83. Langton, 'Artificial Life', in Langton, *Artificial Life* (p. 32).

84. Letter from Turing to J. Z. Young, 8 February 1951 (on p. 517 of *The Essential Turing*).

85. *The Essential Turing*, p. 382.

CHAPTER 11: COLD PORRIDGE

1. *The Essential Turing*, p. 495.

2. *The Essential Turing*, p. 495 (emphasis added).

3. Harlow, J. M. 'Recovery From the Passage of an Iron Bar Through the Head', *Massachusetts Medical Society Publications*, vol. 2 (1868), pp. 328–47.

4. Diane Proudfoot and I pointed this out in our article 'On Alan Turing's Anticipation of Connectionism', *Synthese*, vol. 108 (1996), pp. 361–77. See also our *Scientific American* article 'Alan Turing's Forgotten Ideas in Computer Science' (vol. 280, 1999, pp. 99–103), and the discussion in *The Essential Turing*, pp. 402–32.

5. *The Essential Turing*, pp. 428–9.

6. Letter from Turing to J. Z. Young, 8 February 1951, on p. 517 of *The Essential Turing*.

7. *The Essential Turing*, pp. 422, 424.

8. *The Essential Turing*, p. 424.

9. *The Essential Turing*, p. 429.

10. Farley, B. G., Clark, W. A. 'Simulation of Self-Organising Systems by Digital Computer', *Institute of Radio Engineers Transactions on Information Theory*, vol. 4 (1954), pp. 76–84; Clark, W. A., Farley, B. G. 'Generalisation of Pattern Recognition in a Self-Organising System', in *Proceedings of the Western Joint Computer Conference* (1955).

11. Gold, J. I., Shadlen, M. N. 'Banburismus and the Brain: Decoding the Relationship between Sensory Stimuli, Decisions, and Reward', *Neuron*, vol. 36 (2002), pp. 299–308.

12. Turing first presented his imitation game in 1948 in an NPL report, and then more fully two years later in the philosophy journal *Mind*. His 1952 radio broadcast 'Can Automatic Calculating Machines Be Said to Think?' provided additional information about the imitation game. All three pieces are in *The Essential Turing* (chs 10, 11, and 14).

13. *The Essential Turing*, p. 495.

14. *Contra* French, R. 'Subcognition and the Limits of the Turing Test', *Mind*, vol. 99 (1990), pp. 53–65. French's ingenious attack on the Turing test assumes that the machine is required to try and pass itself off as a member of the judge's own culture, but there is no such restriction to be found in any of Turing's various presentations of the test.

15. Strictly this is an oversimplification. Turing provided a protocol for scoring the test that is based on another form of the imitation game, the man–woman imitation game. This game involves a judge and two contestants, one male and one female; the judge must determine, by question and answer, which contestant is the man. (The male contestant's object in the game, like the computer's, is to try to cause the judge to make the wrong identification.) The performance of the man in the man-imitates-woman game is used as a baseline for assessing the computer's performance in the computer-imitates-human game (see *The Essential Turing*, p. 441). If the computer (in the computer-imitates-human game) does no worse than the man (in the man-imitates-woman game) then it succeeds in the game. For additional discussion see my article 'The Turing Test', in Moor, J. (ed.) *The Turing Test: The Elusive Standard of Artificial Intelligence* (Dordrecht: Kluwer, 2003).

16. *The Essential Turing*, p. 442.

17. *The Essential Turing*, p. 452.

18. The test is reported in Bobrow, D. 'A Turing Test Passed', *ACM SIGART Newsletter*, December 1968, pp. 14–15.

19. The Loebner Turing Test Competition, Dartmouth College, 2000.

20. Loebner, H. 'Why a Loebner Prize', 2009, www.chatbots.org/awards/loebner_prize/why_a_loebner_prize.

21. This is an edited extract from a conversation between Jabberwacky and Sundman at www.loebner.net/Prizef/2005_Contest/Jabberwacky/Jabberwacky_Judge_session2.htm. Chat with Jabberwacky yourself at www.jabberwacky.com.

22. *The Essential Turing*, p. 489.

23. For example by Andrew Hodges in *Alan Turing: The Enigma*, p. 415.

24. *The Essential Turing*, p. 494.

25. *The Essential Turing*, p. 449.

26. *The Essential Turing*, p. 486.

27. *The Essential Turing*, p. 485 (emphasis added).

28. *The Essential Turing*, p. 442.

29. *The Essential Turing*, p. 495.

30. *The Essential Turing*, ch. 11.

31. Letter from Wittgenstein to Malcolm, 1 December 1950, in Malcolm, N. *Ludwig Wittgenstein: A Memoir* (Oxford: Oxford University Press, 2nd edn, 1984), pp. 129–30 and note.

32. Lenat, D. B. 'Building a Machine Smart Enough to Pass the Turing Test: Could We, Should We, Will We?' in Epstein, R., Roberts, G., and Beber, G. (eds) *Parsing the Turing Test: Philosophical and Methodological Issues in the Quest for the Thinking Computer* (Berlin: Springer, 2008).

33. Tversky, A., Kahneman, D. 'Extensional Versus Intuitive Reasoning: The Conjunction Fallacy in Probability Judgement', *Psychological Review*, vol. 90 (1983), pp. 293–315.

34. *The Essential Turing*, p. 495 (emphasis added).

35. French, 'Subcognition and the Limits of the Turing Test'.

36. *The Essential Turing*, p. 484.

37. French, 'Subcognition and the Limits of the Turing Test', p. 17.

38. There is more discussion of French's attack on the Turing test in my chapter 'The Turing Test' in Moor, *The Turing Test*.

39. Searle first presented his famous Chinese room thought experiment in his article 'Minds, Brains, and Programs', *Behavioural and Brain Sciences*, vol. 3 (1980), pp. 417–24 and 450–6; and also in his book *Minds, Brains and Science: the 1984 Reith Lectures* (London: Penguin, 1989). See also Preston, J., Bishop, M. (eds) *Views Into The Chinese Room* (Oxford: Oxford University Press, 2002).

40. Searle, J. R. 'Is the Brain's Mind a Computer Program?', *Scientific American*, vol. 262 (1990), pp. 20–5 (p. 20).

41. Weiskrantz, L., Warrington, E. K., Sanders, H. D., Marshall, J. 'Visual Capacity in the Hemianopic Field Following a Restricted Occipital Ablation', *Brain*, vol. 97 (1974), pp. 709–28; Weiskrantz, L. *Blindsight* (Oxford: Oxford University Press, 1986).

42. For additional discussion of the Chinese room see my 'The Chinese Room from a Logical Point of View', in Preston and Bishop, *Views Into The Chinese Room*.

43. For discussion of more objections to the Turing test, see *The Essential Turing*, pp. 437–8, and my chapter 'The Turing Test' in Moor, *The Turing Test*.

44. Turing's views as reported by Jack Good in conversation with the author, July 2004.

45. *The Essential Turing*, p. 569.

46. *The Essential Turing*, p. 452.

47. Letter from Good to the author, 20 March 2004. Good said 'This gives the essence of the conversation but the precise wording might have been slightly different.'

48. See also my *Artificial Intelligence*, ch. 8.

49. *The Essential Turing*, pp. 452, 569.

50. Michie, *On Machine Intelligence*, p. 51.

51. From Gödel's lecture notes for his 1939 introductory logic course at the University of Notre Dame; in Cassou-Nogues, 'Gödel's Introduction to Logic in 1939'.

52. Gödel in discussion with Hao Wang, reported in Wang, H. *A Logical Journey: From Gödel to Philosophy* (Cambridge: MIT Press, 1996), p. 189.

53. *The Essential Turing*, p. 459.

54. Michie in conversation with the author, February 1998.

55. Gödel in discussion with Hao Wang, reported in Wang, *A Logical Journey*, p. 207.

56. Newman's remark is quoted by Turing on p. 215 of *The Essential Turing*.

57. *The Essential Turing*, p. 215.

58. For a more detailed treatment of these issues see 'Turing versus Gödel on Computability and the Mind', a chapter by myself and Oron Shagrir in Copeland, B. J., Posy, C., Shagrir, O. (eds) *Computability: Gödel, Turing, Church and Beyond* (Cambridge: MIT Press, 2012).

59. *The Essential Turing*, p. 463.

CHAPTER 12: /END////

1. Caroline Davies writing in the *Guardian*, 10 September 2009.

2. The apology appeared on the official website of the British Prime Minister www.number10.gov.uk. Two sheets signed by Gordon Brown and headed 'Remarks of Prime Minister Gordon Brown, 10 September 2009' are now part of the Turing exhibition at Bletchley Park National Museum.

3. *Manchester Guardian*, 11 June 1954; *Alderley and Wilmslow Advertiser*, 18 June 1954.

4. Leavitt, D. 'Alan Turing, the father of the computer, is finally getting his due', *Washington Post*, 23 June 2012, www.washingtonpost.com/opinions/

alan-turing-father-of-computer-science-not-yet-getting-his-due/
2012/06/22/gJQA5eUOvV_story.html.

5. Sara Turing, *Alan M. Turing*, p. 117.

6. Sara Turing, *Alan M. Turing*, p. 117. The coroner's verdict was also reported in *The Times*, 12 June 1954.

7. Statement of Eliza Clayton before the coroner (in the Turing Papers, King's College Library, catalogue reference K 6).

8. Statement of Eliza Clayton before the coroner. There is some additional detail in Clayton's account in Sara Turing's 'Comments by friends on the manner of Alan Turing's death', typescript, no date (in the Turing Papers, King's College Library, catalogue reference A 11).

9. Statement of Police Sergeant Leonard Cottrell before the coroner (in the Turing Papers, King's College Library, catalogue reference K 6).

10. Statement of Police Sergeant Leonard Cottrell before the coroner.

11. Statements of Eliza Clayton and Police Sergeant Leonard Cottrell before the coroner.

12. Statement of Eliza Clayton before the coroner.

13. Statement of Eliza Clayton before the coroner.

14. The Tuesday *Manchester Guardian* was still in the letterbox at the front door but Monday's newspaper was found in the front room downstairs (Statement of Police Sergeant Leonard Cottrell). Turing spoke to a neighbour while out strolling on the Monday, according to a note written by Sara Turing at the top of the post-mortem examination report (in the Turing Papers, King's College Library, catalogue reference K 6). Mrs Clayton mentioned in her statement before the coroner that the remains of a meal of mutton chops were on the dining room table.

15. C. A. K. Bird 'Post Mortem Examination Report', 8 June 1954 (in the Turing Papers, King's College Library, catalogue reference K 6).

16. Statement of Police Sergeant Leonard Cottrell; Statement of C. A. K. Bird before the coroner (in the Turing Papers, King's College Library, catalogue reference K 6).

17. Sara Turing, *Alan M. Turing*, p. 115.

18. Sara Turing, *Alan M. Turing*, p. 115.

19. Sara Turing, *Alan M. Turing*, p. 76.

20. Sara Turing, *Alan M. Turing*, p. 116.

21. Letter from Turing to his parents, 15 March 1925.

22. Furbank in conversation with the author, September 2012; letter from Furbank to Gandy, 13 June 1954 (in the Turing Papers, King's College Library, catalogue reference A 5).

23. *The Inquest Handbook* (London: INQUEST, 2011), Section 4.3.

24. Ferns quoted in *The Daily Telegraph and Morning Post*, 11 June 1954.

25. Sara Turing writing in her 'Comments by friends on the manner of Alan Turing's death'.

26. Eliza Clayton quoted in Sara Turing's 'Comments by friends on the manner of Alan Turing's death'.

27. Letter from Gandy to Sara Turing, quoted in Sara Turing, *Alan M. Turing*, p. 118.

28. Letter from N. Webb to Sara Turing, 13 June 1954 (in the Turing Papers, King's College Library, catalogue reference A 17).

29. Letter from Furbank to Gandy, 13 June 1954; *Manchester Guardian*, 11 June 1954.

30. Letter from Bernard Richards to the author, 20 August 2012.

31. Letter from Turing to Gandy, 11 March 1953 (in the Turing Papers, King's College Library, catalogue reference D 4).

32. Letter from Turing to Maria Greenbaum, postmarked 10 May 1953 (in the Turing Papers, King's College Library, catalogue reference K 1/83).

33. Sara Turing, *Alan M. Turing*, p. 117.

34. Letter from Bayley to Gandy, 14 June 1954 (in the Turing Papers, King's College Library, catalogue reference A 5).

35. Statement of Police Sergeant Leonard Cottrell.

36. Letter from Franz Greenbaum to Sara Turing, 5 January 1955 (in the Turing Papers, King's College Library, catalogue reference A 16); Sara Turing writing in her 'Comments by friends on the manner of Alan Turing's death'.

37. Don Bayley in conversation with the author, December 1997.

38. Sara Turing writing in her 'Comments by friends on the manner of Alan Turing's death'.

39. Burgess, J. L., Chandler, D. 'Clandestine Drug Laboratories', in Greenberg, M. I. et al. (eds) *Occupational, Industrial, and Environmental Toxicology* (Philadelphia: Mosby, 2003, 2nd edn), p. 759.

40. Sara Turing, *Alan M. Turing*, p. 115.

41. Statements of Police Sergeant Leonard Cottrell and C. A. K. Bird before the coroner.

42. United States Army Medical Research Institute of Chemical Defense *Medical Management of Chemical Casualties Handbook* (Aberdeen Proving Ground, 1999, 3rd edn).

43. Bird, 'Post Mortem Examination Report'.

44. Andrews, J. M., Sweeney, E. S., Grey, T. C., Wetzel, T. 'The Biohazard Potential of Cyanide Poisoning During Postmortem Examination', *Journal of Forensic Sciences*, vol. 34 (1989), pp. 1280–4. The US Army *Medical Management of Chemical Casualties Handbook* states that 'approximately 50% of the population are genetically unable to detect the odor of cyanide'. Earlier studies found that about 20% of males are unable to smell cyanide (Kirk, R. L., Stenhouse, N. S. 'Ability to Smell Solutions of Potassium Cyanide', *Nature*, vol. 171 (1953), pp. 698–9; Fukumoto, Y. et al. 'Smell Ability to Solution of Potassium Cyanide and Its Inheritance', *Jinrui-idengaku-zasshi* [*Journal of Human Genetics*], vol. 2 (1957), pp. 7–16).

45. US Army *Medical Management of Chemical Casualties Handbook*.

46. Information from Robert Taylor (a chemist who underwent training in a Ministry of Defence laboratory in the early 1960s).

47. US Army *Medical Management of Chemical Casualties Handbook*.

48. US Army *Medical Management of Chemical Casualties Handbook*. For a literature review regarding this phenomenon see Chiu-Wing Lam, King Lit Wong 'Hydrogen Cyanide', Appendix B15 of Gardner, D. E. et al. *Spacecraft Maximum Allowable Concentrations for Selected Airborne Contaminants*, vol. 4 (Washington: National Academy Press: 2000), pp. 331–2.

49. Bird, 'Post Mortem Examination Report'.

50. Bird, 'Post Mortem Examination Report', and Statement before the coroner. Bird did perform a chemical test to establish that cyanide was actually present.

51. Kirk and Stenhouse. 'Ability to Smell Solutions of Potassium Cyanide'; Fukumoto et al., 'Smell Ability to Solution of Potassium Cyanide and Its Inheritance', p. 8; Andrews et al., 'The Biohazard Potential of Cyanide Poisoning During Postmortem Examination', p. 1283.

52. Bird, 'Post Mortem Examination Report'.

53. Andrews et al., 'The Biohazard Potential of Cyanide Poisoning During Postmortem Examination', p. 1280.

54. Taylor, J., Roney, N., Harper, C., Fransen, M., Swarts, S. *Toxicological Profile for Cyandide* (Atlanta: U.S. Department of Heath and Human Services, Agency for Toxic Substances and Disease Registry, 2006), p. 37.

55. Bird, 'Post Mortem Examination Report'.

56. Sammon, P., Sen, P. 'Turing Committed Suicide: Case Closed', 5 July 2012 (www.turingfilm.com), responding to my 'Turing Suicide Verdict in Doubt', 23 June 2012, where I argued—as I do in this chapter—that we simply do not know whether Turing took his own life.

57. Letter from Greenbaum to Sara Turing, 5 January 1955.

58. Sammon and Sen, 'Turing Committed Suicide: Case Closed'.

59. Turing's Last Will and Testament, 11 February 1954 (in the Turing Papers, King's College Library, catalogue reference A 5).

60. Kilburn in interview with the author, July 1997; Tootill, G. C. 'Informal Report on the Design of the Ferranti Mark I Computing Machine', November 1949, p. 1.

61. Letter from Brigadier G. H. Hinds to F. C. Williams, 11 December 1952; letter from Williams to Hinds, 18 December 1952. The job came not from GCHQ but from the Ministry of Supply, where Brigadier Hinds held a brief for research and development (Wilkes, *Memoirs of a Computer Pioneer*, p. 144).

62. See my *Colossus*, pp. 173–4.

63. Letter from Viscount Portal of Hungerford to F. C. Williams, 30 November 1950; letter from Williams to Portal, 13 December 1950.

64. Corner, J. 'Problem for the Manchester Electronic Computer', 1950.

65. Letter from Portal to Williams, 10 January 1951.

66. Letter from A. C. Ericsson to F. C. Williams, 19 April 1955.

67. Johnson, D. K. *The Lavender Scare: The Cold War Persecution of Gays and Lesbians in the Federal Government* (Chicago: University of Chicago Press, 2004).

68. 'British spies carried out assassinations during Cold War', claims former agent Le Carre', *Mail Online*, 29 August 2010.

PICTURE ACKNOWLEDGEMENTS:

The Publisher and Author apologize for any errors or omissions. If contacted they will be happy to rectify these at the earliest opportunity.

INDEX

Page numbers indicating photographs and diagrams are bold and italicized.